BONES FOR THE ARCHAEOLOGIST

BONES
FOR THE
ARCHAEOLOGIST

by

I. W. Cornwall

B.A. (*Cantab*), PH.D. (*Lond*), F.Z.S., *formerly Reader in*
Human Environment, London University,
Institute of Archaeology

J. M. DENT & SONS LTD
London

Dedicated to
the memory of the late
Sir ARTHUR KEITH
MD, FRCS, FRS,
Master Anatomist, Honoured Teacher
and Kind Friend

First Published 1956
Second Impression 1960
Third Impression 1964
Reprinted 1968
Revised edition, 1974
ISBN 0 460 04229 7

FOREWORD TO THE FIRST EDITION, 1956

by the late Professor F. E. Zeuner

PH.D., D.SC., F.G.S., F.Z.S.

THE INVESTIGATION of an archaeological site is not complete without the study of its natural and artificial environment. Man of the past stood with both feet on the ground, and one of his chief activities was the exploitation of the animal world. It is natural, therefore, that much valuable information can be obtained from the animal bones found on a site. They may be derived from domesticated beasts and tell us about the breeds then reared, or they come from game animals and tell us about hunting activities. Perhaps both groups are present, and their proportion may be an index of the relative importance of hunting and stock-breeding. Moreover, in the Old Stone Age, bones provide crucial evidence for the kind of environment man was living in, for climate and dating.

It is unfortunate, therefore, that no book has been published in the last eighty years from which one can learn the kind of mammalian osteology required by the archaeologist, and, for that matter, the biologist in general—for archaeologists are today nothing but specialist biologists, studying one particular, and in fact, somewhat peculiar, species. This gap in our literature has indeed been awkward not only from the research point of view, but from the teaching angle also. It is one thing to teach students with the aid of material in the class room, but quite another to expect them to learn the matter up without a text-book and, what is worse, to make them use their knowledge after the completion of their training.

This gap has now been filled by the admirable book Dr Cornwall has written. It is admirable in three respects. First, it does contain the matter one hopes to find in it (not all books do); secondly, it has been planned in such a way that even the reader without previous biological training will find it possible to get down to brass tacks; and, thirdly, it is written in an exceedingly pleasant manner which makes reading easy.

I am thus very happy that *Bones for the Archaeologist* is at last appearing in print. It will make life easier for both students and teachers, and I am convinced that it will—as it should—encourage some of the younger generation to take up comparative osteology seriously. We are, indeed, greatly in need of workers in this field.

F. E. ZEUNER

CONTENTS

Foreword by Prof. F. E. Zeuner, 5
List of Illustrations, 9
Preface and Acknowledgments, 15

1. Introduction   19

2. The Animal Kingdom   23
Classification · Nomenclature · Palaeontology · Evolution · The geological record · Animal groups of particular interest.

3. The Vertebrate and Mammalian
        Skeleton as a Whole   36

4. The Skull   45
The human skull as a whole · Bones of the skull in man with comparisons with lower mammals · Some general features of the skull in different mammalian Orders.

5. Dentition   74
Structure of teeth · Growth and wear of teeth · The heterodont dentition. Deciduous ('milk') teeth · Salient characters of the dentition in different Orders, genera and species.

6. The Axial Skeleton   105
Vertebral column · Groups of vertebrae · The ribs · The sternum · The thorax as a whole · Special features of the axial skeleton in different mammals.

7. Shoulder- and Hip-girdles   117
The scapula · The clavicle · Characters of the shoulder-girdle in different mammals · The pelvis · Particular features of the pelvis in different groups of mammals.

8. The Fore-limb   131
'Long' bones and their process of growth · Bones of the fore-limb: humerus, ulna, radius · Special features of the fore-limb bones in the different groups.

9. The Fore-extremity (manus)   146
Carpus, metacarpus, phalanges · Bones of the manus in different mammalian groups.

[OVER

10. The Hind-limb   157
Femur, tibia, fibula, patella · Particular features of the hind-limb bones in different mammalian groups.

11. The Hind-extremity (pes)   170
Tarsus, metatarsus, phalanges, sesamoid bones · The pes in different mammalian groups · A non-skeletal bone: the os penis.

12. Determination of Species from Bones   184
   A. *What part of the skeleton is it? Key to single bones*
   B. *First elimination: possibilities in point of size*
   C. *Second elimination: assignment to an Order*
   D. *Assignment by size to a lower group within the Order*
   E. *Comparison with known material*

13. Fragmentary bones   196
What is (a) determinable, (b) worth great trouble in arriving at a determination? Some commonly found fragments and their determination

14. Bones in the Field and in the Laboratory   204
Properties and structure of bone · Fossilization · Excavation · Measurements in the field · Treatment in the field for preservation · Packing and transport · Cleaning, strengthening, mending and reconstruction in the laboratory.

15. Estimation of Age, Sex and Stature from Bones   218
Age determination in man, (a) from the skull, (b) from the state of the dentition, (c) from ossification of epiphyses in the long bones · Sex determination in animals · Age determination in domestic animals · Sex determination in man—pelvis, skull, thorax · Reconstruction of living stature from bones.

16. Study and Interpretation   238
In the field and in the laboratory · Some questions to which a study of the bones may provide an answer.

    Bibliography   246
    Appendix A. Examples a-t to illustrate the process of determination of whole bones   248
    Index   256
    Appendix B. Classification of Mammalia (based on G. G. Simpson)   260

ILLUSTRATIONS

FIG.   PAGE

1. 'The skeleton hunt', a fanciful tableau of the bones of four common mammals in action   12, 13

2. Some varied living members of the Chordate phylum   38

3. Skeletons of some mammals, primitive and specialized   41

4. Skeletons of four Ungulates   43

5. Skulls of horse and man, in profile   46

6A, B, C. Skull of man in five standard attitudes   49, 51, 53

7A, B. Skull and mandible of dog   56, 58

8. Interior views of the human brain-case   61

9. The skull in various mammalian groups   64

10. Skulls and antlers of deer   68

11. Skulls and horns of the larger bovids   70

12. Skulls and horns of smaller bovids   72

13. Teeth in section to show structure   75

14. Dentition of pig   77

15. Milk dentition still partly retained in a young carnivore   79

16. Dentitions of insectivores   81

17. Four variations on the rodent dental theme   83

18. Dentitions of orang and man   85

19. Dentitions of bear, hyaena, fox   88

20. Dentition of African lion   90

21. Dentitions of four Mustelids   92

22. Dentition of young elephant   94

23. Molar teeth of Proboscidea   96

24. Dentitions of rhinoceroses   98

25. Dentition of horse   100

26. Dentition of hippopotamus   101

27. Dentitions of ox and reindeer   103

28. Thoracic vertebrae of man and horse   106

29. Human vertebrae   108

30. Cervical vertebra of a young ox   110

31. Human sacrum and coccyx   111

32. Atlas and axis (cervical vertebrae 1 and 2) of dog, ox, pig   114

33. Shoulder-girdles and scapulae   119

34. Left scapulae of elephants   122

35. Ungulate scapulae   125

36. Pelves of man and bear for comparison   127

37. Left innominate bones of hare, pig, horse, ox, sheep, red deer   129

38. Humerus of a young pig   132

FIG.		PAGE
39.	Arm-bones of man, anterior and posterior views	134
40.	Bones of the left fore-limb and manus in some mammalian groups	136
41.	Left fore-limb bones in typical ungulates	140
42.	Left fore-limb bones of hippopotamus and rhinoceros	143
43.	Dorsal view of the manus of man, dog, bear, and elephant	149
44.	Dorsal view of the manus in various ungulates	152
45.	Left leg bones of man, anterior and posterior views	158
46.	Hind-limb bones of bear, shrew, hedgehog, beaver, cat and seal	161
47.	Left hind-limb bones in ungulates	164
48.	Left hind-limb bones of hippopotamus and rhinoceros	167
49.	Dorsal views of the bones of the left pes of man, dog, bear, and of the right pes of elephant	174
50.	Dorsal views of the right pes in ungulates	177
51.	Human patella, lateral and posterior views; patellae of dog and ox. The os penis of a wolf	181
52.	A bone for determination	192
53.	Examples (a) to (j) for initial practice in determination of entire bones and teeth	194
54.	Examples (k) to (t), all to the same scale, for practice in determining bones and teeth	195
55.	*Homo sapiens*, plan of vault of skull and ages at which sutures are obliterated	222
56.	*Homo sapiens*, average dates of eruption and replacement of teeth	224
57.	*Homo sapiens*, dates of synostosis of epiphyses with the shafts of the main long bones	226
58.	Deciduous and permanent dentitions of domestic animals	227
59.	Female and male human pelves	230
60.	Typical female and male adult human skulls	233

FIGURE I

'THE SKELETON HUNT'

A fanciful tableau

'The Skeleton hunt', a fanciful tableau of the bones of four common mammals in action. Man (a Primate) rides the horse (a Perissodactyl ungulate) to hunt the stag (an Artiodactyl ungulate) with the assistance of the dog (a Fissipede carnivore). Note the basic mammalian structures common to all, differing mainly in proportions and attitudes, with increasing adaptation of the extremities to speed, in the order: man, dog, deer, horse.

Man directs the enterprise by virtue of his superior
brain and hands able to make implements and use
them; nevertheless, without the horse's superior
fleetness of foot and stamina he would not easily
get within bowshot of such a target. Without
the dog's superior sense of scent, gripping teeth,
and 'dogged' spirit he would be hard put to it to
follow and bring to bay a merely wounded
quarry. The deer's superior agility over rough
country may yet save him should the loosed
arrow miss its mark.

PREFACE AND
ACKNOWLEDGMENTS

ALMOST EVERY EXCAVATION to find the relics of ancient man and of his culture yields, among other natural evidence, the bones of his animal contemporaries, and sometimes those of man himself. Commercial pits for gravel, sand, chalk and brickearth often cut into deposits of the Pleistocene geological period, where, along with stone implements shaped by Palaeolithic man, are found remains of the animals which he hunted and which may, sometimes, have hunted him.

It is now a commonplace that it is the duty of archaeologists and others, who may unearth such bones, to collect them for examination, so that no evidence may be lost which may help to fill in the natural and economic background in which ancient cultures flourished.

It is, perhaps, less well known that the specialists who may best be qualified to examine the material and pass zoological and palaeontological judgment on it are often not particularly interested in its archaeological context and have other work to do besides reporting on the large quantities of bones, human and animal, often collected on archaeological excavations. The result of their natural preoccupation with their own special interests is that there is a dearth of workers in this field, the greater number of archaeologists not having enough anatomical and zoological skill to determine their own bone-finds reliably.

Clearly, the main responsibility for the first sorting over of the material rests with us, the archaeologists. Only when the importance of the case or the special interest of the bones warrants it should we have to apply for assistance and final judgment to the experts.

Not every archaeologist has the need (or the desire!) to make himself his own osteologist, but there should be a sufficient small number of the fraternity with a certain interest and skill in the matter of bones, who would enable the really vast material to be sorted, selected and surveyed without undue delay.

Every excavator, on the other hand, ought to have some slight acquaintance with the subject, for he is the first judge of the material and must decide whether it is worth preservation for study or not. To this end, he should obviously be able to distinguish between human and animal remains and between the fore-limb and hind-limb bones of the same human or animal individual. It would evidently be of value if he could even tell the difference between those of a human infant and those of a hare or cat. Lack of even this minimum of technical knowledge makes it not uncommon for bone remains to be collected in such a way that, if it is attempted at a later time to mend and reassemble them for study, whole limbs and parts of skulls of otherwise well-preserved skeletons are found to be missing.

In view of these facts, a short course of human and animal osteology has been deemed necessary for students taking the Degrees and Diplomas in archaeology of the University of London, and it has, for some years past, fallen to the writer to attempt to cover the required field in lectures and practical demonstrations. Every year at least some few students show special interest in and aptitude for the subject and wish to give it rather more attention than is absolutely required by the syllabuses, but there was in 1956 no book on the rather narrow part of the zoological and palaeontological field which is of chief importance for archaeologists.

Flower's *Osteology of the Mammalia* (1876) is admirable, and still unsurpassed in its way, but contains much that is irrelevant to our subject.

Gray's *Anatomy* and other textbooks of human anatomy are designed for the medical student and deal exclusively with man. The detail, even of the sections dealing with osteology, is too great for our purpose.

The same criticisms apply to veterinary textbooks, which demand considerable labour on the part of the inquirer to select what is relevant to our problems. It is not surprising that, faced with three or four tomes of such scope, most archaeologists decide that life is not long enough for them to become acquainted with the technicalities of bones.

Hue's *Musée Ostéologique* is an atlas of bones by a veterinary surgeon, specifically intended as an aid to archaeologists. Despite some shortcomings, it is a valuable work of reference and should be on the shelf of any student who pretends to recognize animal bones. Since it is frankly an atlas, it lacks explanatory matter which would serve as an introduction to osteology and takes for granted a knowledge of the systematic relationships on which any serious study of bones must be based. Once the reader is familiar with the outline of the mammalian skeleton, Hue frequently provides the comparative material required, though, in the nature of things, he is far from complete—one seems always to want a view of the specimen different from that illustrated!

There is, therefore, room for a book on the particular aspects of human and animal osteology which interest the archaeologist—the study of bones as indices of environment and of the processes of human and animal evolution. In scope it needs to confine itself rather closely to the narrow field with which we are concerned and to concentrate exclusively on the mammals. It is to supply this need, and to digest somewhat the mass of information on comparative anatomy, for archaeologists working far from reference libraries, that this book is primarily designed. It is hoped at the same time that its existence will attract into the field of osteology a few serious students who may fill the gap which at present exists between archaeology and the specialist zoologists and palaeontologists.

It was no part of the original intention to appeal to the interest of the general public, but the cultivation of a knowledge of bones is, after all, no more abstruse than archaeology itself, which has many expert amateur exponents. It may be hoped, therefore, that at least some general readers may be fired in their imaginations with an enthusiasm to follow a science which is also something of an art and a craft, of intrinsic interest as well as an indispensable adjunct to archaeological research.

The illustrations are chosen not so much to provide an atlas of bones as to demonstrate the zoological principles upon which determinations must be based. Their number would have to be enormously multiplied to attempt more than this.

Scales are included in each figure. Where not otherwise stated, they are in inches and centimetres.

No illustrations, however complete, can fully take the place of comparative bone material for the final determination of an unknown species, though they can be useful reminders of the possibilities when the bones are remembered in the round.

*   *   *

MY FIRST DEBT of gratitude is to the late Sir Arthur Keith, whose published works on the antiquity of man first introduced me to ideas of comparative anatomy. His personal interest in this project and encouragement at every point have been invaluable.

The late Professor Zeuner, my immediate master in mammalian palaeontology and the comparative anatomy of the lower animals, introduced me to the environmental outlook and was a very encyclopaedia of information during the years in which I was associated with him. The impetus provided by him is responsible for the central theme of the work, without which it would inevitably have been altogether dry and barren.

The late Dr. J. C. Trevor, of the Duckworth Laboratory, Cambridge, helped me with the quantitative aspect of human osteology and kindly gave permission to reproduce the technique of measurement and the tables for calculation of living stature from long bones. His kindness and practical assistance far exceeded anything I was entitled to expect.

My thanks are also due to his co-author, Professor J. D. Boyd, of the Anatomy School, Cambridge University, and to Messrs. Butterworth & Co., Ltd., the publishers of their article (see footnote, p. 235) for giving their assent, also, to the reproduction here of their data.

To my predecessors, the authors of many books on which I have drawn for inspiration and specific information, I gladly acknowledge my indebtedness. Many of their names are household words: Buckland, Cuvier, Darwin, Falconer, Linnaeus, Lyell, Owen. Others, more modern, are perhaps just as illustrious in their less all-embracing fields: Abel, Broom, Cunningham, Lydekker, Osborn, Soergel, Rütimeyer and many others. Gray, Flower, Zittel and Hue have provided me with most of the substance for my descriptive matter, for which I take the credit only of having selected and edited what seemed most apposite in my context.

My best thanks and admiration are due to my skilled illustrator, Miss M. Maitland Howard, F.Z.S. Artistry and an intimate knowledge of the material itself are uncommon gifts in one person, which I have been fortunate indeed to have had at my disposal. Her technical contribution and tireless industry have alone made this part of the work possible.

Finally, to the staff of my publishers I would express my gratitude for constant helpfulness, many valuable technical suggestions and unfailing patience in seeing the book through the press.

*   *   *

SINCE THIS BOOK first appeared, in 1956, bone-studies have made great advances, especially in the direction of quantitative and statistical treatment of remains from ancient settlements, with a view to elucidating their ecology and economics. A number of synthetic works has also appeared, giving the results of such studies.

On bone determination, an extremely useful and well-illustrated bilingual *Atlas of animal bones* (E. Schmid, 1972) refers to the bones of a short representative list of hunted and domesticated animals, including man, which most commonly occur on occupation-sites. It is particularly valuable in pointing out the details on which their identification may rest.

R. E. Chaplin (1971) deals not only with determination, but with the establishment of a comparative collection, planning technique and execution of the study and interpretation of its results, based on the author's experience as a practitioner in this field.

M. L. Ryder's little handbook (1969) is a practical introduction for beginners in bone-determination.

A standard work on the domestication of animals is Zeuner (1963), re-published in German in 1967, with additional notes and references to its date by Boessneck and Haltenorth.

An up-to-date review of palaeontology is Kurtén's (1968) *Pleistocene mammals of Europe*.

D. Brothwell's *Digging up bones* (1963) is mainly concerned with human material and with pathology.

Two major syntheses are: Brothwell & Higgs (eds.) *Science and archaeology* (1969), which contains a number of papers by specialists on animals and animal materials, and Ucko & Dimbleby (eds.) (1969), *The domestication and exploitation of plants and animals*.

The first European agriculture by J. Murray (1970) assembles quantitative results of bone-studies at numerous Neolithic sites in Europe.

Most have extensive bibliographies of the original literature.

I.W.C., 1974

1

Introduction

‣‣‣

IF ARCHAEOLOGY ITSELF is popularly regarded as a dry-as-dust study, that of fossil and sub-fossil bones may well seem, in the eyes of the general public, to be the quintessence of dryness and dustiness, the preserve of imaginary bearded professors and museum curators.

Like many popular conceptions, this one is superficial and erroneous.

Archaeology today has advanced beyond the stage of being preoccupied exclusively with the material equipment of ancient peoples: it has become part of the wider study of man. Knowledge of an ancient culture through its artifacts alone is incomplete. The study must include its setting in the larger scheme of things—its relation to the natural environment, of which, in the earliest human times at least, it formed an integral part.

Environment is a complex of topography, climate, soil, flora and fauna—factors all variable and interacting. In any given place at any given time some degree of balance in the character of the environment tends to be established and this persists until one or more of the causative factors changes, when evolution towards a new equilibrium begins afresh.

The interplay of these variables has become the subject of study of the special science of ecology. This, of its nature, encroaches over the boundaries of all the natural sciences interested in the above main factors in environment. Thus there have arisen, for example, ecologies of soils, plants and animals.

The ecology of man in later times is called economics, which, because of the complexity of human social organization, has become quite distinct in character from the natural ecologies. Before man became a more or less sedentary animal human ecology was embraced in that of zoology.

If, therefore, a geological or archaeological site yields animal bones in association with the artifacts of man, these often poorly preserved and fragmentary relics may lead to at least a partial reconstruction of the animal environment of the ancient human group, and thus enable us to indicate with some assurance the climatic, floral and faunal background in which the men must have lived.

Investigation of a collection of bones, as of all archaeological materials, is thus detective-work. Its objectives are different from those of Mr Sherlock Holmes— and its results, perhaps, less definitive—but some of the methods of research are not unlike those employed by up-to-date criminal investigation departments, and may even, on occasion, be identical. For instance, the methods of determining the sex, age and stature of fragmentary human remains of the past are the same as those used by police investigators for attempting to identify remains of victims of the more grisly murders.

The identification of animal species from loose teeth and fragmentary bones requires a certain knowledge of anatomy and zoology, of a strictly limited character. The more durable parts only being represented, the soft parts concern us only in so far as they form part of the complete living mechanism of the body and affect the bones at their points of attachment. The field of possible unknown species is further narrowed, for any given place and period, to the list of species likely to be found. New discoveries cannot be excluded, but will probably not be frequent.

The task before us, therefore, is not as insuperably great as it might at first sight appear, nor is it without its own interest for a student with a mechanical turn of mind, able to appreciate the intrinsic beauty of anatomical mechanisms.

Any person wishing to understand the working of the internal combustion engine soon learns to speak fluently in terms of 'gudgeon-pins' and 'big-ends' and 'compression-ratios'. The terminology of bones, for all that it is in Latin, is no more difficult. Lengthy as the terms often seem at first acquaintance, they are, in the long run, less cumbersome in use than 'plain English' periphrases. 'The knob behind the ear-hole' is little plainer, and less accurate, than 'mastoid process'. Moreover, 'mastoid'—unlike 'gudgeon-pin'!—is internationally understood. It is worth the trouble, therefore, to learn the language of the subject, and no apology is made for introducing the technical terms at the very outset of the descriptive section. A literal translation is often given at the first mention of a new term, to assist in remembering it and to show that it is generally simply descriptive.

For earlier Stone-Age times bones and teeth often provide valuable dating evidence also. If, for instance, we find remains of the wild pig associated with a stone industry, we can be sure that the makers of the tools lived in, or near, a temperate forest. Such a forest, in its turn, requires a climate not far removed in character from that of the present day in western Europe. Thus it can only have existed during one of the warmer (interglacial or interstadial) stages of the Pleistocene period. There may be geological evidence enabling the deposit containing the remains to be correlated with the sequence of known Pleistocene climatic events, making it possible for us to tell precisely to which warm interval the implements must belong.

Few animal species are as unequivocal in their requirements as the pig, most being adaptable to a much wider range of environments and hence affording less reliable climatic indications, but if, as is not uncommonly the case, there is available a whole assemblage of animals, the total character of the assemblage and the relative proportions of the species present may lead to useful conclusions.

For archaeological periods from the Neolithic onwards, in which the wild fauna closely resembles that of the present day, remains of man's domestic animals help to reconstruct the history of domestication, the food-habits of the human group in question and something of their economics and social organization.

Remains of man himself are extremely rarely found as fossils in the earliest archaeological periods. They may be of the utmost importance to the study of human origins and evolution and therefore call for specialist treatment. Nobody finding an early human fossil should even remove it from its position as found without first calling in every available expert witness to see it in position and vouch for its authenticity. The study of such material lies altogether outside the scope of this work and is for trained human palaeontologists only.

In the Pleistocene, man was part of his animal environment and strictly dependent on it, competing with the larger carnivores for at least part of his food. When his remains are found in the fossil condition it is because, as with the other animals, a probably violent death overtook him and his remains became scattered and buried by chance in rapidly forming sediments. Whether it is that he was, in any case, a rare animal in those earliest times, or that, because of his superior intellect he was generally able to avoid accidental death, the fact remains that human fossils are notably scarce in comparison with the remains of other mammals.

In later prehistoric times, when men gathered together in some numbers in settlements and towns, the volume of human bone-remains in and about their habitations greatly increases.

These are the raw material of the physical anthropologist who concerns himself with early races and who alone is competent to pronounce on their racial affinities. The anthropologist, however, is seldom himself an excavator, so that, in general, it is through the hands of his archaeological confrères that his material first passes. Our obligation for its condition when it reaches him is a heavy one and can only be properly discharged if we have the necessary outline of anatomical knowledge to recognize broken and fragmentary remains in the field, and are able to take the necessary steps to prevent the further deterioration of the specimens.

To the same end, if, for any reason, it is impossible to recover the human bone material, the archaeologist should at least endeavour to record some measurements in the field (p. 208 ff).

A study of ancient animal and human bones, then, is desirable from many points of view.

To zoology and palaeontology it is essential; in archaeology it cannot be dispensed with when the environments of early mankind come to be described and understood; to several other branches of biological science it affords an historical background, without which their present-day pictures are incomplete; it has an interest of its own for any person able to appreciate the mammalian body as a wonderfully designed working mechanism.

Not least, it appeals to the detective instinct in many of us, when the facts pose questions 'how?' or 'why?' to which we would fain know the answers. Sometimes it is the material, often our knowledge, that is insufficient, when we either cannot reply at all or can, at best, give only very partial answers.

With better-collected material and more workers in the field perhaps our future performance will be more impressive than it has been in the past.

2

The Animal Kingdom

+-

OF ANIMAL REMAINS the archaeologist is generally chiefly concerned with mammalian bones. This is partly because, in dealing with the animal material of the geologically brief human period, only the mammals have evolved to a sufficient extent to make their progress a useful time-indicator. Mammals are also of special interest to the archaeologist because they represent the most important group of food-animals for man, both in the hunting stage of culture and in the later food-producing stages. Their value as indicators of environment has already been mentioned.

The relative importance of mammals in the economy of early man does not, however, exclude the large remainder of the animal kingdom from our interest. Invertebrates, fish, reptiles, amphibians and birds have always, when available, figured largely on the human bill of fare, as they still do today. Where these groups possess hard parts capable of preservation as fossils, their remains, on a site of human occupation, may be just as informative as those of the usually commoner mammals. If found, such evidence should be submitted for report to the appropriate zoological authority.

Even less conspicuous contemporary creatures which, because of their small size, evidently played no part in man's food-supply, may not be without importance as indicators of environment. Among these are Foraminifera, from marine deposits and the often very small shells of land, freshwater and marine molluscs, which may accompany evidences of human occupation in archaeological deposits. These, again, must remain the objects of specialist study while we concentrate on the mammals, but unless the archaeologist recognizes their presence and collects a sample of the material for expert examination any information which they might have yielded will be lost.

It is not altogether out of place, therefore, in a book chiefly about mammalian bones, to begin with a rough outline of the whole animal kingdom, of which the mammals form only a small, if important, part.

In surveying the animal kingdom we are at once faced with the questions of classification and nomenclature, which together form the science of *Taxonomy*, which deals with orderly arrangement of things and their exact naming. To one having small acquaintance with Greek and Latin the scientific titles of zoological groups and anatomical structures are, perhaps, somewhat alarming. The use of Greek and Latin roots and forms is not mere affectation or obscurantism, but provides a relatively exact *lingua franca*, recognized by zoologists the world over, whatever their different mother-tongues.

The animal the English-speaking world knows as a 'squirrel' is to a Frenchman 'écureuil', to a German 'Eichhörnchen', but under the name *Sciurus vulgaris* every zoologist in the world who is concerned with mammals knows the animal in question. Further, this name tells us what 'squirrel' alone does not: that it is the red squirrel, and not, for example, the North American grey species, that is intended. In order that we may share in the exactitude and international comprehension which it confers a sufficient acquaintance with the classification and terminology of zoology is worth making.

Classification

Zoological classification is guided by the anatomical resemblances between animals. While no two individual men are exactly alike (unless they be identical twins), all men have very many physical features in common. They may be divided into geographical *races*, but all living races of men are inter-fertile and form the zoological unit known as a *species*, in the case of modern man labelled *Homo sapiens*.

In the past there have been other kinds of men, differing in their anatomy so much from present-day man as to have been assigned to distinct species. One of these is the extinct Neanderthal species of man, called *Homo neanderthalensis*.* Somewhat different though they were from us, nobody doubts that the Neanderthalers were men, so that they are considered to belong to the same larger zoological group as we do, the *genus Homo*. In the still remoter past lived men differing so much from the Neanderthalers and from us as to have been put into different *genera*, one of which is called *Pithecanthropus** (ape-man).

The genera *Homo*, *Pithecanthropus* and so on are, despite their differences, more alike anatomically than are men, on the one hand, and apes, on the other. The men are, therefore, classified together in a *family*, called the Hominidae, the apes in another, called Pongidae. Parallel zoological families are the Felidae (cats), Canidae (dogs), Bovidae (cattle), Cervidae (deer) and so on.

Now, apes and men, cats and dogs, cattle and deer are, respectively, more closely allied in their structure and habits than are any of the three distinct groups which they form. They are thus considered to belong to three different higher divisions, called *Orders*: the Primates (first among the mammals), the Carnivora (flesh-eaters) and the Artiodactyla (hoofed mammals with an even number of toes) respectively.

These Orders, and others, all share the similarity that their members bear their young alive and suckle them for a while, until they are able to fend for themselves. All belong to the *Class* Mammalia.

---

* Now regarded as only a sub-species of *Homo sapiens*: *H. s. neanderthalensis*. *Pithecanthropus* is now known as *Homo erectus*. The principles which the former names illustrate remain unaltered.

With the mammals, the classes Pisces (fishes), Amphibia (living in either element—water or air), Reptilia, Aves (birds), among others, all have back-bones with a cartilaginous (gristly) 'notochord', at least at some stage of their development, so that they are grouped together in the *Phylum* Chordata, with less obtrusive creatures, like the lancelet (*Amphioxus*) (Fig. 2a) which share this feature, though not having any actual bones.

The phylum Chordata is one of the primary subdivisions of the animal *Kingdom*. Parallel phyla are, for example, the Arthropoda ('joint-footed'—including crabs, lobsters, insects and spiders), the Mollusca (shell-fish, with animals less evidently shelled, like the octopus and cuttlefish), the Echinodermata ('spiny-skinned'—star-fishes, sea-urchins and sea-lilies), the Vermes (worms), the Coelenterata ('hollow-gutted'—sponges, jellyfishes, anemones, corals) and the single-celled Protozoa, a phylum which includes a few groups, like the Foraminifera, which have hard parts.

The animal Kingdom stands opposed to the vegetable Kingdom, which includes all other living things, though 'opposed' only in theory, for the actual boundaries between them, in the range of microscopic and sub-microscopic organisms, are indistinct. When we descend to bodies of extremely small dimensions, like the filter-passing viruses, the distinctions between animal, vegetable and mineral nature become exceedingly fine.

To return to the animals: the subdivisions phylum, class, order, family, genus and species are the main classificatory heads, but others (e.g. sub-classes, infra-orders and super-families) have here and there been interpolated in the full classification to mark distinctive groups within the main divisions. Expert opinions often differ as to the exact arrangement, but the main outlines are well established.

A recent classification of the Mammalia, based on G. G. Simpson, is reproduced in a somewhat abridged tabular form in Appendix B.

Nomenclature

Zoological nomenclature is the systematic naming of animals and groups of animals. It is subsidiary to classification in taxonomy, in that the establishment of a name does not prejudice reconsideration of classification in the light of increased knowledge. Its intricacies are controlled by a code of Rules, internationally agreed.

The foundation of exact nomenclature is taken to be the Tenth Edition, 1758, of the *Systema Naturae* of the Swedish zoologist and botanist Carl Linné, better known under the latinized form of his name, Linnaeus. He first established the binomial nomenclature, whereby the name of an animal species (specific name) consists of that of its genus (generic name) followed by a name (trivial name) differentiating it from other species of the same genus. The generic name is invariably written with a capital, the trivial preferably with a small letter. Thus the lion is *Felis** *leo,* the domestic cat *Felis catus.* The Rules recommend that the small letter for the trivial name should be used even where the name derives from a personal name. Thus Burchell's zebra is properly designated *Equus burchelli,* though the capital is still permissible.

To the binomial designation may be added, without punctuation, the name, or an abbreviation of the name, of the author who first described the species under that name, thus *Felis catus* Linnaeus, or with the abbreviation of the name, 'Linn.' or even merely 'L.' The author's name may be followed by the date of publication, if a matter of priority is in question, thus: '*F. catus* Linn. 1758.'

No names in use before 1758 are valid unless established by Linnaeus in the Tenth Edition or subsequently resuscitated under the Rules. For acceptance as valid, the name created for a new genus or species must be published with an adequate description of the group, preferably with a figure and, since 1931, a particular specimen in a collection must be designated as the 'type' of the genus or species. The first trivial name so published remains valid even though, by later classifiers, the species may be transferred to another genus. The original spelling, even if erroneous, must be adhered to. Thus, the periwinkle, *Litorina littorea* Linnaeus, is correctly so written, (even though, linguistically, the spelling 'Littorina' would be more correct) because the name appears in this form in the Tenth Edition. Similarly *Dama clactonianus* is the correctly-formed name for the Clacton fossil fallow-deer, in total disregard of latinity, because it was originally described as *Cervus clactonianus* but, under the Rules, its later transference to the genus *Dama,* of feminine form, does not justify the alteration of the original adjectival trivial name even to agree in gender with its new substantive.

Nor may the trivial name be changed at a later time even if an apter descriptive name seems preferable. Linnaeus described the common hare of Sweden, which grows a white coat in winter, by the name *Lepus timidus.* For a long time his name was commonly applied to the equally timid brown hare of milder climates, under the misapprehension that this was the species referred to by Linnaeus. Later, the variable hare was described as a species distinct from the brown hare and called *L. variabilis,* until it was shown that it was in fact this species, and not the brown hare, which Linnaeus had first described. The apter description *variabilis* thus became a synonym, because Linnaeus' name for the variable species had priority. The new name, *Lepus europaeus* was, therefore, applied to the brown hare.

The priority rule is observed without regard to the meaning of the name first given. The mammoth, for example, was described by Blumenbach as *Elephas primigenius* ('first-born'), but the name remains valid though later work on the development of the elephants has shown the species to be a comparatively late, extinct end-product of evolution, not an original form, as the name implies.

* Now transferred to a new genus, *Panthera.*

The International Rules, and numerous appended recommendations not having the force of agreed Rules, are complicated and are revised, amended and emended to correct abuses and misunderstandings which arise from time to time. Enough has been said to show that nomenclature, like classification, is systematic.

Palaeontology

The archaeologist is concerned not so much with living animals (save as comparative material) as with the bones representing those long dead. Though for the later periods of archaeology the wild fauna is little different from that which would be flourishing in the present (save for the depredations of man in historical times), the domestic animals of the prehistoric period differ both from their wild ancestors and from the highly bred races of today. These differences are of the greatest interest to the student of the history of domestication.

In Pleistocene times, however, there lived numerous species of animals which, today, are altogether extinct or, like the lion, for example, no longer inhabit Europe. In studying the evolution of living wild forms the zoologist has to take into account the evidence from fossil remains of extinct species, the field of the palaeontologist. The full description of the Animal Kingdom has, therefore, to include fossil material also, so that a time-dimension is introduced into descriptive zoology as well as the spatial dimensions expressed in the present and past geographical distributions of species.

Living animal species represent the very numerous terminal shoots of the genealogical tree of life. Somewhere, each springs ultimately from the common trunk. Each carries, in its anatomical structure and habits, some indications of its relationship to the rest. The numerous dead twigs and branches of the tree represent the extinct species, genera and higher grades, the actual forerunners, or the more or less close relations, of the living. Thus, if we are to study anatomical structures for the purpose of determining the species represented in the bones from archaeological sites, it is of value to know something of the historical status of the main groups represented.

Evolution

It was Lamarck (d. 1829) who first propounded the theory that all living species had developed by slow stages from more primitive and simpler forms, some of which had been preserved for us as fossils from earlier geological periods. Charles Darwin in *The Origin of Species by Means of Natural Selection* (1859), suggested that the survival to propagate their kind of those individuals best able to adapt themselves to the environment afforded a possible means by which evolutionary changes had taken place in the past. The work of geneticists has shown that the mechanism of variation and inheritance is not quite so simple as the early evolutionists had supposed, since it still remains to be shown, for example, that individually acquired characteristics, imposed by the environment, either physical or mental, can be inherited by the offspring. It is, nevertheless, clear that the process of natural selection expounded by Darwin is capable of perpetuating in the species any heritable variation favourable to survival.

If we still do not understand fully how evolution takes place, the fact that living things have evolved in the past, and are still doing so, may be taken as established. This being so, we can expect the study of fossil forms to lead us to some indications of the course taken in the evolution of the living species.

There is another approach to the problem. Study of the development of living individuals from the fertilized ovum up to maturity has shown that the individual's development (ontogeny) resembles, if without exactitude, the evolution of the species (phylogeny). Thus, the human embryo, beginning as a single cell, passes through stages reminiscent, in succession, of living invertebrate, lower vertebrate, mammalian and generalized Primate forms, before it eventually develops into a recognizably human foetus. Even after birth, the human infant retains characters, such as the powerful grasp of the hands and the inturned sole of the foot, which appear useless in a terrestrial animal destined eventually to walk erect, but which are essential to survival in the infant ape, in view of the arboreal habits of its mother and its own future destiny. It may be concluded from this, among other evidence, that man had an arboreal ancestor. .

The Geological Record

The history of the development of life on earth, of which evidence is preserved in the rocks laid down in past geological ages, bears a very striking resemblance, when tabulated, to the zoologist's table of the animal kingdom, based on living species only. Of course the geological record is very incomplete. Conditions for the preservation of fossils did not always exist when extensive parts of the sequence of the rocks were being formed, and generally only those animals with durable hard parts are represented, even when conditions for preservation were suitable. In very rare instances, as in the famous lithographic limestone of Solenhofen, Bavaria, even the impress of the soft parts and trails of living animals stranded on the then soft mud are preserved. The question of the preservation of fossils is more fully treated below (p. 204).

All life is dependent, for its maintenance, development and propagation, more or less directly on its inorganic environment. The essentials for most living forms are atmospheric oxygen, water below boiling-point and above freezing-point and inorganic salts. How life first arose, given these things, we do not know—and, perhaps, never shall know. As far as the evidence goes, all living things have had living predecessors, probably in the first stage mere microscopic specks of naked protoplasm, but even these composed of highly complicated chemical substances which we cannot yet reproduce in our laboratories. Nor do we know of what life consists or how it could have begun spontaneously, though there are many modern theories.

The geological record is necessarily blank on the subject of creatures so little apt for petrifaction and preservation, but it is supposed that the first living things were unicellular plants, like the present-day algae and bacteria, capable of synthesizing the mineral substances of earth, air and water into compounds suitable for their nutrition.

The early geological periods from which fossils have survived show only marine creatures, but already in such variety and complexity of organization as to demand vast preceding aeons and millions upon millions of generations for their elaboration. The first animal was perhaps an organism not greatly differing from the unicellular plants, which, by feeding on them, was able to divert the ready-made proteins of the vegetable kingdom to its own uses, without the necessity of compounding them for itself. This short-circuit conferred on the creature able to compass it an ecological advantage leading to multiplication of the species and the development of new and more efficient exploiters of the available resources. The animal which first preyed on another animal secured a further advantage over the rest of its kind, and so on.

Before about 500 million years ago recognizable organic remains in the rocks are exceedingly rare and their interpretation is often uncertain, yet with the Cambrian period, beginning about that time, the seas were already plentifully populated by animals with hard parts—primitive representatives of all the living phyla save only the Chordata and one other, the Bryozoa, which is unimportant in this context. Thus it seems likely that the span of time for living creatures about which we have no direct evidence is at least twice as long again as that which has elapsed since the early Cambrian.

In the Ordovician, ending about 350 million years ago, the first vertebrates, jawless fishes, appear. By the end of the next period, the Devonian, say 270 m.y.a., true bony fishes were present in great variety and from them, probably by way of the lung-fishes, had developed the first vertebrate air-breathers, the Amphibia. Primitive Reptiles, the first mainly terrestrial class of vertebrates, had appeared by the end of the Carboniferous, about 225 m.y.a.

Exploitation of marine environment in the Palaeozoic era led some species to grow big and strong, mobile and aggressive. Others remained sedentary or sluggish but developed heavy shells or armoured carapaces. More, again, were scavengers, adapted to nourish themselves with materials which the larger and more active rejected or excreted. Still more survived the slaughter of the weak and defenceless by remaining small, inconspicuous and exceedingly prolific, so that, if their tens of millions perished, a few contrived to survive to perpetuate their kind through sheer weight of numbers. Thus, the waters became so filled with life that they could no longer contain it. Some species, colonizing the shallows and beaches to escape their natural enemies and find other living-space, learned to survive intermittent deprivation of their natural element between tides and became increasingly independent of salt water. It was not the strong and swift predator of the Devonian seas which took the great step on to dry land, but an unspecialized, soft-bodied lung-fish, an extremely unimportant member of the marine community. So, also, in the terrestrial sphere, at the transition from the Palaeozoic to the Mesozoic, it was the reptiles which began to diversify and proliferate and fill the new unexploited land environment, but even before they had reached their climax the next great change had already taken place and their successors were in being. Before the end of the Carboniferous a comparatively obscure, generalized Order of reptiles had appeared, the Theromorpha (beast-shaped). The more enterprising Orders became highly specialized for a particular way of life, during the Permian and throughout the succeeding Mesozoic era (Triassic, Jurassic and Cretaceous periods).

The climax of reptilian diversity was reached in the Jurassic, ending about 110 m.y.a. Many species developed, some of enormous size and fantastic form, both in the vegetarian and the carnivorous ways of life. Some were sluggish and heavily armoured, others of enormous bulk and probably chiefly aquatic in habit. The larger flesh-eaters had terrifying arrays of teeth. Some of the smaller and lighter species had a bipedal gait and probably could run rapidly. Others, again, took once more to the seas and preyed predominantly on fish; still more developed wings and invaded the air.

During all this time there existed alongside the dominant reptiles small primitive mammals, derived as early as the Triassic probably from the Theromorpha. Until the end of the Cretaceous, about 70 million years ago, they remained inconspicuous, small in size and unimportant, but apparently climatic and other environmental changes at about this time caused the extinction of whole Orders of specialized reptiles and gave the mammals their opportunity. The development of the typical mammalian coat of hair facilitated maintenance of a fairly high body-temperature despite fluctuations in the temperature of their surroundings, and this permitted continuance of physiological activity in colder seasons. Abandonment of the egg-laying habit and the prolongation of the care of their young to a more advanced stage of development also favoured survival. When the decline of reptilian competition opened varied environments to its occupation the Class was able to profit from the change and soon filled every available biotope with types specially adapted to exploit them.

All this did not happen at once. In the Palaeocene, Eocene and Oligocene, the opening periods of the Tertiary era, up to about 30 m.y.a., some of the beasts look very strange to our eyes, being primitive and unspecialized, partaking in one species of the characters of several of the Orders which are today quite distinct in our minds. By the end of the Oligocene, however, even the eye untrained in zoology can recognize and distinguish in restoration primitive carnivores, horses, elephants, rhinoceroses, deer and so on which, if unfamiliar in detail, nevertheless clearly show basic features which we know in their living descendants.

As with the reptiles, already long before the maximum diversity and specialization of the Class was attained, some seemingly unimportant, unspecialized branch, probably in this instance from the Insectivore Order, had taken the next major evolutionary step, forsaking the dangerous and overcrowded ground for the trees and giving rise to a new Order, the Primates. The early representatives of the Order to which we belong resembled our tree-shrews, tarsiers and lemurs.

Before the end of the Oligocene there are already, branched from this modest stem, distinct monkeys and small apes, the latter probably ancestral to the living gibbons. During the 30 million years or so of the Miocene and Pliocene, the later Tertiary periods, the fauna assumes an increasingly modern appearance, though some families, such as that of the giraffes, for example, appear to have attained a development and variety which they have since lost. Specialization has increased: whales, seals, manatees and otters have adopted in their own degrees the aquatic way of life from which there can be no evolutionary retreat. Terrestrial quadrupeds such as horses and cattle have lost three or more of their primitive five toes in favour of hooves, highly adapted to their way of life, but in a corresponding degree useless for any function save locomotion. Even the comparatively adaptable living apes have become so specialized for life in the forest that they can progress but clumsily on level ground; the cats have all but lost their molar teeth, so that, if an animal diet should fail, they must starve. Examples could be multiplied. Only man, among the higher mammals, has retained most of his primitive, generalized equipment. If he is but a poor swimmer compared with a seal, inferior as a climber to a monkey or a gibbon, far slower afoot than a horse and vastly weaker than an elephant, he can outdo most animals in any activity save their own specialities and out-manipulate and outwit them all.

We have no positive evidence of Hominids until the last few million years—though recent work suggests that man's family may have been separated from that of the apes as far back as the Oligocene. The living apes exhibit their own peculiar specializations of teeth and jaws, which are found in their remote fossil ancestors also. If man's ancestors were already by then distinct, we still lack most of the intervening links in the chain of evolution.

Primitive, but undoubted, men first appear perhaps half a million years ago, from whom we can trace some probable lines for our own descent. If one may argue from the course which evolution has taken with other groups, the primitive stem which gave rise to man divided from that of the living great apes early in the course of their own differentiation, so that we may expect to find our common ancestor not later than the Miocene and perhaps much earlier.

From this brief sketch of zoological evolution can be drawn some basic principles applicable, *mutatis mutandis*, to man as much as to the rest of the animal kingdom. In the geological record we have seen palaeontological history repeating its revolutions, first with invertebrates and fishes, then with amphibia and reptiles, then with the mammals as a whole and finally with the Primates and man. The process, as in human history, is one of foundation, development, climax, decline and extinction, or at most a much modified survival. A branch insignificant in numbers and influence in contemporary life has its origin near the root of the currently dominant stem, while this becomes more and more floridly differentiated and specialized towards its apogee. When conditions change or a new vacant environment is opened up, the groups unable to adapt themselves sufficiently rapidly to new conditions are overtaken in the race for dominance. The more plastic and generalized branches survive, flourish in their turn, throw out a profusion of new shoots, each in succession more closely adapted to the particular environment, each in its turn doomed to extinction or relegation to obscurity at any serious change in its conditions of life.

Too great specialization is thus seen, in the long view, to carry its own threat of stagnation, or even extinction, for the group—and yet, while conditions remain unchanged, there is a premium on a high degree of specialist adaptation, which the large majority of groups inevitably pursues. In man, the generalized body and limbs have been to a large extent preserved. The specialization on which his evolution has been centred is in the development of brain, reason and intellect. Out of this our whole complex society has grown. Not only have we adapted ourselves to our environment, we have to some extent learned to control it and alter it to our own advantage. If one may look forward to the future development of humanity it seems likely that it is in the structure of human society that adaptive changes must follow the mechanization of the environment and the breakneck speed of technical advance with which humanity has not yet learned to keep pace.

It may appear that we have digressed rather far from the subject of mammalian bones, but the whole question of physical specialization and adaptation in the mammals is most apposite to our study.

It is a fact that most living creatures are most wonderfully adapted, physically, to live the sort of life which their species has adopted. Whatever the mechanism of adaptation, the form of the adapted structure is closely related to its function. Thus, a sharp-edged cheek-tooth could scarcely belong to an animal whose principal diet was grass, which such a tooth would be quite unfitted to masticate. Nor could an animal without upper incisors possibly contrive to live on flesh, even if otherwise fitted to obtain it. So, from the special structures shown by bones and teeth, we may be able to determine the species to which they belonged, or at least the larger group.

Animal Groups of Particular Interest

Though, theoretically, the archaeological student of bones is interested in any animal remains which may be found in association with archaeological objects and structures, in practice the field of his interest is concentrated upon the Mammalia and, within this Class, on a comparatively small number of genera and species in any Order.

In the Old World, for example, we can afford to ignore completely those groups whose past and present distribution is confined to the New, geographically separated from us at least since early Tertiary times. In Europe, many of the long list of Australasian, Asiatic and African mammals may similarly be omitted as being unknown in our human environment, even in the Pleistocene. Again, in studying a Neolithic or later site, the extinct Pleistocene species may be discounted.

Thus we can construct, for a given geographical region and archaeological period, a list of the zoological groups likely to be encountered and to prove informative, to which our osteological study may be confined.

For Western Europe, such a list, based on Simpson's classification (see Appendix B),would perhaps read as follows:—

Infra-class Eutheria ('true beasts').
 Cohort Unguiculata: the 3 Orders Insectivora,
   Chiroptera and Primates.
  Glires: the Order Rodentia.
  Mutica: perhaps the Order Cetacea.
  Ferungulata: the Orders Carnivora, Proboscidea, Perissodactyla, Artiodactyla.

Taking these Orders one by one and subdividing, the significant lower groups may be much reduced in numbers, as follows:—

INSECTIVORA. The only members of this, the most primitive Order, likely to be of interest to the archaeologist are the genera *Talpa* (mole), *Sorex* (shrews) and *Erinaceus* (hedgehog).

CHIROPTERA ('hand-winged', bats). These are rarely found as fossils, save in caves, and should, in any case, be studied by a specialist. The list for Western Europe would probably include only living European species.

PRIMATES. Apart from man, the only fossils of possible interest to archaeologists are very rare Pleistocene monkeys and even rarer anthropoid apes. These would certainly be confined to the earlier Pleistocene. Man we shall study in some detail because his remains, as burials or cremations, are not uncommon from the Mesolithic onwards. The study of Pleistocene human remains, or of other extinct Primates, is a subject for the expert palaeontologist.

RODENTIA. There are very many possibly significant genera and species in this varied and widespread Order. Their detailed study is a specialist matter, but acquaintance with some of the genera of larger bodily dimensions would not be out of place; among these are, *Castor* and *Trogontherium* (beavers), *Sciurus* (squirrel), *Lepus* (hare), *Myodes* (lemming), *Arctomys* (marmot). At least rodent remains should be recognized as such by the student.

CETACEA (whales, dolphins, etc.). Occasionally, through chance, cast-up specimens, members of this Order became the food animals of prehistoric man at coastal sites. Owing to their marine habit they were never economically or environmentally important until man became a seafarer.

CARNIVORA. Many extinct and living species are of interest, mainly terrestrial (the Fissipedia—'divided feet') but some aquatic (Pinnipedia —'paddle-footed'—seals, walruses, etc.). The latter, like the whales, are likely to be encountered only on coasts and by estuaries. Carnivores are regularly associated with man from the earliest times, representatives of the Families Ursidae (bears), Canidae (dogs, wolves, foxes), Mustelidae (marten, badger, stoat, weasel, otter (*Lutra*)), Felidae (lion, lynx and other cats). Hyaenidae (hyaena, especially in caves). The Viverridae (e.g., civet, mongoose) appear in Europe only in the south and east, within human times. The Procyonidae are almost entirely New World (raccoon), but isolated specimens attributable to the family are known from the late Pliocene and earliest Pleistocene in Europe, e.g., *Parailurus* from the Red Crag. We shall have to examine members of most of these groups.

PROBOSCIDEA. In Africa, the extinct *Dinotherium*, really a Pliocene type, was the contemporary of early man, and in Europe *Mastodon* similarly survived into the First Interglacial (horizon of the Cromer Forest Bed). However, we are generally concerned here only with the true elephants, the temperate-climate species, *Elephas meridionalis*, *E. antiquus* and *E. trogontherii* and the cold-climate mammoth, *E. primigenius*, now all extinct.

PERISSODACTYLA (ungulates with an odd number of toes). Only two Families of this decadent group concern us in this context, the Equidae (horses) and the Rhinocerotidae (rhinoceroses). One extinct genus of Equidae, *Hipparion*, the three-toed 'horse', just survives into human times, though properly Pliocene. The true horses (*Equus*), including asses and onager, survived in the wild state in Eastern Europe up to recent historic times, but, in the West, became extinct before the end of the Pleistocene. The domesticated horse arrived from the Near East with Bronze-Age invaders.

The Rhinocerotidae have all been extinct in Europe since the Pleistocene. Three temperate-climate species and one of cold periods are of importance: *Dicerorhinus etruscus*, *D. kirchbergensis* (=*merckii*, *leptorhinus*), *D. hemitoechus*, and the woolly rhinoceros, *Tichorhinus antiquitatis*. They are valuable as indicators of climate and environment; the first is limited in time to the Pliocene and First Interglacial.

ARTIODACTYLA (even-toed ungulates). This extremely widespread and varied Order embraces all the larger herbivores, apart from the above. Two sub-Orders interest us:—(1) the Suiformes ('pig-shaped'), represented in our region by *Sus scrofa*, the wild pig, requiring temperate forest, and *Hippopotamus amphibius*, a member of our freshwater fauna up to the Last Interglacial. The presence of the latter is a guarantee of a climate with mild winters. (2) the Ruminantia. The Families Cervidae (deer) and Bovidae (cattle) include many genera, of which the following are of importance to us in Western Europe: Cervidae. *Dama clactonianus*, an extinct fallow-deer, is dated with some certainty to the Great Interglacial. *D. dama* occurred in the Last Interglacial, died out, and was, it seems, re-introduced by the Romans. *Cervus elaphus*, the red deer, is properly a forest animal. Its modern confinement to mountain and moorland is the work of civilization. *Megaceros eurycerus*, the giant deer, ranges from the early Pleistocene up to the Alleröd period of the early Postglacial, at which time it was very plentiful, especially in Ireland. *Alces*, the elk, is a bark-feeder and, therefore, an exclusively forest animal. In Britain it is known in the Mesolithic but survives today in eastern and northern Europe. *Rangifer tarandus*, the reindeer, is a dweller in arctic and sub-arctic surroundings, it is, therefore, certainly indicative of cold climate wherever it is found. *Capreolus caprea*, the roe-deer, is today confined in Britain to Scotland. It is another forest species, was not uncommon in the south at least as late as mediaeval times, and survives on the Continent.

Bovidae, sub-fam. Bovinae, includes two important genera: *Bos* (cattle, both wild, *B. primigenius*, and domesticated, *B. taurus*) and *Bison*, *B. priscus*, the extinct large-horned bison, and *B. bonasus,* the European living bison, still just surviving in the wild state in the forest reserve of Bialowieza, Poland.

Sub-family Caprinae. The genus *Capra* (goat) both wild, e.g., *C. ibex*, and domesticated, *C. hircus,* are almost indistinguishable* save by fairly complete skulls or horn-cores from *Ovis* (sheep), which is unrepresented by any European wild species. The mouflon, *Ovis musimon*, of the Near East is probably, in part, the ancestor of domesticated breeds. *Ovibos moschatus*, the musk-ox, is a former representative of the sub-arctic fauna in Western Europe. It is now restricted to sub-polar regions. *Rupicapra*, the chamois, is today confined to the Alpine region. In the Pleistocene it was more widespread and occurs with Upper Palaeolithic remains. So also for the saiga-'antelope', a branch of the same sub-family, *Saiga tartarica*. This is a cold-steppe dweller, now occurring only in Siberia.

* But see Boessneck's recent work referred to on p. 145.

3

The Vertebrate and
Mammalian Skeleton as a Whole

THE SKELETON OF THE CLASS MAMMALIA is a somewhat specialized and improved version of the generalized vertebrate skeleton. Most vertebrates have a largely ossified internal skeleton, conferring rigidity on the body and limbs yet permitting free movement at the articulations of the bones. This *endoskeleton* is in contrast with the *exoskeleton* of the arthropods, which forms a hard, jointed, chitinous armour enclosing the musculature and soft parts. Such an exoskeleton has the disadvantage that it must periodically be shed as a whole and be renewed in a larger size to enable the animal to grow. The endoskeleton, therefore, if not affording comparable protection, represents a practical advance in organization, in that it permits greater latitude of movement at the joints, economizes material and does not interfere with the continuous growth of the body to its adult proportions. It also has important protective functions.

Some descriptive terms used in anatomy must be introduced here. They greatly facilitate exact description and prevent mistakes and misunderstandings which, without them, could be avoided only by continual explanation and circumlocutions.

The body in the vertebrates is, save for the viscera (internal organs), bilaterally symmetrical about a median plane. This plane passes roughly along the sagittal (fore-and-aft) suture in the roof of the skull and is called the *median sagittal plane* (abbreviated to M.S.P.). Other planes parallel to it and structures lying in such a plane are also described as *sagittal*.

A structure relatively further to one or other side of the M.S.P. is described as *lateral*. One which is relatively nearer to it is called *medial*.

The terms *anterior*, *posterior*, *superior* and *inferior*, though widely used when their meaning is not in doubt, may be ambiguous, according to the attitude of the animal or part of the animal described. What is the 'anterior' surface of the trunk in man, standing erect, becomes the 'inferior' surface in a quadruped on all fours and might be regarded as the 'superior' in a sloth, which habitually suspends itself upside down! What is meant by the 'superior' surface of the hand depends on the attitude in which it is held. In human anatomy these terms are used to denote the relative situation of structures, on the understanding that the subject is standing erect, arms at the sides and palms of the hands to the front. Where we are dealing with quadrupeds as well as man the terms *dorsal* (towards the back), *ventral* (towards the stomach), *cranial* or *oral* (towards skull or mouth) and *caudal* or *aboral* (towards the tail or away from the mouth) are more exact. *Transverse* (athwart the body, at right angles to the M.S.P.) is a useful term. It refers to orientation rather than position.

In describing the limbs, the terms *proximal* (close to) and *distal* (distant from) are used to convey the position of structures relative to the vertebral column. Thus the proximal end of a femur (thigh-bone) is that which articulates with the pelvis, the distal end that which meets the tibia (shin-bone) at the knee-joint. The proximal phalanx ('joint') of a finger is the bone next the joint at the knuckle.

Special descriptive terminology is also necessary for hands, feet and teeth.

Hands, feet, paws, hooves, flippers or parts of the wings (in a bat or a bird) are collectively described as *extremities*. The fore-extremity is called the *manus* (hand) and the hind-extremity is called the *pes* (foot). This terminology is not affected by the special form taken by the extremities in a particular case. The manus, whatever its attitude, has a *palmar* and a *volar* (back of the hand) aspect and surface; the pes a *plantar* (sole) and a *dorsal* (back).

In teeth, the five ordinary aspects are described with reference to the M.S.P., the tooth-row being considered as extended in a straight line laterally from it. The surface of a tooth facing the M.S.P., in this conventional attitude, is described as *mesial* (towards the middle); that facing away from the M.S.P. is the *distal*. The surface presented to the tongue is the *lingual*; that facing the cheek the *buccal*. The chewing-surface is called the *occlusal* (closing against its opposite number), a term which is unambiguous whether the tooth belongs to the upper or lower set. The aspect from the root-end of a tooth, not frequently described, is the *radical* aspect. These terms are equally applicable to dentitions as different as those of man and elephant.

'Prone' describes the position of the whole body lying face downwards, 'supine' that when it is lying on the back. The terms are extended to the palm ('face') of the hand when the forearm is bent upwards to a right angle with the upper arm and the palm turned respectively downwards and upwards ('in pronation' and 'in supination').

A joint between two bones is said to be *flexed* when the bones form an angle, *extended* when their shafts lie more or less in the same straight line. In addition to flexion and extension, the limbs in less specialized mammals, particularly in the Primates, can be *abducted* (arms spread, legs straddled) and *adducted* (arms at the sides, legs together) as well as somewhat *rotated* on their own axes. These latter movements are very restricted in most quadrupeds.

The main axis of the vertebrate body originated as a mere cartilaginous rod, the notochord. In a primitive aquatic Chordate like

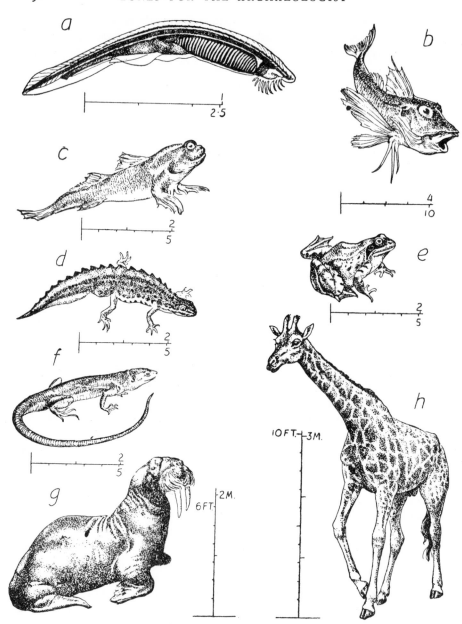

FIG 2.   Some varied living members of the Chordate phylum:
(a) *Amphioxus* (pp. 25, 39), a lower Chordate; (b) Gurnard (p. 39),
a marine fish; (c) Mud-skipper (p. 39), a fish of partly terrestrial
habit; (d) Crested newt, a tailed amphibian (p. 39); (e) Frog (p. 39),
a tailless amphibian; (f) Lizard (p. 39), a reptile, altogether terrestrial; (g) Walrus (p. 40) a marine mammal; (h) Giraffe, a specialized
terrestrial mammal (pp. 40, 105).

Amphioxus (the lancelet) (Fig. 2a) this constitutes the whole skeleton. In the true vertebrates the notochord is superseded, at least in the adult individual, by a chain of ossifications which have taken place round it. These ossifications are the bony bodies of the *vertebrae*. Dorsally from the body of each vertebra springs an arch enclosing a large foramen, or opening, through which the spinal chord passes. The conjoined arches of the vertebrae form a jointed bony tube enclosing this nervous axis of the body, protecting it from injury while permitting a small amount of movement between adjacent vertebrae and providing foramina (holes) for the passage of nervous and vascular (vessel) branches between each pair, leading to other parts of the body. The whole structure is called the *vertebral column*, and is prolonged posteriorly in most species into a more or less well-developed tail.

To some of the vertebrae are attached on each side *ribs*, which curve round the sides of the trunk and meet ventrally, either directly or through costal (rib) cartilages (gristly prolongations of the actual bony ribs) with the *sternum* (breast-bone). Together, these structures form a capacious bony cage, called the *thorax,* which encloses, protects, and to a variable extent supports, the vital organs—heart and large blood vessels, lungs and digestive organs. The skull, vertebral column, ribs and sternum form the *axial skeleton.*

To the axial skeleton are attached two pairs of appendages, in higher vertebrates the limbs, in fishes forming fins. These constitute the *appendicular skeleton.* Limbs are evidently derived from fins by the processes of evolution. Some reptiles, such as the snakes and slow-worm (really a lizard) have secondarily lost the limbs. Even some mammals, especially those which have adopted a permanently aquatic habit, such as whales and seals, have much modified limbs, and the former have only useless vestiges of the hinder pair.

Among living fishes the gurnards (Fig. 2b), bottom-feeding sea fishes, 'walk' on the extended rays of the pectoral (breast) fins, and the partly terrestrial mud-skippers (Fig. 2c), progress when out of the water in a series of hops, propelled and supported by the pectorals. Rayed fins are not the true intermediates. Lobe-fins of Coelacanths preceded tetrapod limbs.

Another step in limb development is seen in the amphibia, e.g., newts and frogs, and in some lower reptiles. In the newt, the limbs are little used in progression, even in the water, the tail, as in fishes, being the principal organ of propulsion. Out of water newts can do little more than crawl on their bellies, propelled, but not really supported, by the weak limbs (Fig. 2d). The frog is, of course, much better adapted to land life (Fig. 2e). Both fore and hind limbs stand out at right angles to the trunk, the bend at the knee and elbow being, in both cases alike, in a transverse and dorso-ventral plane. This condition is also seen in the tortoises and lizards. For a terrestrial quadruped the arrangement is obviously ill suited, mechanically, to rapid or sustained progression, and is uneconomical of muscular energy owing to the lateral distance of the point of support from the load.

A further development is to bring the points of support by the extremities well under the body. It was first achieved in the more active reptiles by a rotation of the forelimb at the joint with the shoulder-blade, so that the elbow pointed backwards, and a similar forward rotation of the hind limb at the hip to bring the knee forward. This is generally accompanied by a further rotation of the distal segment of the fore-limb (forearm) so as to bring the manus to point in the direction of progression, as does the pes already. A mammal in which this second rotation has apparently once more been reversed is the walrus (Fig. 2g), in which the manus is turned backwards when the animal is ashore. In all the mammals with which we are concerned the permanent attitude of the fore-limb includes this second rotation or, in some species with separate movable forearm bones, it is attainable voluntarily by the movement of pronation of the manus.

The Mammalian Skeleton

The Class Mammalia includes such diverse terrestrial animals as horses and men, elephants and pygmy shrews, giraffes and tigers. Some are specially adapted to marine and arboreal or aerial life, such as whales and manatees on the one hand and monkeys, squirrels, flying phalangers and bats on the other. Despite their enormous differences in size, form and habits, all conform to a common pattern, pointing to their original derivation from a single ancestral mammal which had developed that pattern at an early stage. The original placental mammal was doubtless a terrestrial quadruped, probably of small size. It had four more or less equally developed limbs with five toes in manus and pes and probably put the whole sole of the foot to the ground in walking. It had a coat of hair to assist maintenance of a constant high body-temperature and a longish, unspecialized tail. Characteristic anatomical details included only seven cervical (neck) vertebrae, a brain large in size for its stature in comparison with the contemporary reptiles, forty-four rather simple permanent teeth in four characteristic functional groups and a number of soft structures which do not greatly concern us in this context, such as a diaphragm muscle separating the thoracic from the abdominal cavity, a four-chambered heart and mammary glands.

The structure of all living and extinct placental mammals is based on this generalized pattern. Very great changes in bodily size and proportions have taken place in some orders and families and specializations for particular habitats and ways of life have been adopted, but such changes in the basic pattern as have occurred have all been in the direction of simplification, degeneration, and even loss, of some of the structural units. Whalebone whales, for example, living in the sea and feeding on plankton, chiefly small crustaceans, have no need of a hairy coat, teeth, claws or even of hind limbs. All these struc-

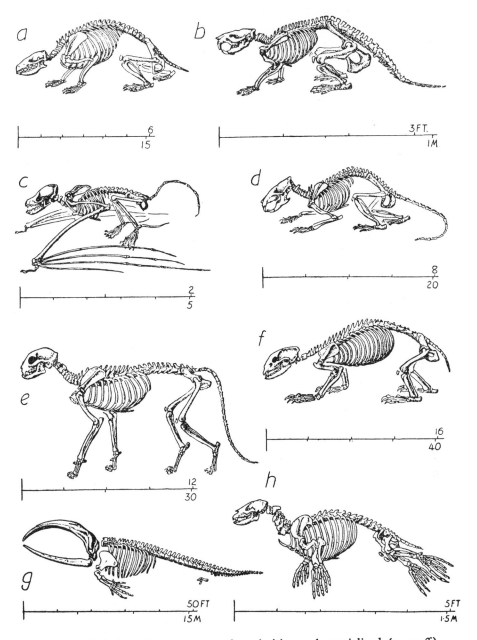

FIG 3.   Skeletons of some mammals, primitive and specialized (p. 42 ff),
(a) Insectivore (hedgehog); (b) and (d) Rodents (beaver, rat);
(c) a Chiropter (bat); (e), (f) Fissipede carnivores (cat, badger);
(g) a Cetacean (Greenland whale); (h) a Pinnipede carnivore (seal).

tures have degenerated almost to vanishing point, though vestiges of them are found in very young individuals and, in the case of the hind limbs, persist even in adulthood, though useless and not even visible externally. Nevertheless, the whales, with their seven cervical vertebrae, warm blood and mammary glands, speak eloquently of their true mammalian nature and ancestry. In land mammals the most usual reductions attendant upon specialization are in the numbers of toes and of teeth and in the posture and development of the limbs.

The Orders which are least specialized, and which, therefore, most closely resemble in structure and habits the original generalized quadruped mammalian ancestor, include the Insectivora, the Primates, many rodents and some of the less specialized carnivores, such as bears and badgers. All these have the full complement of toes and walk habitually sole to the ground—the *plantigrade* gait (Fig. 3, a, b, d, f). Their dentitions, however, are all somewhat specialized and reduced, particularly in the case of some of the rodents, and few have the complete dentition of forty-four teeth—the mole, among the common insectivores, is an exception.

The next stage in terrestrial limb-specialization is that of the *digitigrades*, the toe-walkers, including most of the Carnivora, e.g., cat (Fig. 3e) and dog. The rise to the toes has been accompanied by a great increase in length of the foot-bones and this 'higher-geared' lever enables the animal to run more quickly and leap further than the comparable plantigrades. In the matter of teeth, a high degree of specialization for flesh-eating is the rule, generally associated with severe reductions, especially loss or degeneration of molars, these grinding teeth being inessential for a purely flesh diet.

In parallel with the improved speed afoot of the flesh-eaters, their prey, the larger herbivores, have carried the process of limb-specialization a stage further, engaging 'top gear', as it were, by rising to the very tips of the extremities, the nails of the toes, which have become much modified as hooves. These Ungulates, or hoofed mammals, are without exception *unguligrade*, hoof-walkers (Fig. 4), using the last inch of length in their limbs to increase their speed and relying mainly on flight to escape predators. Extreme specialization of herbivorous teeth and reduction in number of toes has been attained in this group by the horse.

Ungulate specialization, with the accompanying increase of terrestrial speed and agility, depends on reduction in adaptability to any other limb-function save progression. The horse, an animal of the dry steppes, is ill-adapted for boggy or rocky ground and could, by no stretch of the imagination, dig a hole or climb a tree, activities which are commonplace in the carnivorous dog and cat, respectively. Without grass, cattle cannot survive in nature, but a bear can make a livelihood out of berries, roots, fish and small game where more substantial fare is lacking.

Specialization, entailing, first, loss of full function and, ultimately, of the bony structural units themselves, is a long process and once achieved by a species is virtually irreversible. We have already glanced at the whales, a highly successful retrogressive adaptation to the conditions of life of a fish. The fishes at least have ventral fins and, should some watery cataclysm destroy all terrestrial life, it is not inconceivable that

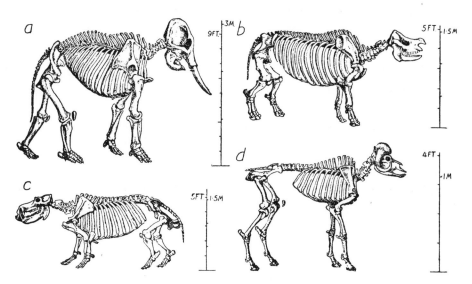

FIG 4.   Skeletons of four Ungulates: (a) elephant, (b) rhinoceros, (c) hippopotamus, (d) musk-ox, showing reduction of toes with increasing
specialization—5 toes, 3 toes, 4 toes, 2 toes respectively (p. 42).

their progeny should eventually repopulate the dry land, as once it did before. An air-breathing leviathan, lacking all but functionless vestiges of the hind limbs and their connections with the trunk, even though less remotely related to a four-legged terrestrial form, would clearly never compass that feat of evolution-in-reverse.   Even the almost exclusively aerial Chiroptera, the bats, would be better suited for the role.

It was not the highly-specialized ungulate stem, nor even those of the adaptable carnivores or successful rodents which gave rise to man, the most advanced mammalian experiment of Nature to date. Far back, some small insectivore with omnivorous habits and teeth, with all five toes, a plantigrade gait, a collar-bone and separate forearm bones gave rise to the Primates. Progress in physical evolution demands plasticity of structure. Such a beast as we have imagined for the Primate ancestor has all the structural essentials of man—the only changes necessary for the transmutation are of proportion and degree, not of kind.

Man's particular specialization is in brain. Reason is essentially flexible and adaptive and we have not yet seen the limits of its achievements even in the most unpromising physical and mental environments. Nevertheless, the giant intellect unsupported by a manipulative hand would have been impotent to construct tools and inanimate engines. The hand, in its turn, depended on erect posture, emancipating the forelimb from the relentless task of locomotion, to which in most quadrupeds it is the slave. Indeed, it seems now that we have, in the South African fossil Australopithecines, a stage possibly parallel with the direct line of human evolution where the erect posture and the free hand have been attained while the brain still lags behind.

And so, save for his adaptable hands and brain, man is a rather primitive and unspecialized mammal. In view of this, and because our own bodies are somewhat familiar to us all, human anatomy makes a good starting-point for many comparative considerations of mammalian structure.

In describing human bone-anatomy reference has from time to time been made to other, lower, members of the mammalian Class. Among others the dog is much used in comparison, the reason for this choice being that the dog is not only a beast familiar to everybody, but at the same time is a fairly typical and not too highly specialized quadruped which may, with reservations, be taken as representing many others.

4

The Skull

As the leading part of the bodily axis, the skull has three important functions:—

1. To enclose and protect the brain, relatively large in the mammals, the highly-developed nerve-centre and control of the whole organism. This delicate organ governs not only the voluntary actions of its owner but also all the many automatic unconscious and instinctive motions of the body and limbs. Its mechanical support and protection from outside injury are therefore vital functions.

2. To accommodate the specialized sense-organs, those of smell, sight, hearing and taste, the sense of touch being unequally distributed over the whole body, but developed in a particularly high degree on the surface of the face and in the mouth-parts, especially the tongue. The location of the most sensitive receptors at the extreme anterior end of the animal is obviously an important feature.

3. To carry the feeding apparatus. The mouth and jaws, aided to a variable extent by the fore-limbs, are chiefly concerned in seizing, holding, cutting up and masticating food, the presence of which has first been perceived by the sensory organs. Apart from taking food, the mouth-parts are, in many quadrupeds, the only available instruments for grasping and manipulating inanimate objects.

The proportions assumed by a mammalian skull depend on the relative importance of these three functions in the life of the animal. In most quadrupeds the more primitive of the senses, touch and smell, are very highly developed. Smell is often particularly acute and is used both to locate and distinguish food and to warn of the approach of enemies or friends, besides being a source of general information about the surroundings. Touch comes into play only on contact or near-contact. In quadrupeds much dependent on smell and touch, e.g. those of nocturnal habit, the exploring nose is relatively long. Much of the behaviour of lower mammals consists of automatic or instinctive responses to stimuli, so that the cerebral part of the skull does not need to be very large to suffice in its role of brain-case. Consequently, the sensory and feeding part of the skull, the facial part, is large in proportion to the cerebral part.

In arboreal animals, the emphasis is on the sense of sight rather than on smell, so that a long snout which partially interrupts the field of vision would be rather a liability than an asset. Motor dexterity and intelligence are more helpful than an acute sense of smell, so that, in the Primates, the snout tends to be short and the brain-pan relatively large. The correlation of terrestrial quadruped habit and the development of the muzzle is well seen in the baboons, which, of all the monkeys, are the least arboreal and have the longest snouts. This is evidently a re-adaptation in an animal of arboreal ancestry to life in open country. The shortening of the muzzle consequent on raising the nose far from the ground

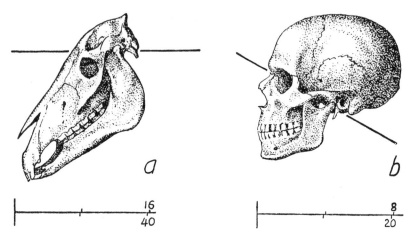

FIG 5. Skulls of horse and man, in profile, to show difference in cerebral and facial development. The line in both cases passes through the point of junction of frontal and nasal bones (nasion) and the anterior margin of the foramen magnum (basion). The brain-case lies above it, the face and jaws below it.

is most clearly seen in modern man, with his large brain, small nose and vertical face. Though terrestrial in habit, his presumably arboreal ancestry has promoted an erect posture and fostered reliance on sight and sound to the almost complete exclusion of the sense of smell. On returning to the ground, his ancestors, unlike the baboons, never again dropped their noses to pick up scent. The hands being free, the jaws are no longer needed for fighting, catching and holding prey. The cerebral part of the skull is very large, occupying some two-thirds of the area of the lateral profile, while in the horse, a highly specialized terrestrial ungulate, the proportion of brain-pan to the whole profile is less than one-fourth.

Thus, the relative proportions of the cerebral and facial parts of a skull are some guide to the cerebral status and habits of the animal. The boundary between the parts is roughly taken as a straight line drawn between the junction of frontal and nasal bones and the anterior margin of the foramen magnum (Fig. 5).

In quadrupeds the direction of progress is a continuation of the main axis of the body. The cerebral part of the skull necessarily lies in this line and the facial parts, prolonged into a more or less long snout, lie in front of it. In man, on the other hand, and to a lesser extent in the great apes, because of the erect posture the base of the skull has acquired a flexure, so that the facial parts, instead of lying in the same general line as the vertebral column and the cerebral part of the skull directly attached to it, tend to come rather ventral to it. In this way, the face continues to be directed forwards on the new line of progress, though the main axis of the body has been raised to the vertical position.

Though this striking difference appears, superficially, to rest on some basic difference in structure, the impression is mistaken, for it is due entirely to differences of proportion and form in the homologous bones. If we compare, bone for bone, the skulls of man and of a dog—a fairly generalized quadruped—it will readily be seen that this is so (Figs. 6 and 7).

The human skull as a whole (Fig. 6 p. 49)

The skull consists of two main parts, articulated together, the *cranium* proper and the *mandible* (lower jaw).

The cranium may be conveniently divided into two regions, the *cerebral,* containing the brain, and the *facial* parts. The cerebral part has a vault, or roof, and a base, side walls and a strongly-curved posterior (dorsal) wall. The facial parts are well defined externally, but internally their boundaries are less distinct, some bones contributing both to the brain-case and to the orbits (eye-sockets) and nasal structures. The two latter are, strictly, part of the face.

The vault of a human cranium, deprived of the base and face, a condition not uncommon in fossil skulls, is called a *calotte* (Fr. skull-cap), *calvarium* (plur. *calvaria*) or *calvaria* (plur. *calvariae*). The Oxford Dictionary gives both of the latter alternatives.

The cranium is formed of numerous bones, meeting, generally, edge to edge and there joined, but not in youth fused (synostosed), with their neighbours at more or less complexly denticulate *sutures* (seams). The general course of these sutures is very constant among different individuals, though the detail varies greatly.

Sutures, save for those of the vault which have special names, are known by a designation compounded of the names of the bones meeting at those sutures, e.g. 'sphenotemporal' suture, 'fronto-malar' suture or 'inter-nasal' suture.

Some skull sutures are obliterated in later life by synostosis of the adjacent bones. When the course taken by synostosis in a species has been well studied it is possible to estimate the age of an individual by study of the degree of obliteration of sutures (p. 222).

The cranial bones are not solid, but have relatively thin *inner* and *outer tables* of dense bone with a cancellous (spongy) bony tissue between them, called the *diploë*. This arrangement has the functional advantage of great strength and resistance to external pressure while saving weight. Some slight yielding or elasticity at the open sutures between the bones also has a protective effect.

The thickness of the bones of the brain-case is variable, being less where they are deeply protected by muscles and soft tissues, as at the nape of the neck and at the temples, greater where it is reinforced by little save the thin scalp, as in the vault. The thickness, even of the vault, also varies greatly among individuals, according to age, sex and build.

The most striking feature of the cranium in man is the extensive, almost globular, brain-case, wider behind and narrowing somewhat to the temples in front. The forehead (*frontal region*) rises more or less steeply from the brows. Behind there is a narrowing (*post-orbital constriction*) on each side of which lies a considerable depression (*temporal fossa*), bounded on the vault above by a pair of arched lines (*temporal lines*) and bridged by a horizontal bony arch (*zygomatic arch*) meeting the side-wall of the brain-case again above the ear-hole (*external auditory meatus*). These side-walls (*temporal region*) are more or less vertical and form, where they meet the transverse curve of the vault, something of a blunt angle. The back of the cranium (*occiput*) is rounded both in the sagittal and a horizontal transverse plane.

Below the brows are the large, conical, forward-facing eye-sockets (*orbits*), between which the more or less prominent bony bridge of the nose bounds from above a pear-shaped nasal opening (*apertura piriformis*). Below this the dental arch, closely set with teeth, surrounds a somewhat hollowed open-horseshoe-shaped bony palate, which terminates sharply behind at the posterior opening of the nasal cavity (*posterior nares*).

The base of the cranium shows a complicated array of prominences (*processes*) for muscular attachments and openings (*foramina*) for the transmission of vessels and nerves. The most striking of these latter is the great opening (*foramen magnum*), by which the spinal chord issues from the base of the skull and which is flanked by two rounded articular processes (*occipital condyles*) for the attachment of the skull to the vertebral column. The mandible articulates at two shallow depressions (*glenoid fossae*) just in front of the ear-holes.

In describing or measuring the human skull it is considered as being poised in its natural attitude of carriage. This attitude is assumed when the upper margins of the two ear-holes and the lowest point of the margin of one* orbit (*infra-orbital point*) are all brought into the horizontal plane. The plane defined by these three points is called the *Frankfort plane*, the definition having been internationally agreed at an anthropological congress held in that city.

The four true-profile views of the skull from points in the Frankfort plane are called the *norma facialis* (full face view), the two *normae laterales sinistra et dextra* (left and right side views) and the *norma occipitalis*

---

* Owing to slight asymmetry it may not be possible to bring *four* points (including both infra orbital points) into a single plane.

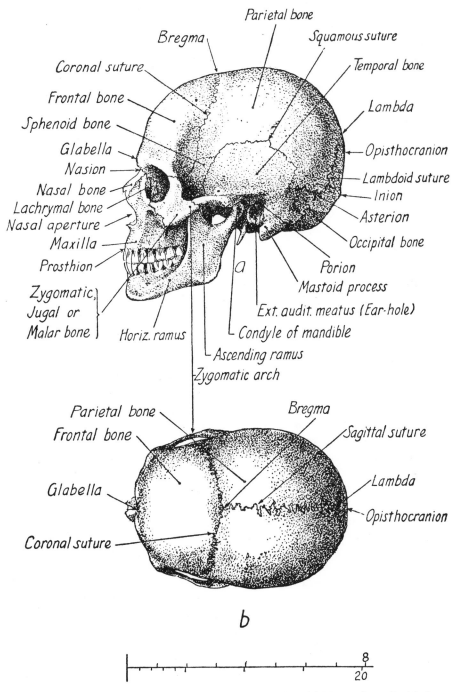

FIGS 6A, B, C. Skull of man in five standard attitudes: (a) Norma lateralis (sin.),
(b) Norma verticalis.

(back view). The remaining two views, at right angles to these, from points in the M.S.P. respectively above and below the skull, are the *norma verticalis* and the *norma basalis*. (Fig. 6). True comparison of skulls is possible only when they are viewed or represented in the standard attitude from defined viewpoints.

CRANIOMETRIC POINTS

In measuring, describing and comparing skulls the physical anthropologist uses a number of points of reference readily identifiable in most specimens, which have received special names. Some of those most commonly used are defined below. Their positions are indicated in Fig. 6. Some definitions apply only to skulls oriented in the Frankfort plane.

POINTS IN THE M.S.P.

Nasion. The point of junction of the fronto-nasal and inter-nasal sutures, the root of the nose.

Glabella. The most anterior point *in the midline* at the level of the supra-orbital ridges, when the skull is in the Frankfort plane.

Bregma. The point of junction of the coronal and sagittal sutures.

Lambda. The point of junction of the sagittal and lambdoid sutures.

Opisthocranion. The most posterior point of the skull oriented in the Frankfort plane.

Inion. The most prominent point of the external occipital protuberance.

Opisthion. The midpoint of the posterior margin of the foramen magnum.

Basion. The midpoint of the anterior margin of the foramen magnum.

Prosthion. The lowest point of the alveolar margin of the maxilla between the upper incisor teeth.

Pogonion. The most anterior point of the mental (chin) eminence.

Akanthion. The most prominent point of the anterior nasal spine.

BILATERAL POINTS

Porion. The uppermost point on the margin of the external auditory meatus (ear-hole).

Pterion. Owing to individual variations, this is a region rather than an easily definable point. It lies in the temporal fossa, close to the junction of the coronal with the spheno-parietal suture. In a few human individuals, and in increasing numbers of individuals of the species as we descend the Primate scale, there is a contact between the temporal and frontal bones, excluding the typically human contact between sphenoid and parietal. The pterion region is, thus, somewhat unstable and a pterion point almost impossible to define exactly.

Asterion. The point of junction of the lambdoid, temporo-occipital and squamosal sutures.

Gonion. The most lateral point of the angle of the mandible.

The list is not exhaustive. There are many other named and defined points used for particular measurements, but these are not so useful as the above for describing the position of skull-features.

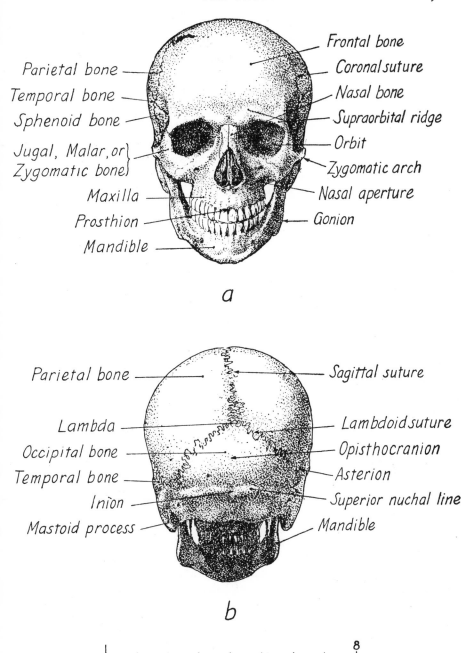

Frontal bone
Coronal suture
Nasal bone
Supraorbital ridge
Orbit
Zygomatic arch
Nasal aperture
Gonion

Parietal bone
Temporal bone
Sphenoid bone
Jugal, Malar, or Zygomatic bone
Maxilla
Prosthion
Mandible

a

Parietal bone
Lambda
Occipital bone
Temporal bone
Inion
Mastoid process

Sagittal suture
Lambdoid suture
Opisthocranion
Asterion
Superior nuchal line
Mandible

b

8
20

FIG 6B.   (a) Norma facialis (frontalis), (b) Norma occipitalis.

Bones of the skull in man, with comparisons with lower mammals

BONES OF THE CEREBRAL PART:
FRONTAL, PARIETALS, OCCIPITAL, SPHENOID,
ETHMOID, TEMPORAL

The *frontal bone* forms the forehead region and the fore part of the vault as well as the superior margins of the orbits and portions of their roofs. It articulates with the facial bones in front and is separated from the parietals behind by the *coronal* (crown) suture, which crosses the vault from side to side. At the brows it may bear more or less strongly developed *supra-orbital ridges*, in modern man bipartite on each side.

The frontal bone is the product of synostosis (bony fusion) of two equal frontal bones meeting in the M.S.P. These are separate at birth but meet, and generally begin to fuse, in the second year of life. The *metopic* (forehead) *suture* at which they are joined is normally completely obliterated by the eighth year, but may, rarely, persist in the adult. The two bones are separate to a later stage of development in most lower mammals and so remain, for example, in the adult dog.

The *parietals* are a pair of bones, somewhat rectangular, meeting in the midline at the *sagittal suture*, forming the middle part of the vault of the brain-case. Anteriorly they join the frontal bone at the coronal suture and are bounded behind by the *lambdoid* (λ-shaped) *suture*. On the sides of the cranium their inferior margins are overlapped from below by the temporal bones in the arched *squamous* (scale-like) *suture*, so called because of this overlap.

The *occipital bone* forms the whole of the back wall of the cranium and the posterior part of the basal axis also. It is pierced below by the *foramen magnum*. It includes the two *occipital condyles* by which the skull is supported on the first cervical vertebra and affords an area for the attachment of *nuchal* (nape) muscles (see below).

The occipital, a single bone in adult man, represents four or more bones which are separate in youth and of which the homologues in lower mammals remain separate. The squamous part (shaped like a fish-scale) wedges between the two parietals, to which it is locked at the lambdoid suture. In some animals the point of this wedge forms a separate bone, the *inter-parietal*, and indeed it is rarely, even in man, present as a separate bone. The squamous part corresponds with the *supra-occipital bone* in the dog. (Fig. 7.)

Next come two *condylar parts*, bearing the occipital condyles, which correspond to the *ex-occipital bones* in the dog. In the dog and especially in the ruminants there is a strong *par-occipital process*. Lastly, the *basilar part* forms the anterior margin of the foramen magnum and part of the basal axis of the cranium, corresponding to the dog's distinct *basi-occipital bone*. In man, the condylar parts unite with the squama about the fourth year, the basilar part not being joined with these until the sixth year.

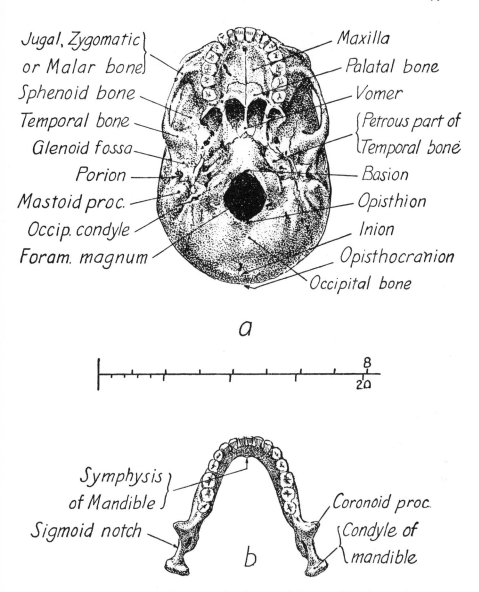

Jugal, Zygomatic or Malar bone

Sphenoid bone

Temporal bone

Glenoid fossa

Porion

Mastoid proc.

Occip. condyle

Foram. magnum

Maxilla

Palatal bone

Vomer

{Petrous part of Temporal bone

Basion

Opisthion

Inion

Opisthocranion

Occipital bone

a

8
20

Symphysis of Mandible

Sigmoid notch

Coronoid proc.

{Condyle of mandible

b

FIG 6C. (a) Norma basalis, (b) occlusal view of the mandible (vertical to the molar occlusal plane).

MUSCULAR IMPRESSIONS. The frontal and parietal bones bear, each, a pair of more or less strongly marked temporal lines. At the external angular process of the frontal, where it meets the malar bone, the *inferior temporal line* begins as a ridge, becoming less prominent as it passes upwards to cross the coronal suture. It arches across the parietal bone from near the middle of its anterior margin to its postero-lateral angle, where it may be seen to join a ridge, in prolongation of the zygomatic arch, which crosses the temporal bone from above the ear-hole. This line marks the limit of the area of origin of the fan-shaped *temporal muscle* which, in life, occupies the temporal fossa. The fibres of this muscle converge to a tendon which is inserted at the *coronoid process* of the mandible. The action of the muscle is to close the jaws, so that its area of origin is some measure of the power of the jaws. The *superior temporal line* marks the limit of extent of a tendinous sheet, or fascia, associated with the muscle.

About the middle of the squamous part of the occipital bone is a more or less well-marked prominence, the *external occipital protuberance*. This marks the point of attachment of the strong nuchal (nape) ligament. Arching upwards and laterally from this point is a pair of lines marking the margin of the area of attachment of the nuchal muscles and their fascia, the *superior* and *highest nuchal lines* respectively. A little below runs the *inferior nuchal line,* marking the boundary between the insertions of the deep and superficial muscles of the neck. The strength of the pro-tuberance, the area enclosed by the nuchal lines and the impressions of the muscle-insertions all help to estimate the strength of the neck musculature.

In quadrupeds, owing to the skull and its often very long muzzle being hinged on the vertebral column like a bascule of the Tower Bridge, the nape musculature has to be very strong and the area for its insertion on the occipital bone correspondingly extensive and rugged. Since the brain-case itself is comparatively small, the occipital area is often increased by massive bony outgrowths and ridges. (Fig. 7.)

The *sphenoid bone* forms the middle part of the base of the cranium, part of the lateral walls in the temporal fossa and of the internal walls of the orbits. Below, it has various processes for the attachment of muscles and soft structures. It is a bone of complicated form, having a basal part, in the axis of the cranium, and pairs of greater and lesser wings. It is represented in youth by separate parts and corresponds with the follow-ing bones in the dog:—the *basisphenoid* and *presphenoid,* both in the basal axis, a pair of *alisphenoids* (greater wings) and of *orbitosphenoids* (lesser wings).

The *ethmoid bone* plays a part, small in man, in closing the anterior wall of the brain-case. This it does by means of the *cribriform* (sieve-like) *plate,* which is pierced by numerous fine foramina admitting fibres of the olfactory nerve (nerve of smell) to the brain (Fig. 8). For the rest, its *perpendicular plate,* connecting with the sphenoid behind, forms the up-per part of the bony support for the *nasal septum* (partition), the cartila-ginous sagittal wall dividing the nostrils. The orbital plates fill small spaces in the medial internal walls of the orbits. It is connected with a pair of paper-thin, much convoluted bones, the *superior nasal conchae,* forming the lateral walls of the nostrils, and upon these are spread part of the delicate mucous membranes of the nasal cavity in which the smell-receptor nerve-endings are located.

The dual role of the ethmoid bone is explained by the fact that, in man, it and the superior nasal conchae represent a whole group of bones which never fuse in the dog, for example. These are the *mesethmoid* (ossified septum) a pair of *ethmo-turbinals* (conchae) connected above with the cribriform plate and a pair of *orbito-ethmoids* (orbital plates).

The *temporal bones,* on each side, form the lower part of the lateral walls of the brain-case, meeting the parietals above, the occipital behind and the sphenoid in front, closing the gap in the base between the occipital and sphenoid. Once more, these are single bones in adult man, which are formed from separate parts in early youth and correspond with permanently distinct bones in the dog.

The *squamous part* overlaps the edge of the parietal above and sends forward a slender zygomatic process forming the posterior part of the zygomatic arch. The *mastoid part* is of cellular structure within and lies behind the ear-hole, bearing the *mastoid* (nipple-like) *process,* at which is inserted a neck-muscle (sterno-cleido-mastoid) important in the maintenance of erect head-carriage. The *tympanic* (drum) *part* forms the floor of the *auditory meatus* (ear-hole) and supports the ear-drum, while the *petrous* (stony) part in the base of the skull contains the rest of the apparatus of hearing. The petrous part is very dense and is often preserved in fossil skulls when much else has perished. These parts correspond in the dog, respectively, with the *squamosal bone,* the *periotic* (surrounding the inner ear) *bone,* which includes also the mastoid part, and the enormously developed *tympanic bulla* (bubble), which is evidently associated in the dog with a very much more acute sense of hearing than is at man's disposal.

THE FACIAL BONES:
NASALS, MALARS, LACHRYMALS, MAXILLAE, PALATINES, VOMER

In man the *nasals* are a pair of small bones about 1 inch long articulated side by side with the frontal, between the orbits, forming the bridge of the nose. In quadrupeds, as in the horse or pig, they are often very large (for example, 12 inches and 8 inches respectively), corresponding with the large muzzle and highly developed sense of smell (Cf. Fig. 5).

Malar, jugal or zygomatic (yoke) *bones.* The first of these three terms is usually used in human anatomy; 'jugal' is more generally found in zoological and comparative works. 'Zygomatic' appears to serve for both to some extent. This pair of bones in man forms the lateral and inferior margins of the orbits and supports the cheeks. Each has a meeting at the fronto-malar suture with the external angular process of the frontal, joins the maxilla below in the maxillo-malar suture, crossing the cheek-bone, and lies alongside the nasal medially. Laterally and poster-

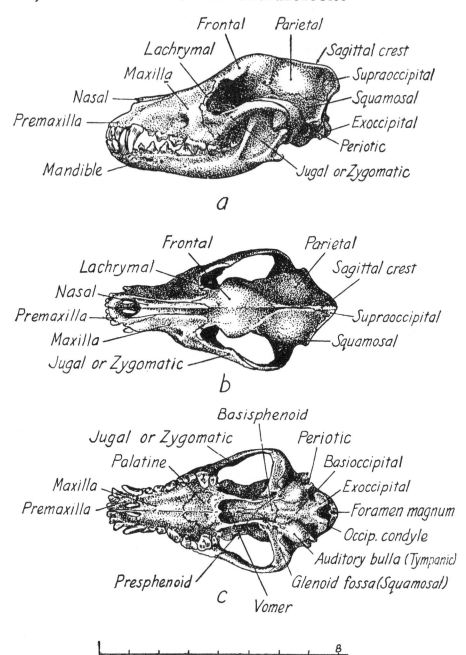

FIGS 7A and B. Skull and mandible of dog, for comparison with the corresponding views of the human skull in Fig 6: (a) lateral, (b) vertical, (c) basal views.

iorly it sends out a short stout process which joins the zygomatic process of the temporal bone, completing the zygomatic arch across the temporal fossa.

Lachrymal (tear) *bones*. These are so called because they are grooved to carry the tear-duct, leading from the orbit into the nasal cavity. In man they are small, extremely delicate bones situated just within the medial border of the orbit and forming part of its medial wall. In the dog and other Carnivora they just reach the actual border and a very narrow area on the cheek. In the Ungulata, however, they widely transgress the orbital border and occupy a considerable area on the cheek before it. They are thus of some systematic value, though insignificant in appearance and, in man, at least, only preserved in very perfect skulls.

The *maxillae* are the largest bones of the face and form a pair, united in the M.S.P. below and behind, together forming the major part of the bony palate and supporting the upper set of teeth, which are set in their *alveolar* (socket) *margins*. Above, a process on each side forms the medial border of the orbit, save where the lachrymal does so, embraces the nasal bone by its lateral border and meets the frontal alongside it. The maxillae frame the nasal aperture anteriorly, save for the small part of its superior margin formed by the two nasals. They afford points of attachment and support on their medial walls for the *superior nasal conchae*, of the ethmoid group of bones (see above) and to the *inferior nasal conchae* related to the maxillae themselves. In the M.S.P. they embrace the vomer posteriorly, which is an ossification of the lower part of the nasal septum.

In the dog the maxillae are very strong and much elongated in the sides of the muzzle, as are the nasals in its roof. The anterior portion of the alveolar margin, bearing the upper incisors and forming the lower border of the nasal aperture, is, here, a pair of separate bones, the *premaxillae*. These have been overgrown and obliterated by the maxillae in the shortening of the human face, but are constantly present as distinct bones in lower mammals. The inferior nasal conchae in man correspond with the *maxillo-turbinals* in the dog.

The medial and posterior part of the bony palate is formed by the conjoined *palatine bones,* which have each a perpendicular part, forming the lateral wall of the *posterior nares* (hinder nasal opening). Towards the midline, above, these curve in to meet the *vomer,* an unpaired bone connecting with the presphenoid behind and continuing into the mesethmoid above. Below, the vomer rests, in the M.S.P., on the maxilla and palatines, but is not actually united with them.

This completes the enumeration of the cranial bones, save for the *hyoid* bone or bones, which form supports for parts of the neck and throat structures, and for the *auditory ossicles* of the middle ear. These are all unimportant in the present context, being seldom preserved, or at least recovered, in archaeological circumstances, though they are of

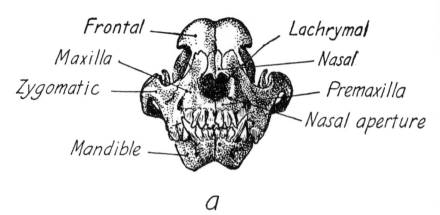

Frontal — Lachrymal
Maxilla — Nasal
Zygomatic — Premaxilla
— Nasal aperture
Mandible —

a

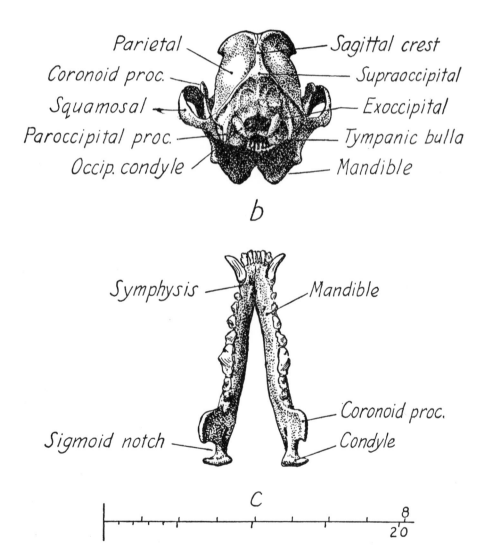

Parietal — Sagittal crest
Coronoid proc. — Supraoccipital
Squamosal — Exoccipital
Paroccipital proc. — Tympanic bulla
Occip. condyle — Mandible

b

Symphysis — Mandible

Sigmoid notch —
Coronoid proc.
Condyle

c

FIG 7B.   (a) frontal and (b) occipital views, (c) mandible.

evolutionary importance, being homologous with some of the bony gill-arches in fish, adapted to their special functions in higher vertebrates.

To these, the bones of the cranium proper, must be added the mandible, completing the description of the skull.

The *mandible*, carrying the lower set of teeth and worked often by very powerful muscles, is the strongest and most solidly-constructed of the bones of the skull. For this reason it is frequently well preserved in archaeological deposits. It consists of two symmetrical halves meeting in the M.S.P. and there fused, in man, during the first year of life. Each half has a *horizontal ramus* (branch) and an *ascending ramus*. The latter is bifurcated above by a deep rounded notch (*sigmoid notch*) into processes lying roughly in a sagittal plane, of which the anterior is called the *coronoid process* and the posterior the *head* of the mandible. This head is elongated transversely and presents a rounded, somewhat almond-shaped *condyle* which articulates with the *glenoid fossa* of the temporal bone, at the base of the skull, just in front of the ear-hole. This joint is the hinge of the mandible. The coronoid process affords attachment for the insertion of the temporal muscle which closes the jaws.

The upper part of the horizontal ramus contains the *alveoli* (sockets) of the teeth, while its lower border projects somewhat forward in the *mental* (chin) *eminence*.

The line of bony union of the two mandibular halves in the midline is termed the *symphysis*. The sagittal section of a mandible in this region is of value for comparative purposes in determining the relationship of a fossil human specimen with the apes on the one hand and with modern man on the other.

Corresponding with the very great development of the facial part of the skull in lower mammals, the mandible is often extremely massive, requiring powerful muscles to drive it. Since the large jaws are frequently combined with a relatively small cranial part, and since the principal jaw muscle, the temporal, originates there, it is often the case that the area of the cranial part is insufficient to accommodate the muscles. Outgrowths of bone, taking the form of strong ridges and prominences, are added with increasing age and strength, often quite masking the exterior of the brain-case, to give the necessary increased area. In the dog (not an extreme case) these take the form of a *sagittal crest*, (Fig. 7) arising on the sagittal suture near the front of the parietals and ending in a great prominence on the supra-occipital where the temporal muscles border on the area for the equally powerful nuchal group. Lesser crests run laterally downwards from this protuberance along the lambdoid suture, to meet that prolonging the powerful zygomatic arch in the mastoid region of the periotic bone.

In the cats these ridges are even more pronounced and the zygomatic arches more widely spread. Nor is this condition confined to the carnivores. Animals like the horse, rhinoceros or elephant have very small brain-cases in comparison with their bodily bulk. The jaws and teeth are commensurate in size and weight with the large intake of food necessary for their maintenance, so that they require very large muscles indeed. In the elephant, for example, the brain-case is completely enclosed by enormous over-growths of bone, coarsely cellular in structure to save weight, which render the true form of the adult cranium unrecognizable from without but at the same time provide the necessary areas for the jaw and neck musculature (Fig. 9.)

FEATURES OF THE CEREBRAL CAVITY
(INTERIOR OF THE BRAIN-CASE) (Fig. 8.)

In a human cranium of which part is broken or cut away the internal features of the brain-case will be visible. The greatest value of these for the present purpose is to assist in the mending or reconstruction of a broken skull. The study of internal details for their own sake is a matter for trained anatomists and anthropologists.

To display the internal features, the vault of a cranium may be sawn off in a plane parallel to the Frankfort Plane, perhaps half an inch above the superior margin of the orbits. Such a cut will pass through, or close below, the apex of the occipital squama.

Interior of the vault. The interior of the skullcap, thus separated, shows a number of characteristic features. Depending on the age of the individual, the sutures may or may not be visible internally. On the midline of the frontal bone is a prominent *frontal crest*, separating the frontal lobes of the cerebrum (fore-brain) which occupy the fossae to either side. The base of this crest is marked by the beginning of the *sagittal sulcus* (groove) which crosses the vault in the midline between the cerebral hemispheres and, in life, accommodates a large blood-sinus (channel). The sulcus continues along the sagittal suture and crosses on to the apex of the occipital bone. It is well marked here in the section of the separated skull-cap, on the thickening of the bone which separates the occipital poles of the hemispheres.

To either side, and mounting the interior of the vault towards the sagittal sinus, may be seen the impressions of the meningeal vessels, which convey blood to and from the membranes investing the cerebrum. The impressions are most deeply grooved on the parietals, about half an inch behind the coronal suture, and the general direction of their ramifications is upwards and backwards. The position of a cranial fragment bearing these impressions is, therefore, fairly easily ascertained. Another feature, well seen in the section of the walls of the vault, is the thinning of the bones inside the temporal lines (i.e. where they are covered and protected by the temporal muscle). The line itself is seen in section on the frontal bone, perhaps one inch in front of the coronal suture. The line and the thinning of the bones in the temporal fossa are also useful indications for interlocating fragments and rebuilding a broken skull.

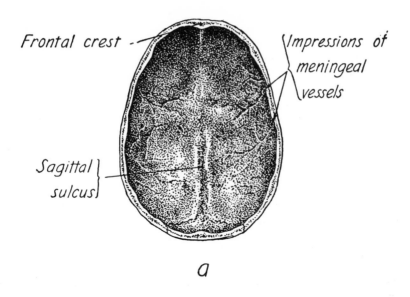

Frontal crest

Impressions of
meningeal
vessels

Sagittal
sulcus

a

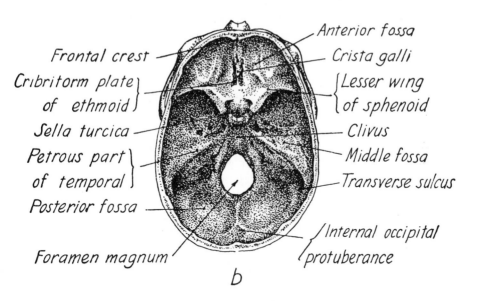

Frontal crest

Cribriform plate
of ethmoid

Sella turcica

Petrous part
of temporal

Posterior fossa

Foramen magnum

Anterior fossa

Crista galli

Lesser wing
of sphenoid

Clivus

Middle fossa

Transverse sulcus

Internal occipital
protuberance

b

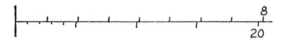

FIG 8.   Interior views of the human brain-case: (a) vault, (b) base.

VERTICAL VIEW OF THE BASE OF THE SKULL. This is somewhat complicated, as is the basal view. Only a few features need be mentioned here.

The base of the cranial cavity is seen to be divided, on each side, into three large, well-defined depressions, the *anterior, middle and posterior fossae*. In the midline, separating the two anterior fossae, is seen the lower part of the *frontal crest*, already noticed in the vault, which rises in the floor of the frontal midline as a narrow prominence, the *crista galli* (cock's comb). On either side of the crista, and extending a little behind it, is seen a *cribriform plate of the ethmoid*, pierced by many fine foramina, like those in the sifter of a pepper-pot. The floors of the anterior fossae form the roofs of the orbits, and the lesser wings of the sphenoid (orbitosphenoids), which contribute to them, are well seen to be separated from the greater wings (alisphenoids) by the *superior orbital fissure*, transmitting vessels and nerves to the eye-mechanism.

The middle fossae are bounded in front by the lesser wings of the sphenoid and behind by the petrous parts of the temporal bones (periotics), which extend forwards and medially across the base of the cranial cavity. In the midline is seen a small, saddle-shaped depression on the upper surface of the sphenoid bone, called the *sella turcica* (Turkish saddle), bounded by two processes, respectively before and behind it, termed the *tuberculum* (pommel) and *dorsum sellae* (back). Behind the dorsum there is a steep incline down to the foramen magnum, the *clivus* (slope), formed in part by the basisphenoid and in part by the basioccipital.

The posterior fossae lodge the two hemispheres of the cerebellum (hind-brain), concerned with reflex muscular co-ordination, which is covered in life by a membrane, the *tentorium cerebelli*, which also supports the occipital lobes of the cerebrum. In the dog, unlike man, this membrane is ossified in its posterior part and forms a shelf-like septum (partition) crossing the occipital bone transversely. Above the tentorium, branches of the large blood-sinus run laterally, in large *transverse sulci* (grooves), crossing on to the mastoid part of the temporal bone on each side. These transverse sulci, with the posterior part of the sagittal sulcus and the midline thickening below of the occipital bone between the two cerebellar fossae, contribute to a prominent, right-angled cross, thus +, in the middle of the cerebral surface of the occipital squama. The point of intersection of the limbs of the cross forms an *internal occipital protuberance*, nearly coincident with the external occipital protuberance already noticed. Thus the bone here is very thick, perhaps, in a male subject, more than 10 millimetres, while in the cerebellar fossae and in the fossae above for the occipital poles of the cerebral hemispheres it may be a millimetre or two only. The thinning in the lower part of the occipital bone is accentuated by the presence of the external muscular impressions in the nuchal region, so that, in lightly-built youthful or female skulls, the bone in the fossae may be so thin as to be translucent. The 'cross' of the occipital bone is thus highly characteristic, as well as being frequently preserved in buried, or even cremated, skulls, owing to its comparatively massive and dense structure. Its development enables an estimate to be made of the age and possibly the sex of an individual, from a skull-fragment no more than 1 inch square.

Some general features of the skull in different mammalian Orders

INSECTIVORA. Most members of this Order are small in size and burrowing or nocturnal in habit. In general shape the skull tends to be low and flat in outline, broad at the occiput, prolonged into a more or less long and narrow snout anteriorly. The orbits are not even partially closed off from the temporal fossa and open posteriorly into it. The cerebral hemispheres are small, smooth and unconvoluted, so that the bones of the containing vault are plain within. The mandible is long and narrow, with a short ascending ramus and a well-developed angular process. The auditory bulla and palate are incompletely ossified. The shrews, mole and hedgehog are typical and familiar examples of the Order (Fig. 9a).

CHIROPTERA. The bats are closely related to the insectivores, though specialized for aerial, not terrestrial, life. As might be supposed, the muzzle tends to be much shorter and the skull-vault somewhat higher. There is a well-marked sagittal crest and a pronounced post-orbital constriction. The small European bats are all insectivorous and closely resemble the insectivores in other skull-characters.

RODENTIA. The members of this Order are generally small (but note the beaver) with burrowing and herbivorous habits, often good climbers and swimmers. They are possibly derived from primitive insectivores, though now often highly specialized in some of their characters—in particular the teeth (see below, p. 80). Rodents are very varied and numerous.

The cerebrum is smooth and unconvoluted, the vault low, the muzzle long and the nasal cavity large, consistent with the acute sense of smell. The orbits open posteriorly into the temporal fossa. There is often a large paroccipital process, infra-orbital foramen and anterior palatal foramina. The jugal bone is well developed. The lachrymal extends considerably on the cheek in front of the orbit. The mandible has only a small coronoid process, sometimes none, but the angle is greatly developed. The mandibular condyle is not extended transversely, but is of a rounded oval shape, fitting in a groove, adapting it for antero-posterior movement. There is often a prominent masseter crest on the horizontal ramus.

CARNIVORA. These are very variable in size and habits (e.g., the weasel and the lion). The brain is relatively large and the hemispheres of the cerebrum convoluted. In the more advanced types the snout is

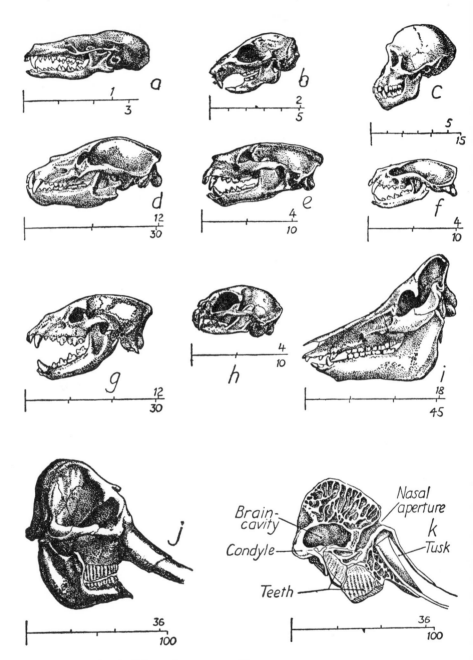

FIG 9. The skull in various mammalian groups:
(a) mole (insectivore): (b) squirrel (rodent); (c) chimpanzee
(primate); (d) bear, (e) badger, (f) otter, (g) hyaena, (h) cat—all
carnivores; (i) pig, (j) Indian elephant (ungulates), (k) shows the
skull of the elephant in section.

shorter in proportion to the cranial part (e.g., cats). The zygomatic arches are strong and wide-spreading. Most have strong sagittal and occipital crests to support the powerful jaw-muscles. The more primitive, e.g., Mustelidae, have low, elongated skulls with the orbits far forward and comparatively short muzzles (Fig. 9 e, f), the higher types a steeper profile. The auditory bulla is more or less inflated (cf. in the dog) and both it and the bony palate are completely ossified.

Three Orders of Ungulates, the hoofed mammals, are of importance in the present context—the Proboscidea, Perissodactyla and Artiodactyla. All show a great degree of specialization in particular directions.

The primitive ungulate skull was small, the cerebrum only slightly furrowed. It had a low, flat roof and a prominent sagittal crest.

PROBOSCIDEA. Judging from the comparatively completely retained elements of manus and pes, the Proboscidea represent the most primitive of the three Orders, but the skull in the adult is different beyond recognition from the primitive ungulate skull described above (Fig. 9 j, k). The brain-case itself increases but slightly in size during the growth of the individual, but a very large area is required for the attachment of the large tusks and trunk and an additional area for that of the strong muscles required to support so massive a head on the vertebral column. Consequently, an enormous growth in thickness of the cranial and facial bones is demanded and is fulfilled by the formation of great air-cells in the diploë separating their inner and outer tables. A thickness of up to 12 inches is thus locally acquired, composed of a coarsely cellular tissue of bone which is immensely strong, in view of the comparatively small weight of solid bone-substance laid down. In the process, individual bones become fused with their surroundings, and scarcely recognizable. The nasal opening is raised far in front of, and to a higher level than, the brain-case. The premaxilla, housing the tusks, and the maxilla and mandible, in which the great molars are set, become enormously developed. The occipital condyles become large masses of bone so voluminous as, together, almost to equal the volume of the brain. The area for the nuchal musculature is pushed forward almost to the line of the frontal poles of the cerebrum.

PERISSODACTYLA. This Order, having an odd number of toes, is represented, for our purposes, by the rhinoceroses and horses. The former are the less specialized.

In comparison with the rest of the skull, the cranial cavity is small and the facial, especially the nasal, bones are greatly developed. The occiput is steep and large in area and the occipital condyles are convex transversely. The base of the skull, from basion to prosthion, is almost straight. There is a large temporal crest.

The nasals, in the living representatives, stand out free above the nostrils, but in the extinct *Tichorhinus* (woolly rhinoceros) the mesethmoid cartilage, forming the nasal septum, was completely ossified and supported the nasals from below. This was evidently a functional adaptation for the support of the very long anterior nasal horn of this beast.

The nostrils open laterally and extend backwards, sometimes beyond the premaxillary-maxillary suture.

In the Rhinocerotidae there is no post-orbital process and the small orbit is completely open to the temporal fossa. In the more recent genera of the Equidae, however, the orbit is surrounded with a complete ring of bone, formed by the junction of the post-orbital process with the zygomatic process of the squamosal. The latter process takes a very large share in the formation of the zygomatic arch in all perissodactyls and, in the horse, even forms part of the inferior margin of the orbit.

As in the Proboscidea, though to a lesser extent, the large expansion of the face, and the weight of the nasal horns in the rhinoceroses, has demanded a commensurate growth of musculature and of the skull area for its attachment. The occipital region is very extensive and the temporal crests rise to meet it, so that an acute angle is formed at the summit of the supra-occipital. A considerable development of air-cells is here necessary, covering the small brain-case and completely masking its external shape. In the horses these outgrowths are present, but much less developed.

The mandible, in both families, is long and massive, tapering anteriorly to the symphysis, very wide at the angle, which is rounded. The condyle stands high above the teeth and is very wide transversely. The coronoid process is slender and recurved.

ARTIODACTYLA. The even-toed Order of ungulates is subdivisible into the Suiformes, a sub-Order of more generalized, pig-like families and the longer-legged, more lightly built and highly diversified Ruminantia.

In the former, the skull is somewhat reminiscent of that of the carnivores and perissodactyls, but in the latter the frontals develop extensive air-cells and often bear horns or antlers, especially in the males.

In both sub-Orders some families have the face somewhat bent down upon the cranial axis, so that the nose points downwards, instead of forwards, when the axis is horizontal. This is the case in the Suidae (pigs) and the Bovidae (cattle), while in the Cervidae (deer) the face and basal axis are almost in the same straight line.

For the present purpose only two families in the sub-Order Suiformes are of importance, the Suidae and the Hippopotamidae. In both, the brain-case is small and the face very large. The junction of the parietals and supra-occipital is marked by a high transverse occipital ridge, hollowed transversely behind. In the pigs there is a long par-occipital process. The long muzzle narrows anteriorly and the small nasal opening is almost at its extremity. A small post-orbital process does not meet the zygoma, so that the orbit is open posteriorly. The lachrymal extends beyond the orbit for a considerable distance on the cheek. The mandible has a high ascending ramus, a small coronoid process and a transverse condyle.

The hippopotami have the facial parts enormously developed (Fig. 26). In front of the orbits the face narrows, but is laterally expanded in the broad muzzle. The orbits project outwards laterally and are almost, or entirely, enclosed behind. The mandible is massive, with a low ascending ramus and an angle greatly expanded and everted. The horizontal rami converge at first, but the symphysial portion is expanded again laterally corresponding with the wide muzzle above.

The sub-Order Ruminantia is divided into several families, of which only two, the Cervidae (deer) and Bovidae (cattle) are of concern to the European archaeologist. The former are characterized by the possession of annually grown and annually shed antlers, generally only in the males. The Bovidae have permanent hollow horns, generally in both sexes, though those of the male are much the larger. These are supported upon bony outgrowths of the frontal bones, the so-called 'horn-cores'.

Cervidae (Fig. 10). The bones of the skull are notably thin and brittle. The cranial and facial axes lie nearly in a straight line, so that, in the normal attitude of carriage, the nose is directed forwards and not downwards. The parietals form the greater part of the cranial vault, but the frontals contribute to the narrow anterior portion. The squamosals are large. The orbits are large, prominent and completely surrounded by bone. There is often an unossified space on the cheek, between the frontal, nasal, lachrymal and maxillary bones, and in front of the orbit a so-called lachrymal fossa, which has nothing to do with tears but, in life, lodges a gland.

Antlers. The most striking feature of the family is the antlers, generally borne only by the males, though in *Rangifer* (reindeer) the female also has them. They arise from *pedicles*, short bony processes of the frontal bones, and are developed anew and shed each year. The antlers are true bony growths, being invested during development by skin and having a copious blood-supply. At this stage the antlers are said to be 'in velvet' owing to the close, short, velvety hairs covering the skin. Once fully grown, the blood-supply is interrupted, the skin and vessels die and are gradually rubbed off by the animal. The antlers then consist of bare bone, on the surface of which the ramifications of the nutrient vessels can still be traced. After the rutting season, during which the stags fight fiercely for possession of a group of hinds, the antlers are shed, separating from their pedicles, to be regenerated in the following year. In the first year the antler consists of a single prong. In each subsequent year another point (tine) is added, so that the age of the animal can be estimated by the development of the antlers. Among recent species the form and character of the antlers is distinctive, though there is considerable individual variation. The 'anatomy' of antlers is

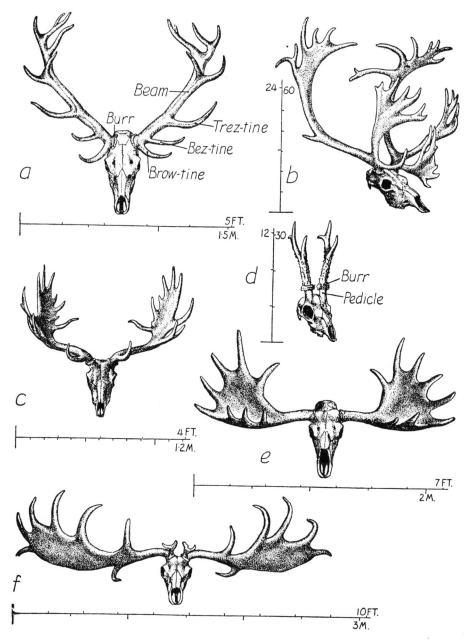

FIG 10.   Skulls and antlers of deer (Cervidae):
(a) red deer (*Cervus elaphus*), (b) reindeer (*Rangifer tarandus*), (c)
(Clacton fallow deer (*Dama clactonianus*), (d) roe deer (*Capreolus
capreolus*), (e) elk (*Alces alces*), (f) giant Irish deer (*Megaceros eurycerus*). (Skulls *not* similarly oriented. Drawn to display antlers fully.)

simple. Immediately next the pedicle is the 'burr', or 'coronet', below which the antler separates from its pedicle when it is shed. The main stem of the antler is called the 'beam', from which spring the branches, called 'tines' or points'. From below upwards the tines are called the 'brow-', 'bez-', and 'trez-' tines. The bez is developed last. Above the trez the points have no special names, being known to the deer-stalking fancy as so many 'points on top'.

Distinguishing features in the antlers of the species with which the archaeologist may meet are as follows:—

Dama spp. (fallow deer) (Fig. 10c). The antler is very smooth and the marks of the blood-vessels shallow. The brow-tine springs from the beam directly above, almost in contact with, the burr. A bez-tine is generally absent and the antler tends to be markedly palmated above the trez.

Cervus elaphus (red deer) (Fig. 10a). The antler tends to be rather rough and is much larger when fully grown than in *Dama*. The brow-tine is borne on the beam at a little distance above the burr, a bez-tine is usual, save in the British insular race, *C.e. scoticus*, in which it is absent. Even above the trez the tines are clean cylindrical points, without a trace of palmation.

Megaceros (giant deer) (Fig. 10f). In this extinct species, sometimes erroneously called the 'Irish elk', the beam is very large and strong with a surface quality similar to that of *C. elaphus*. It tends to be somewhat recumbent in attitude, or even drooping, in old individuals. There is generally no distinct bez-tine and, close above the trez, the equivalents of the points on top are enormous tines peripheral to a very extensive, somewhat horizontal palmation. It is this palmation which gave rise to the 'elk' misnomer, though *Megaceros* is more closely related to the red deer or perhaps to *Dama*.

Alces (elk) (Fig. 10e). The short, stout beam is borne horizontally and the antler is widely palmated, though with nothing like the enormous spread of a fully-grown *Megaceros*. The numerous points surrounding the palm turn upwards. The difference from *Megaceros* is in the shortness of the beam and the less unwieldy and more regular development of the palm and tines.

Capreolus (roe deer) (Fig. 10d). The animal is much smaller than our other deer, scarcely taller, but much more lightly built, than a goat. The antler is borne upright and consists only of the beam and two or more points on top A brow-tine is lacking. Both the burr and the rest of the antler are very irregular and deeply channelled by the blood-vessels, so that the species is readily recognized, even from a small fragment.

Rangifer (reindeer) (Fig. 10b). Antlers are borne by both sexes. The attitude of the beam is characteristic, sweeping backwards and upwards in a curve from the point of origin of the brow-tine. This arises some little distance above the burr, is very long and may be bifurcated or

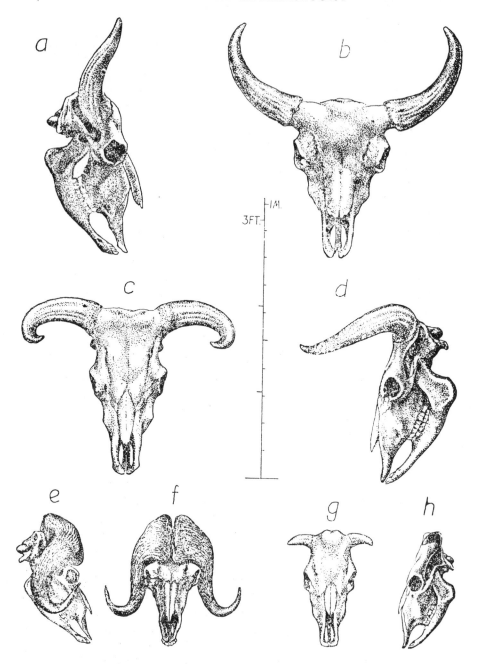

FIG 11.   Skulls and horns of the larger bovids:
(a), (b) *Bison priscus* (Pleistocene bison), (c), (d) *Bos primigenius*
(Urus, urochs), (e), (f) *Ovibos moschatus* (musk-ox), (g), (h) Celtic ox
(the so-called *Bos longifrons*). All on the same scale.

even palmate. Most of the branches and tines, even the brow-tine, are more or less palmate. One or two tines may branch from the beam in a posterior direction. In quality, the surface of the antler is very smooth, the marks of the nutrient vessels being only slightly grooved.

Bovidae (Figs. 11, 12). This large and varied family is characterized by the hollow permanent horns generally borne by both sexes. In consequence of the presence of the horn-cores, the frontal part of the skull may be much expanded and full of air-cells communicating with those of the horn-cores themselves. The frontals form the greater part of the cranial vault, the parietals becoming small and, in the extreme case of the genus *Bos* (cattle), being entirely relegated to the occipital area. The orbits are prominent and completely closed posteriorly. The facial axis is bent down at a considerable angle to the basi-cranial axis, so that, in the normal carriage of the head, the nose is directed downwards. The occipital area is small and sloping forwards and there are large paroccipital processes. In oxen a lachrymal fossa is wanting.

The genus *Bos* includes both our domestic cattle and their presumed wild ancestor, *Bos primigenius* (Ur, Urochs) (Fig. 11c, d) which only became extinct on the continent of Europe in the seventeenth century A.D. This species had horns which were often enormous in old bulls (e.g., the Sutton Hoo horn, 9 inches in diameter across the mouth*). Borne wide apart at the summit of the skull, these curved outwards, forwards and upwards. Among domesticated breeds the Longhorn types are closest to the wild species in horn development, but many breeds, past and present, in particular the small Celtic ox (the so-called *Bos longifrons* (Fig. 11g, h), though it is no more than a race of *Bos taurus*) are of the Shorthorn type, with generally small, stumpy, often downturned horns.

The skull of *B. primigenius* is said to be distinguished from those of domestic cattle by having a 'strut' of bone near the base of the horn-core, supporting it where it is weakest, close to the margin of the temporal fossa. The feature is not easily recognized in most fossil material.

Bison (Fig. 11a, b), for our purposes, includes two species. First is the Pleistocene *B. priscus*, with horns very large in the bulls and up-turning in a more or less coronal plane—not bearing forwards as in *Bos*. The angle between the occipital and frontal planes in lateral view is much more acute in *Bos* than in *Bison*. The face is shorter and wider, the orbits often very prominent laterally.

The living European bison, *B. bonasus*, now survives only in zoological collections, but is only recently extinct as a wild species in eastern Europe. It has rather small horns of the same form and carriage as the extinct Pleistocene species.

Ovibos moschatus, the musk ox (Fig. 11e, f), a member of the Caprinae,

* This is now thought to be an error of reconstruction—parts of *two* decorated horns having been combined as one!

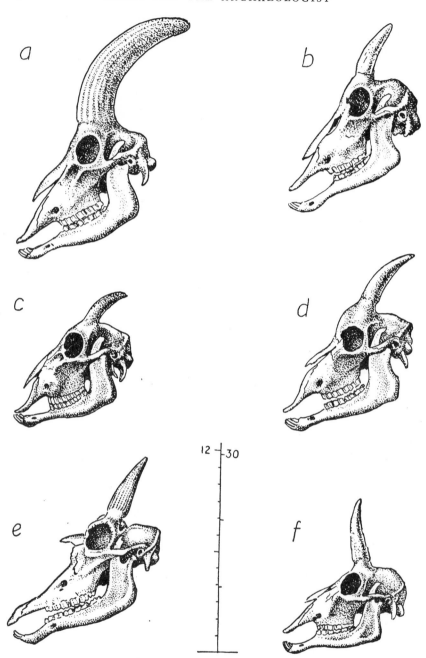

FIG 12.   Skulls and horns of smaller bovids:
(a) *Ovis musimon* (♂) (mouflon ram), (b) *Capra ibex* (♀) (ibex),
(c) *Ovis aries* (domestic sheep), (d) *Capra hircus* (domestic goat),
(e) *Saiga tartarica* (saiga 'antelope'), (f) *Rupicapra rupicapra* (chamois).
All on the same scale.

the sub-family of the Bovidae which includes the sheep and goat, has unmistakable horn-cores, of which the massive, flattened bases almost meet in the midline, forming a sort of casque. The horns curve, at first, steeply downwards laterally, before turning forwards and upwards in fine sharp points.

The closely related sheep (*Ovis*) (Fig. 12a, c) and goats (*Capra*) (Fig. 12b, d), are practically indistinguishable in most parts of the skeleton, but are readily identified when comparatively complete skulls and horn-cores are available. The course of the coronal suture is a distinguishing criterion, bowed forward at the bregma in sheep and practically straight transversely in goats. The course of the lambdoid shows the opposite condition—straight in sheep and bowed forward in goat. In the sheep the sub-orbital crest (a small ridge running forwards and downwards from the inferior margin of the orbit) is entirely on the jugal (malar, zygomatic) bone. In the goat it is on the jugo-lachrymal suture or even entirely on the lachrymal bone. This is due to the presence of a lachrymal fossa in sheep, whereas the goat has none. Sheep horn-cores are of sub-circular section and strongly curved to support the often large horns which are coiled in a short helix of considerable amplitude. In goats, however, they are relatively slightly curved and of markedly sub-triangular section with a sharp antero-lateral keel. The helical twist is present but is long and of very small amplitude, rather resembling an Archimedean screw.

Far less common are *Saiga tartarica*, the saiga antelope (Fig. 12e), and *Rupicapra*, the chamois (Fig. 12f). The former has rather short, fairly straight and upright conical horn-cores, originating close together forward, above the orbits, and diverging somewhat laterally, In the chamois the horns curve sharply backward distally and are less divergent near their bases. The curvature is less clear, however, in the bony core.

5

Dentition

‣‣‣

TEETH ARE OF GREAT IMPORTANCE to the palaeontologist and archaeologist for two reasons. First, they are very variable and often specialized and are, therefore, of systematic value for differentiating between species and higher groups of mammals. The teeth are closely related to the food habits and therefore to the environment occupied by the animal. Secondly, since they are formed of extremely dense and hard materials, they are often preserved when little else has survived decay. Many extinct species of animals are known to the palaeontologist only by their teeth, but these are enough clearly to indicate their zoological relationships.

Structure of teeth

The teeth of most mammals are composed of three distinct substances of differing hardnesses:

(1) Enamel, a very dense, hard and brittle outer casing, resistant to wear, generally forming a complete envelope to the part of the tooth exposed above the gum;

(2) Dentine (or ivory), of which the greater part of the body and roots of a tooth consist. This is secreted by the living pulp which forms the core of the tooth. Dentine is fairly hard but tougher and more resilient than enamel.

(3) Cement is a softer, more granular, bone-like substance, covering the dentine of the roots and sometimes also more or less investing the enamel walls and crown, filling folds and valleys in it.

A typical tooth consists of a *crown* covered with enamel and a *body* and *roots* of dentine, separated by a more or less well-defined *neck*. The root or roots of most adult teeth are pierced by fine canals which admit vessels and nerves to the pulp-cavity, the space for the living part of the tooth. In immature teeth, the pulp-cavity is widely open at the root, and so remains into maturity in some teeth of certain species which grow continuously throughout the life of the animal.

Some typical teeth are illustrated in Fig. 13.

Growth and wear of teeth

The enamel crown is first laid down by the surrounding tissues deep in the jaw. This is called the *germ* of the tooth. Since the crown is of non-living tissue and will not be surrounded by living tissue when in use, it must be elaborated, once and for all, in its full dimensions and

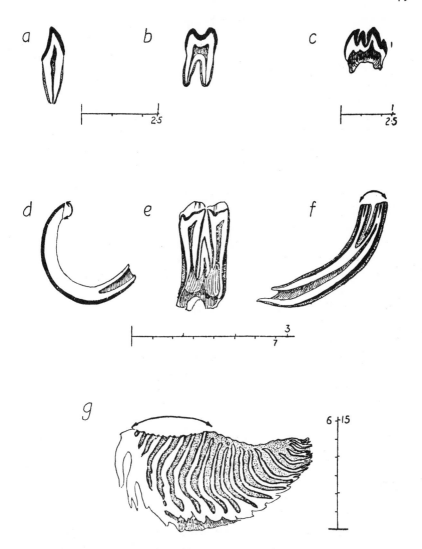

FIG 13.   Teeth in section to show structure:
(a), (b) canine and molar of man, (c) pig, unworn molar, (d) beaver, incisor, (e) ox, unworn molar, (f) horse, incisor in early stage of wear, (g) elephant, partly worn lower molar. The drawings are semi-diagrammatic, showing enamel in full black, dentine white and cement stippled. Pulp-cavities in section are shaded in line. Extent of worn surface indicated by arrows.

complexity. The pulp inside the crown then deposits dentine within and below the enamel, closely following its folds, if any, forming the body of the tooth. The tooth moves up in the jaw and cuts the gum and the roots are gradually laid down in step with the eruption of the crown. By the time that the crown has risen into line with the other teeth and is in use, the roots are completed and shortly close save for the narrow nerve-canal.

In species where the tooth-wear in life is severe, the enamel capping the cusps and eminences of the crown may be worn through to the dentine. Once exposed, this 'inlier' (to use a stratigraphical term), being softer, wears more quickly than the surrounding enamel, so that the edge of the enamel stands out in relief. Any pits or valleys in the enamel filled with 'outliers' of cement wear more quickly than either enamel or dentine, so that, in such a case, the three substances maintain a rough, rasp-like chewing surface, however hard the wear. If the wear of the uncovered dentine threatens to expose the underlying pulp, this may retreat within the body of the tooth, laying down a thickness of secondary dentine behind it. This process compensates, to some extent, for the wear and prolongs the life of the tooth.

Special adaptations to function and drastic attrition are seen in the continuously renewed, open-rooted incisors of rodents (Fig. 13d), in which the enamel is concentrated upon the buccal surface of the tooth so that, in wear, a sharp chisel-edge is constantly maintained.

An unspecialized mammalian grinder has a comparatively low and wide (*brachyodont*) crown and distinct roots which become closed when the tooth is fully erupted. The teeth of many vegetable-feeders, by contrast, tend to be markedly high-crowned (*hypsodont*), the enamel deeply folded and the folds filled with cement. They are thus enabled to sustain a lifetime's hard wear. The elephants show an extreme development of this adaptation.

Teeth with rounded or conical eminences on the chewing-surface (*bunodont*) (Figs. 13e, 14) are less specialized, more primitive and suitable for dealing with a varied diet.

Where the separate cusps come to be grouped in linear ridges the tooth is said to be *lophodont* (Figs. 13g, 23a). These ridges may run transversely, as in some rodents and in the Proboscidea, or they may be oblique, forming V- or W-shaped crests. When somewhat worn the enamel pattern of these on the chewing surface often comes to resemble a series of crescents—the *selenodont* (Fig. 27) pattern of many ungulates.

The complete set of teeth present in an animal is termed the *dentition*.

A feature of the mammalian dentition is its division into four more or less distinct functional groups of teeth:—

INCISORS, for nibbling, biting off or gnawing food;

CANINES, long pointed teeth, particularly developed in the carnivores for seizing and holding their prey, but also developed as formidable weapons by, for example, the pigs;

PREMOLARS, transitional in function between the predominantly cutting and grasping front teeth and the grinding cheek-teeth, partaking of both, and often developed to assist in that one of the two main functions which is the more important in a particular animal group. Thus a

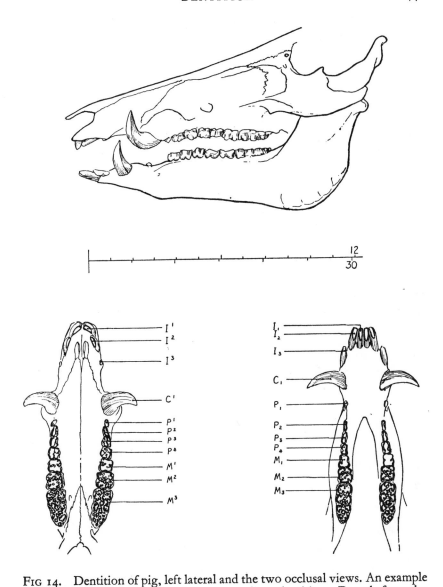

FIG 14. Dentition of pig, left lateral and the two occlusal views. An example
of the complete adult mammalian dentition. Dental formula:

$$\frac{3 \cdot 1 \cdot 4 \cdot 3 \cdot}{3 \cdot 1 \cdot 4 \cdot 3 \cdot} = 44.$$ All the teeth are somewhat worn.

Compare the section of an unerupted unworn pig's molar in Fig. 13.
Only the worn edges of enamel are in black. Unworn enamel surfaces are rendered in line.

seal's premolars are somewhat hooked, caniniform teeth, assisting in
the important task of catching and holding smooth and slippery prey,
while those of a horse are scarcely to be distinguished from the molars,

which they assist in the foremost duty of grinding up often tough, dry, vegetable food;

MOLARS, or grinders, more or less adapted for crushing and comminuting the food. These are relatively of slight use to flesh-eaters, but form the most important group in confirmed vegetarians—especially the grass-eaters.

This differentiation of the teeth by function gives rise to the typically mammalian *heterodont* (several kinds of teeth) dentition. In fishes and reptiles, the teeth are numerous, more or less simply spiked or conical and all of similar shape—the *homodont* dentition. Some mammals which have reverted to a fish's way of life have secondarily re-acquired a homodont dentition (e.g., some of the Cetacea).

The primitive mammalian dentition consists of 44 teeth. Many more specialized groups, both living and extinct, have fewer than this, but only very exceptionally more. A few of the less specialized living animals retain the complete dentition, e.g., the pig (Fig. 14).

Since the teeth are repeated symmetrically on each side, though the upper and lower sets may differ in some cases, it is necessary to describe only one side of the mouth. This is briefly done by means of a *dental formula*, in which each group of teeth, above and below, on one side, is enumerated in order, beginning from the midline in front. Thus, the full mammalian dentition of 44 teeth, consisting on each side, above and below, of 3 incisors, 1 canine, 4 premolars and 3 molars, may be rendered by the formula:

$$I\frac{3}{3}, C\frac{1}{1}, P\frac{4}{4}, M\frac{3}{3} = \frac{11}{11} \times 2 = 44$$

This may be further simplified by taking the grouping as understood, omitting the arithmetic, and writing the formula:

$$\frac{3 \cdot 1 \cdot 4 \cdot 3}{3 \cdot 1 \cdot 4 \cdot 3} = 44$$

Following this scheme of abbreviated description, individual teeth are often designated also by a letter for the group to which they belong and a numeral, superscript for an upper tooth, subscript for a lower, giving the position of the tooth within the group and in the mouth. Thus I^1 means a first incisor of the upper jaw, P^2 a second upper premolar, M_3 a lower third, or last, molar.

DECIDUOUS ('MILK') TEETH. Preceding the permanent adult dentition, most mammals have, in youth, a more or less complete set of milk teeth, which are shed as the jaws grow to their adult size and the permanent teeth are erupted.

Some milk teeth are the precursors of the corresponding permanent teeth. The three permanent molars, however, have no precursors and the milk molars occupy the positions later taken by the premolars, which are unrepresented in the deciduous dentition. Milk teeth are

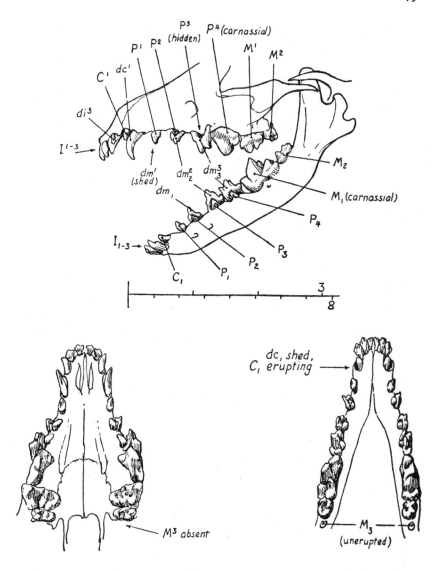

FIG 15. Milk dentition still partly retained in a young carnivore. Arctic fox (*Alopex lagopus*) aged about 6 months, left lateral and the two occlusal views. The deciduous incisors have all been shed save DI³ on the left side. Above, the milk canines are still in use, only the points of the permanent teeth yet showing. DM¹ has been replaced by P¹, while DM²⁻³ remain, the former only precariously rooted. Below, both deciduous canines have been recently shed, their alveoli still showing, but all three milk molars are in position, straddling the emerging cusps of their premolar successors.

distinguished in abbreviation either by the prefix 'D' (deciduous) (e.g., DM^1) or, more briefly, by the use of a minuscule letter instead of a capital, e.g., m^1.

The full milk dentition thus reads:—

$$i\frac{3}{3}, c\frac{1}{1}, m\frac{3}{3} = \frac{7}{7} \times 2 = 28.$$

As with the permanent dentition, this is more or less curtailed in most species.

The order of eruption and stages of replacement of the deciduous by the permanent dentition vary greatly as between one species and another, but, when they are known, afford a valuable means of determining the age of immature individuals from the state of the dentition. Some commonly useful data are given below (p. 227). An example of a milk dentition in the process of replacement is shown in Fig. 15.

Salient characters of the dentition in different Orders, Genera and Species

INSECTIVORA. The complete dentition is often somewhat reduced. Incisors, canines and the more anterior premolars are generally simple, pointed teeth and hard to distinguish from one another. The more posterior premolars tend to resemble the molars, which are strong, conically cuspidate teeth, the cusps of one set occluding with the valleys of their opponents. These molars are admirably adapted for crushing the chitinous exoskeletons of insects, which form the principal food of the Order.

Hedgehog (*Erinaceus europaeus*) (Fig. 16a, b, c) $\frac{3 \cdot 1 \cdot 3 \cdot 3}{2 \cdot 1 \cdot 2 \cdot 3}$. $= 36$ P4 is molariform, M3's reduced in size.

Mole (*Talpa europaea*) (Fig. 16d, e, f) Complete dentition. C^1's somewhat enlarged, in adaptation to a diet largely of earth-worms, larvae and more soft-bodied prey rather than adult insects.

Shrews (*Sorex* spp.) $\frac{3 \cdot 1 \cdot 3 \cdot 3}{1 \cdot 1 \cdot 1 \cdot 3}$. $= 32$ (Fig. 16g, h, i). All the teeth have red-brown points when fresh. I^1 and I$_1$ are both much enlarged and procumbent, the former with 2 points, the latter with 4. The canines are small and pointed, like the smaller incisors. The molars have very sharp cusps.

The Water-shrew (*Neomys fodiens*) has one less upper P and the other teeth differ in detail, e.g., the large I$_1$ is single-pointed and the cusps of the teeth are uncoloured.

The Scilly shrew is a distinct species of a continental genus, *Crocidura*.

RODENTIA. In their general structure primitive, all rodents have a typical, highly-specialized gnawing dentition, consisting generally (Simplicidentata) of a single pair of curved, rootless incisors (I1)

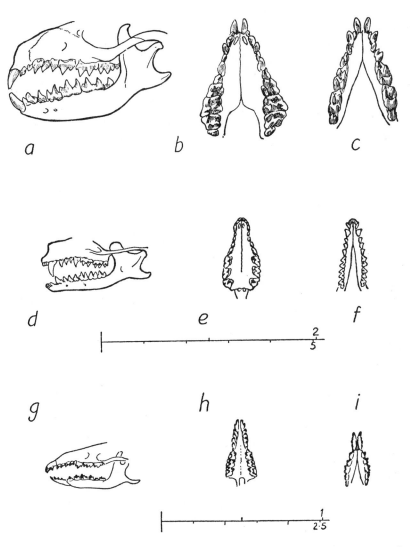

FIG 16. Dentitions of insectivores: (a, b, c) hedgehog, (d, e, f) mole, (g, h, i) shrew, all somewhat magnified. Mole and hedgehog on the same scale. Left lateral and the two occlusal views in each case. Only the mole has the complete dentition of 44 teeth.

above and below. Hares and rabbits belong to a distinct sub-Order (Duplicidentata)* characterized by a second pair of incisors (I^2) on the lingual side of the main incisors, in the upper jaw only.

Canines are absent, premolars reduced in numbers, degenerate or wanting altogether, as in the true mice and rats (Fig. 17a, b, c). All three molars are well developed and, in the more specialized groups,

* More recently distinguished as a full Order, the Lagomorpha.

have only thin enamel on the crowns, which is soon worn through in use, exposing a pattern of transverse or diagonal ridges of enamel alternating with dentine, forming an efficient rasp.

The chisel-like incisors (Fig. 13d) are maintained in sharp condition by use, owing to the slower wear of the thick enamel coating of the buccal surface. They are unrooted, the pulp cavity always wide open at the base, and grow continually during the life of the animal. If, through accident, one of them should be lost, its opponent incisor continues to grow in a circle until the animal is prevented from feeding and dies of starvation or there is actual perforation of the skull by the advancing edge.

The food of rodents is as varied as their species and habits, but is mainly vegetarian. Squirrels and rats (Fig. 17 g, h, i and a, b, c) will, however, take birds' eggs and their young. The omnivorous and cannibal habits of rats and mice are proverbial. Squirrels, rats and the true mice (Murinae) have rooted molars of comparatively simple enamel pattern; the numerous voles (Microtinae) (Fig. 17d, e, f) have hypsodont, rootless, prismatic molars with a complex enamel pattern, adapted to their tough and fibrous diet of grasses, etc. In rabbits and hares 3 pre-molars survive above and 2 below. The cheek-teeth are prismatic and rootless. The M^3 is degenerate, a mere peg.

Among larger rodents extinct in western Europe the beaver (*Castor fiber*) (Fig. 17 j, k, l) and its giant Lower Pleistocene forerunner, *Trogontherium cuvieri*, have enormous gnawing incisors and 4 equal prismatic cheek-teeth to a side, of which the first is a P4. The Old-World porcupine (*Hystrix*) is a rare Pleistocene fossil found only on the Continent. The rooted cheek-teeth include P4, likewise. Lemmings (*Myodes*), of the vole family, now living in northern Europe, extended far to the south during the Pleistocene glacial periods, as also did the marmots (*Arctomys*, *Spermophilus*), relatives of the squirrels, with similar teeth. They are alpine and cold-steppe species, respectively, today. These and other rodents, mostly small in size, sometimes afford valuable climatic and environmental evidence when found with the cultural remains of early man and should not be overlooked, though their determination and study are a matter for a specialist.

PRIMATES. In man, anthropoid apes (Fig. 18) and Old-World monkeys the dental formula for the adult dentition is $\dfrac{2 \cdot 1 \cdot 2 \cdot 3}{2 \cdot 1 \cdot 2 \cdot 3} = 32$. The teeth are unspecialized, rooted and the crowns of the cheek-teeth are provided with a fairly simple pattern of low, blunt cusps. Cement is absent from the crowns and is found only covering the roots. The teeth have a distinct neck between crown and root. The dentition is rather primitive and generalized, adapted to a mixed diet, though most primates, and particularly the great apes, are mainly vegetarian and frugivorous.

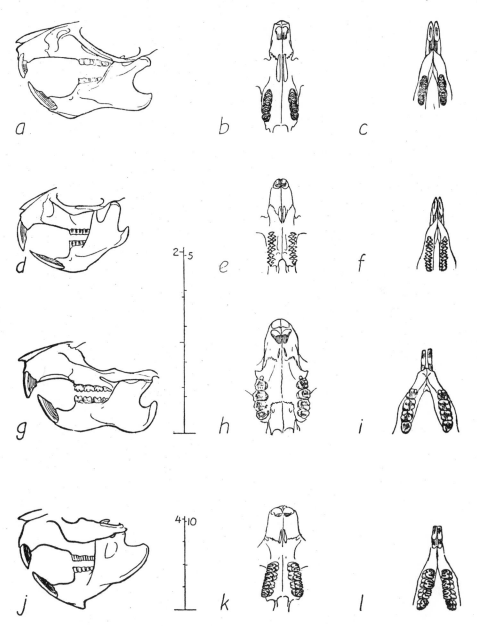

FIG 17. Four variations on the rodent dental theme: (a, b, c) rat, (*Rattus norvegicus*, (d, e, f) vole (*Arvicola terrestris*), (g, h, i) squirrel (*Sciurus vulgaris*), (j, k, l) beaver (*Castor fiber*). The first three all on the same scale.

The incisors are small, more or less spatulate and chisel-shaped, though without a very sharp edge. The canines are stronger, with sub-conical crowns, high, pointed teeth standing well out above the chewing surface of the rest of the set in monkeys and apes, especially in the males. In modern man they are not enlarged and only exceptionally so in the case of one extinct species of the Hominidae *H. erectus modjokertensis*). The 1st lower premolars are sectorial teeth in all living, and most extinct, monkeys and apes, but are small and bicuspid in man. The three molars have more or less square or rectangular crowns with 4-5 principal cusps and M_3, both above and below, tends to be somewhat smaller than the rest.

Occlusion of the teeth in Primates. I^1 is a wide spatulate tooth which opposes I_1 and the mesial half of I_2. Otherwise the teeth above and below are of corresponding mesio-distal dimensions, so that each meets half of two teeth in the opposing set and the point of C_1 lies in front of that of C^1. M^3 is a smaller tooth than M_3, so that, though the upper row begins half a tooth ahead in mesio-distal length, both sets end on the same line. In primitive races of modern man, both living and fossil, the incisors normally meet in an edge-to-edge bite. The prevailing shearing over-bite of the upper incisors of modern civilized peoples is a late development and is unusual in British human remains even of as late a time as the Roman period of these islands.

Movements in mastication and consequent wear. In the monkeys and apes, with prominent canines, neither an antero-posterior nor a lateral motion of the jaws in mastication is possible, save to a very limited extent. The same cusps and valleys of the opposing teeth meet at every bite, so that the wear is irregular and localized. In man, however, there is no such restriction and, with motion in any direction permitted, the wear of the teeth tends to be equal over the whole chewing surface. In time, all cusps tend to be ground down to a common level. Even wear is thus, even though only a single tooth may be available, indicative of small canines and, therefore, probably, of human ownership. It is not distinctively human, however, in that it will also be found in the tooth of any higher primate individual or species not provided with enlarged and interlocking canines, as, for instance, in some female anthropoid apes.

Differences between human and simian dentitions. Individual teeth in apes are larger and more powerful, in accord with the strongly developed jaws. On the whole, the crowns of simian cheek-teeth are low and the cusps prominent. In man, the crown as a whole is high and the cusps small and but slightly elevated. In the living great apes this feature is seen clearly in the gorilla, less clearly in the chimpanzee and orang, in that order. Canines are enlarged in the apes, especially in the males, and the 1st lower premolars are constantly of sectorial type.

The dental arcade in man, as may be seen (Fig. 18 e, f), is parabolic in form, owing to the straight face, small teeth and wide cranial base

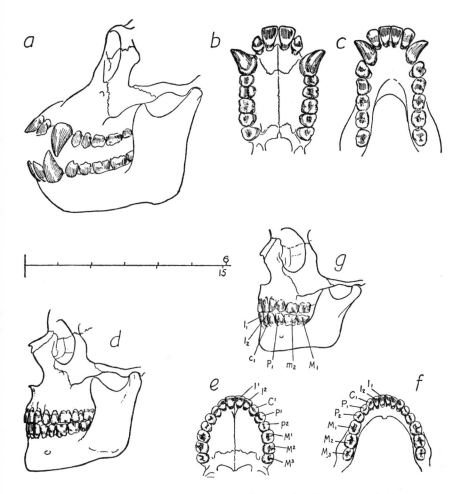

FIG 18. Dentitions of orang (a, b, c) and man (d, e, f). Left lateral and two occlusal views. Dental formula: $\dfrac{2.1.2.3.}{2.1.2.3.} = 32.$ (g) is the left lateral view of a human child aged about 10. Both permanent incisors are in use, but the canine is still the milk tooth. P^1 has replaced m^1 in both jaws, m^2 is still in use and only M^1 of the permanent molar set is yet erupted.

for the articulation of the mandible. In apes (Fig. 18b, c), where there is a distinct muzzle and a narrower skull-base, the premolars and molars form straight parallel rows, the incisors a straight, or but slightly curved, transverse row, so that the palate-shape is not parabolic but rectangular. It is elongated antero-posteriorly with the large canines situated at the anterior angles. There is usually a distinct *diastema* (space) above, between C^1 and I^2, below, between C_1 and P_1, necessary in each case for the accommodation, when the jaws are closed, of the point of the opposing canine. There is hardly ever such a gap in the tooth-row in man—or, indeed, in female apes with small canines.

Whereas in man the lower border of the mandible extends in a chin eminence in front of the line of the incisors, in apes there is no chin and the lower incisors are more or less procumbent. This difference seems to follow the shortening of the muzzle in man and the smallness of the teeth, resulting in a reduction of the alveolar perimeter and palatal area, while the body of the mandible has not been commensurately reduced.

Milk dentition in man and replacement by the permanent teeth. As usual, the permanent molars have no precursors and there are no deciduous premolars. The permanent premolars replace the two milk molars in each side of the jaw. The formula for the milk dentition thus reads:

$$i\frac{2}{2}, \ c\frac{1}{1}, \ m\frac{2}{2}, \ = \frac{5}{5} \times 2 = 20 \ (\text{See Fig. 18g}).$$

The crowns of the permanent teeth are calcified often long before their eruption, e.g., I's and C's at age 6 months, M_3's by age 10 years, although the former erupt only between the 7th and 12th years and the latter not until between 17 and 25. Before they cut the gum and replace their precursors, if any, the roots of the milk teeth, below which they may be situated, begin to be absorbed, until only the crown remains, and this is eventually pushed out and shed.

Differences between man and apes in the times of the eruption of the teeth have not been closely studied, but it has been established that, in apes, the permanent canines erupt later, after M_2, whereas in man they appear before the M_2's. The c_1 in apes is a pointed conical tooth and projects above the rest of the tooth-row. The m_1 is sectorial, like its premolar successor, with a marked mesial cusp. In man the c_1 is spatulate and blunt and does not rise above the general level of the other teeth, while the m_1 is molariform, with 4-5 more or less equal cusps.

The usual times of eruption of milk and permanent teeth are given in Chapter 15. An example of a youthful human dentition may be seen in Fig. 18g.

CARNIVORA (Figs. 19, 20, 21). In their skeletons as a whole, the members of the Order are comparatively primitive, but they have a dentition highly specialized for catching living prey, cutting up the flesh and cracking the bones.

While a vegetable-feeder needs efficient grinders to break open the insoluble cellulose cell-walls of plant tissues, so that the gastric juices may attack the contents, a flesh-eater need comminute the food very little, since the stomach acid can dissolve each morsel completely from without.

Incisors are small, often with several pointed cusps rather than a cutting edge (Fig. 19b, c), and the full complement of $\frac{3}{3}$ is generally present. Their function is to nibble and tear the last shreds of soft tissue from bones and their comb-like array of points forms an efficient instrument for scraping and gripping. The more lateral incisors may be caniniform (Fig. 20b).

Canines are evidently important to seize and hold active and struggling prey and to deliver a rapid quietus, so that these teeth are strong, pointed and interlocking. For the rest, efficient shears and bone-crackers are the whole requirement and, in pursuit of this ideal, the grinding function of the cheek-teeth has largely given place to larger and better cutting teeth, so that, in the most specialized carnivores, the complete dentition is severely reduced.

The P_1's may be somewhat caniniform, but P2-4 in both sets are generally markedly cutting teeth. This is especially the case with P^4, which is generally very large and strong, consisting of two or three main cusps united by sharp cutting edges. This is the upper *carnassial* (flesh-tooth). In the lower jaw the opponent of P^4 is M_1, the lower carnassial, a tooth of similar shape, whose points and edges fall closely within those of P^4, forming the lower blade of a pair of shears (Fig. 20a). M^1 is often a considerable tooth with a strong cusp lingually to the two main cutting cusps. M^{2-3} are progressively smaller and less important and, indeed, the latter may be altogether missing. Below, even M_2 is absent in some species (e.g., hyaena, Fig. 19f) and M_3, when present at all, is a comparatively insignificant little vestige (e.g., fox, Fig. 19g, i).

Most carnivores are of moderate size, but range from the large bears and cats, on the one hand, to very small, but fierce, hunters like the familiar ferret and weasel.

The bears, dogs and cats show progressive dental specialization, in that order.

Bears (Ursidae, Fig. 19a, b, c). Dental formula: $\frac{3 \cdot 1 \cdot 4 - 1 \cdot 2}{3 \cdot 1 \cdot 4 - 1 \cdot 3}$. The incisors are small but tricuspid, strong and with long single roots. Canines are very strong, with enormous roots but not unduly long in the crown or sharply pointed. P^1 is a small pointed tooth close behind the canine, P^{2-3} are often missing, leaving a considerable *diastema* (gap in the tooth-row): if present they are small. P^4 is a somewhat narrow tricuspid tooth, not unlike a molar. M^{1-2} are frankly grinders, low-crowned, multi-cuspidate when unworn, showing a complex pattern of worn cusps later in life. M^3 is lacking. In the lower jaw, P_{1-3}, if present, are small; P_4 is narrow and the closest approach in the mouth to a sectorial tooth. The three molars are all large, functional grinders, though M_3 is considerably shorter than M_2 and this suggests incipient reduction of the molar set.

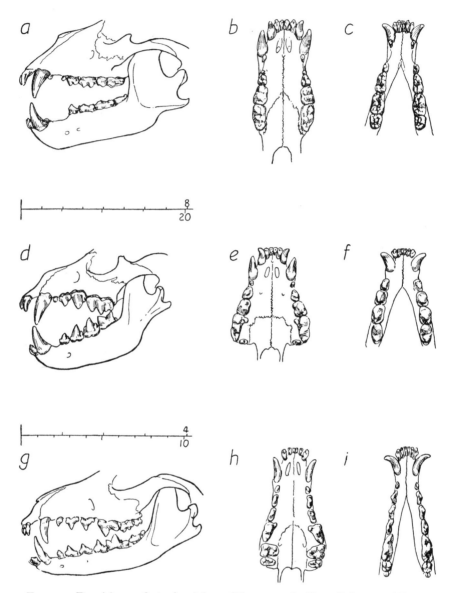

FIG 19.   Dentitions of: (a, b, c) bear (*Ursus arctos*), (d, e, f) hyaena (*Crocuta crocuta*), (g, h, i) fox (*Vulpes vulpes*). Left lateral and two occlusal views. Bear and hyaena on the same scale.

Despite the reduction in the premolars and the loss of the M³, this is a comparatively complete, primitive and unspecialized dentition for a family of carnivores. In fact the bears, apart from the polar bear (*Thalassarctos*), are often somewhat omnivorous and vegetarian in habits, eating berries and fruits, roots, honey in season, subsisting on fish, frogs, rodents and other small game when larger prey is hard to come by.

Of the two bears which concern the archaeologist the cave-bear (*Ursus spelaeus*) is distinguished as to the dentition from the surviving brown bear (*Ursus arctos*) by its enormous size and the absence even of a vestige of P^1.

Dogs (Canidae). $\frac{3 \cdot 1 \cdot 4 \cdot 2}{3 \cdot 1 \cdot 4 \cdot 3}$. These are represented for the present purpose by the wolf (*Canis lupus*), the red fox (*Vulpes v.*) (Fig. 19g, h, i) the arctic fox (*Alopex lagopus*) (Fig. 15) and the domestic dog (*C. familiaris*) (Fig. 7). All are members of the sub-family Caninae and have closely similar dentitions, complete save for M^3, but markedly specialized for the carnivorous way of life.

The incisors are small, somewhat spatulate and tricuspid save for I^3, which is larger and somewhat caniniform. The canines are large and strong in wolf and dog, slenderer and even more acutely pointed in the foxes. The P_1's are small and sub-conical, P_2's and P_3's of increasing size; long, narrow sectorial teeth with the main cusps united by sharp cutting edges. P^4 is the upper carnassial and an exclusively cutting tooth, unlike that of the bears. P_4 is the largest of the lower premolars, but much smaller than P^4. M_1 is the lower carnassial, an even longer cutting tooth than P^4, which it opposes. M^1 is a considerable tooth, with a strong lingual cusp affording something of a grinding surface. M^2 is much reduced in size and M^3 is missing altogether. Below, M_{2-3}, are respectively smaller than M^{1-2}, the last, especially, being a mere peg of a tooth, obviously vestigial.

Differences between wolf and dog are only of the slightest, the canines in wolf tend to be longer, and it is stated that the length of P^4 exceeds or is equal to that of M^{1-2} in wolf, while in dog it is shorter or equal, but Reynolds[*] is not enthusiastic about either of these criteria.

Living as they do, exclusively on flesh, the dogs, though having a dentition even more nearly complete than the bears, show the emphasis on grasping, tearing and flesh-cutting teeth to the almost entire exclusion of the grinding function. Indeed, anyone who has watched a domestic dog feeding on meat knows how the toughest cartilage and the smaller bones are quickly cut up between the carnassials and unceremoniously gulped down without further mastication. In nature, many dogs hunt in packs, or at least parties, and it is clear that, in the presence of competition, the ability to cut up and swallow quickly ensures a fair share of the common quarry. Chewing and cracking large bones is good economy as well as a leisurely pastime—the dessert which follows the feast. The dogs are not averse to carrion and the leavings of larger, more particular, or less hungry, hunters. It was this characteristic, no doubt, which led readily to their domestication, apparently as camp-followers of Mesolithic man.

[*] Reynolds, S. H., 1909. *A Monograph of the British Pleistocene Mammalia*, (3) The Canidae. Palaeontographical Society, London.

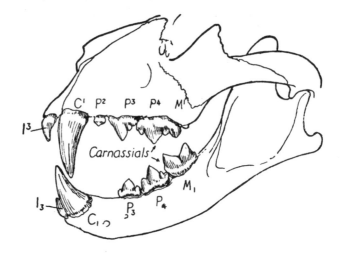

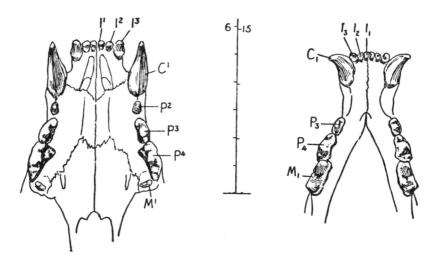

FIG 20. Dentition of African lion—a highly specialized carnivore. Left lateral and two occlusal views.

The domestic dog has the complete adult dentition soon after the age of 6 months (Fig. 57, Chapter 14).

Cats (Felidae). One extinct sub-family, the Machairodontinae (sword-toothed) concerns the archaeologist only as a Pliocene survival into the First (Günz-Mindel) Interglacial of the European Pleistocene. *Machairodus latidens* (broad-toothed), the sabre-toothed 'tiger', is a rare and striking fossil, the enormous dagger-like upper canines with sharp, denticulated distal edge being most frequently preserved and instantly recognizable. They were apparently used for stabbing rather than biting. The rest of the teeth are unmistakably cat-like.

Of the surviving sub-family Felinae, still of wide distribution and comprising numerous species, the cave-lion (*Felis spelaea*) (like the African lion, Fig. 20, but larger), lynx (*Lynx lynx*), leopard (*F. pardus*), European wild cat, (*F. sylvestris*) and domestic cat (*F. catus*) (Fig. 9h) must be mentioned in the European context. All are closely alike in their dentition, save in point of size: $\dfrac{3 \cdot 1 \cdot 3 - 2 \cdot 1}{3 \cdot 1 \cdot 2 \cdot \quad 1}$. The incisors are small, forming an even, closely-set row both above and below. The canines are large and stout, relatively higher in the crown, stouter and more acutely pointed than in the dog or bear. They are readily distinguished at a glance from the canines of these by the presence of a shallow longitudinal channel or flute in the enamel on the buccal surface (Fig. 20a).

P^1 is wanting. P^2 is a small and P^3 a larger, strictly sectorial tooth. P^4 is enormous and forms the upper member of the carnassial shears. M^1 is a degenerate vestige of the molar set. Below, both P_{1-2} are wanting, P_{3-4} are cutting teeth and M_1, very large, is the lower carnassial. There is no trace of M_{2-3}. All the cheek-teeth are narrow and of sectorial type, the lower set closing within the upper with a shearing action all along the row, not only between the carnassials. The cusps of one set close alongside the valleys of their opponents, making a very efficient scissor-like cut. Degeneration of the sub-conical anterior premolars, of nearly all the grinding molars and the exclusive development as cutting teeth of the survivors makes the feline dentition the most highly-specialized and efficient carnivorous equipment known.

Weasel family (Mustelidae) (Fig. 21). This includes the marten (*Martes*), the polecat (*Mustela putorius*), stoat (*M. erminea*) (Fig. 21g, h, i), weasel (*M. nivalis*) and the domesticated ferret (*M. furo*), the otter (*Lutra*) (Fig. 21d, e, f) and badger (*Meles*) (Fig. 21a, b, c), all still surviving in the British Isles. The glutton or wolverine (*Gulo*) (Fig. 21 j, k, l) is now restricted to arctic lands, but was formerly a member of the glacial faunas of W. Europe. The general dental formula is $\dfrac{3 \cdot 1 \cdot 4 - 3 \cdot 2 - 1}{3 \cdot 1 \cdot 4 - 3 \cdot 2}$. The muzzle is rather short and broad. Incisors are small, the canines slender and sharp. P1, if present, is generally small, the rest of the premolars sectorial with one main cusp, though P^4, the carnassial, may have a subsidiary lingual cusp. M^2 is a considerable grinding tooth, as well as possessing a cutting edge, but M_2 is generally vestigial. In the badger (*Meles*), both M1's are large and developed as grinders. This unspecialized condition corresponds with the animal's plantigrade gait and relatively omnivorous habits.

Hyaena family (Hyaenidae). The cave hyaena (*Crocuta crocuta*) (Fig. 19 d, e, f), is the sole representative of interest. The dental formula is

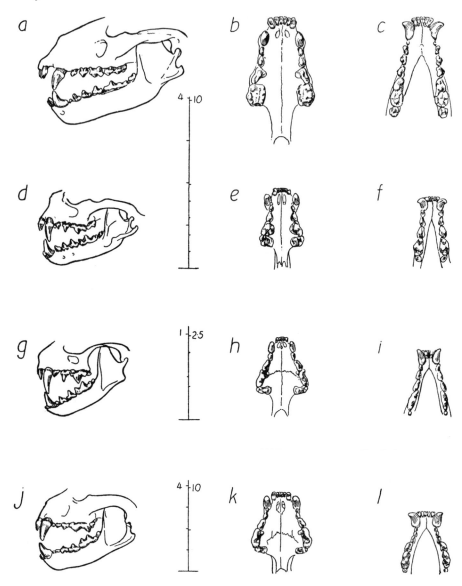

FIG 21.   Dentitions of four Mustelids: (a, b, c) badger (*Meles meles*), (d, e, f) otter (*Lutra lutra*), (g, h, i) stoat (*Mustela erminea*), (j, k, l) glutton (*Gulo gulo*). The first two on the same scale.

$\frac{3 \cdot 1 \cdot 4 \cdot 0}{3 \cdot 1 \cdot 3 \cdot 1}$. Owing to its cave-dwelling habits it is a common fossil of Pleistocene cave-earths. A carrion-feeder, it has very powerful jaws and large, stout teeth. Canines are very strong and have a prominent long ridge on the lingual surface, premolars increasing in size and complexity from P1 —4 with subsidiary cusps. P^1 is very small, P_1 is missing. The carnassials, P^4 and M_1, are enormous bone-crackers. The upper molars are altogether absent.

PROBOSCIDEA. The dentition in this Order is peculiar and much specialized, consisting in modern species of incisor tusks and cheek-teeth only.

Dinotherium $\frac{0 \cdot 0 \cdot 2 \cdot 3}{1 \cdot 0 \cdot 2 \cdot 3}$. The large lower tusks curve downward and backwards. There are no maxillary tusks. The cheek-teeth are lophodont (Fig. 23a), bearing $2-3$ (3 in M1) transverse ridges, the upper almost square, ridges mesially convex, the lower rectangular, elongated mesio-distally and with slight distal convexity of the ridges. There is no cement on the crowns.

Mastodon arvernensis had upper incisor-tusks with only vestiges in youth of the lower. The cheek-teeth (cf Fig. 23b) are bunodont and brachyodont, the cusps arranged in rough transverse groups with a little cement in the valleys of the crowns.

The true elephants (*Elephas*) concern us more than these, which properly belong to a period (Pliocene) before the emergence of man, but just survived into the earliest human times.

Elephas $\frac{1 \cdot 0 \cdot 0 \cdot 3}{0 \cdot 0 \cdot 0 \cdot 3}$. The incisors form the characteristic maxillary tusks and of the rest of the tooth-row only the three molars remain in living species of elephants. In some of the extinct species, however, there were, in addition, two premolars preceding the molars in succession. The tusks are without enamel, rootless and, like the incisors of rodents, grow throughout the lifetime of the animal.

Seeing that the crown of an elephant-tusk is conical and grows by continuous laying down of dentine on the surface of the pulp-cavity, elephant-ivory has a characteristic, and easily recognizable, structure. In transverse section a tusk is seen to be built up of successive concentric layers of dentine, like an onion. Viewed in longitudinal section there is seen to be a succession of cones nesting closely one within the other, repeating the form of the pulp-cavity and increasing in diameter towards the base.

There are, further, two series of sub-radial structures to be seen in the transverse section, numerous rays of denser dentine, arising at the centre and curving away right- and left-handed to the circumference. Not only do these two sets cross the concentric zones of dentine referred to above, but they intersect with each other, giving a symmetrical reticulated pattern similar to 'engine turning' on a watch case. This is best seen on a piece of turned and polished ivory, such as a billiard ball, but it may easily be recognized even in fossil ivory and is very characteristic. Decay of ivory results in annular lamination of the concentric zones with radial and circumferential cracks, so that it tends to break up into more or less rectangular prismatic crumbs, exceedingly difficult to reconstruct owing to the regular similarity of the fragments.

The cusps of the cheek-teeth are laterally confluent just below their apices, forming transverse ridges of extraordinary height, the whole of the crown being thrown into deep alternating ridges and valleys, well seen in the longitudinal section of the tooth (Fig. 13g). The limbs of these folds have become so compressed as to be parallel, so that each ridge is a thin, more or less flat plate of dentine clothed with enamel,

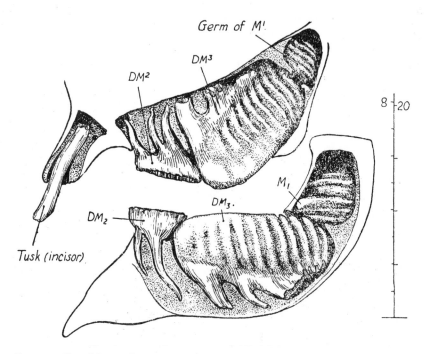

FIG 22. Dentition of young elephant, exposed to show the process of tooth-replacement. The last two milk molars are in use: the developing germs of the first permanent molars are buried in the jaws behind.

called a *lamella*. The valleys between adjacent lamellae are completely filled with cement, which thickly invests the entire tooth.

When the crown is worn in use, a complicated structure is revealed of transverse edges of enamel surrounding transversely elongated islands of dentine, each separated from the adjacent enamel-ringed island by a more or less narrow band of cement. The worn surface of the crown thus forms an efficient rasp, constantly kept sharp in wear owing to the differential abrasion of the constituent substances, in accordance with their differing hardnesses.

The elephant is exclusively vegetarian and requires enormous quantities daily of foliage and herbage for its maintenance. As we have seen, digestion of plant-matter depends on efficient crushing of the cell-walls so as to expose the nutritious contents. The rasp-like character of an elephant's grinders ensures adequate trituration and is an admirable adaptation to the animal's requirements.

The mode of succession of the teeth in elephants is characteristic, and unique among mammals (Fig. 22).

A milk dentition of three deciduous molars precedes the permanent teeth. These are shed in the living Indian elephant (*E. maximus*) in the second, fifth and ninth years respectively. In more primitive genera (e.g. the Miocene *Tetrabelodon*) the last two of these were replaced in the orthodox manner, from below, by two premolars, but in the true elephants the milk teeth are succeeded in order *from behind* by the premolars (if any) and by the three molars. Each tooth is larger and with more enamel plates than its predecessor, moving forward in the jaw to replace that in front and only coming fully into wear when the worn-out remnant of the preceding tooth is shed. Thus, no more than two cheek teeth on one side of upper or lower jaw are at any time simultaneously in use. For relatively long periods there is one only. Added to the great height of the crowns, this method of replacement greatly prolongs the maintenance of efficient grinders during the long life of the animal (at least sixty years in Indian elephants).

The upper teeth acquire in use a longitudinally convex grinding surface, the lower, one which is concave (Fig. 13g), so that isolated upper and lower molars are readily distinguished at a glance.

This rather detailed description of the dentition in elephants is necessary because of the importance of fossil teeth of different species as indications of environment and date, when found, as they not uncommonly are, in association with the artifacts of Palaeolithic man.

The following extinct species are distinguished:—

Elephas meridionalis, the Southern elephant, occurs in association with the works of the earliest known Europeans in deposits of the First (Günz-Mindel) Interglacial period. The other species are thought to be descended from this.

The teeth (Fig. 23c, d) are comparatively low in the crown, broad transversely, with few, widely-spaced lamellae with thick enamel. The first milk-tooth (m2) has 3 lamellae, the last molar (M3) up to 14.

E. antiquus, the Straight-tusked elephant, is the typical temperate-forest species of the Interglacial periods. The teeth (Fig. 23e, f) have rather low, narrow crowns, lamellae more numerous than in *E. meridionalis* but well spaced, each tending to be thicker in the middle of the tooth than at its lingual and buccal extremities. The enamel figure on the worn surface thus often resembles a narrow lozenge (*loxodont* pattern). M^3 has up to 20 lamellae, M_3 perhaps one more.

E. trogontherii (associated with the giant beaver, *Trogontherium*) is an earlier Pleistocene parkland or steppe type, of lineage distinct from *antiquus,* intermediate between *meridionalis* and the mammoth. The tooth is higher and wider than in *antiquus,* the lamellae more numerous and

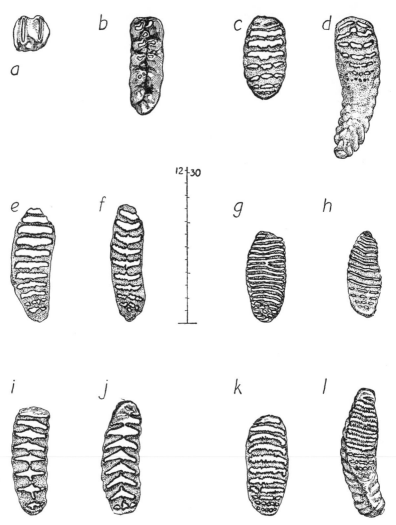

FIG 23. Molar teeth of Proboscidea, occlusal views, semi-diagrammatic to distinguish enamel (black), dentine (white) and cement (stippled on worn surfaces). (a) *Dinotherium* (upper molar), (b) *Mastodon* sp., (c, d) *Elephas meridionalis* (upper and lower), (e, f) *Elephas antiquus* (upper and lower), (g, h) *Elephas primigenius* (upper and lower), (i, j) African elephant (upper and lower), (k, l) Indian elephant (upper and lower). All on the same scale.

closely-packed, parallel-sided and without the typical lozenge-figure of *antiquus* on the worn surface. Gradations are known between *meridionalis* and *primigenius* and a maximum number of lamellae cannot be certainly assigned.

E. *primigenius*, the mammoth, with strongly-curved tusks, has up to 27 lamellae in the M₃'s. The crown is very high, the lamellae wide transversely, thin, close and crowded (Fig. 23g, h), making an extremely rough, durable chewing-surface when worn. Even the milk molars have 4 lamellae instead of the 3 usual in other species. These are adaptations to a tough, gritty diet of the grasses, herbs and stunted conifers of the loess-steppe and taiga zones during glacial periods. Most elephants are by preference browsers, taking a diet largely of foliage. The environment of the mammoth contained few leafy trees so that this species, more than any other, was probably a grazer, save in winter, when pine-shoots provided a tough and perhaps not very palatable diet.

Of the two surviving species of elephants, the Indian, *E. maximus* (Fig. 23k, l) is clearly related on the evidence of the teeth to the *trogontherii-primigenius* lineage. The African, on the other hand, appears to stand closer to the *antiquus* line, the narrow teeth (Fig. 23i, j) with comparatively few lamellae of marked lozenge-section constituting common features. The immediate ancestry and history of the African elephant is, however, something of a mystery, for it seems to appear comparatively recently in that continent and is unknown as a Pleistocene fossil.

PERISSODACTYLA (Odd-toed ungulates). *Rhinoceroses* (Rhinocerotidae). The more recent members of this ancient and widespread family, which alone concern the archaeologist, have the dental formula: $\frac{0 \cdot 0 \cdot 4 \cdot 3}{0 \cdot 0 \cdot 3 \cdot 3}$. Incisors and canines are wanting. The premolars are molariform. The upper cheek-teeth, save for P^1 which is vestigial when present at all, are more or less square in section parallel to the chewing surface and, in the cold-climate *Tichorhinus*, markedly hypsodont. They consist of a stout buccal mesio-distal ridge from which spring two lingually- and distally-curving ridges almost enclosing anterior and posterior fossae. These, however, remain open lingually and posteriorly unless worn right down close to the gum. The M^3 lacks the posterior lingual ridge and is, in consequence, nearly triangular in plan. The lower cheek-teeth are narrower bucco-lingually and consist of two somewhat crescentic ridges, running at first mesiodistally and then bent inwards lingually, partly enclosing two fossae, which are, however, more open lingually than in the upper set.

Differences between the upper cheek-teeth of the various species are recognizable, but the lower are more difficult to distinguish.

Dicerorhinus etruscus, D. hemitoechus (Fig. 24b) and *D. kirchbergensis* (*merckii* Auctt.) (Fig. 24a, d) warm- or temperate-climate species, have lower crowns, little or no cement covering the walls and lining the fossae and differ chiefly in details of the chewing-surface relating to the disposition of promontories which invade the anterior fossa from the three adjacent ridges. *Tichorhinus antiquitatis,* (Fig. 24c, e), the woolly rhinoceros, differs from the rest in the high crown, the plentiful cement (present also in well-preserved specimens of the lower cheek-teeth) and

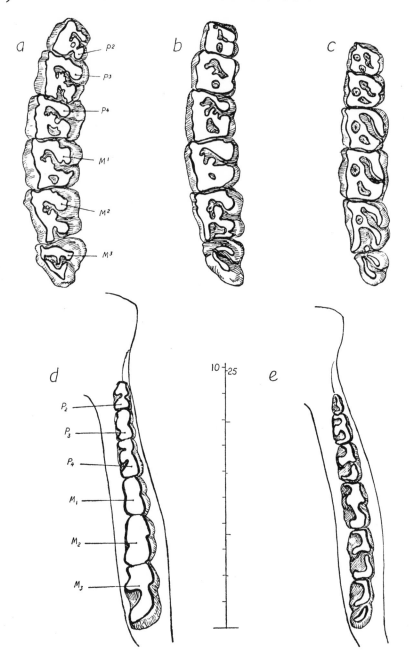

FIG 24.   Dentitions of rhinoceroses, right upper (a, b, c) and lower (d, e)
teeth. (a, d) *Dicerorhinus kirchbergensis* (*merckii* Auctt.); (b) *D.
hemitoechus*, (c, e) *Tichorhinus antiquitatis* (woolly rhino.). All three
upper sets are half-worn, as is (e) belonging to the same individual
as (c), (d) belongs to a much older individual than (a) and the teeth
are deeply worn.

the meeting of two of the above-mentioned promontories to isolate the buccal part of the anterior fossa as a distinct cement-lined pit, even at an early stage of wear. The last feature is quite specific and enables any reasonably complete upper tooth of this species to be identified at a glance.

Height of crown and presence of much cement are adaptations, as in the mammoth, to the steppe and tundra-dwelling habit and tough diet (including willow and coniferous shoots) of *Tichorhinus*, as opposed to the forest and savannah environments of the temperate species.

Horses (Equidae). Sub-family Equinae. $\dfrac{3 \cdot 1 \cdot 4 - 3 \cdot 3}{3 \cdot 1 \cdot 4 - 3 \cdot 3}$. The incisors (Figs. 25, 13f) both upper and lower, are long and curved and there is a deep depression in the enamel of the crown ('mark') which shows as an isolated cement-lined pit in the earlier stages of wear, disappearing when the wear reaches the floor of the pit. Short, conical canines are present in both sexes in *Hipparion* (a survivor into Pleistocene times of a typically Pliocene three-toed genus). Canines are present only in the stallion in *Equus,* the true horses. P_1 is rarely present as a vestige (Fig. 25b), and is shed early. P_2-4 are molariform, scarcely to be distinguished from M_1-3, which are prismatic, hypsodont, with much cement embedding the walls of the enamel crown as well as almost completely filling the deep pits in the chewing surface. *Hipparion* (Fig. 25d, e, f) differs from *Equus* in the lower crowns of the six cheek-teeth, more complex folding of the enamel and, especially, in the isolation of the lingual column, which, when worn, presents a more or less oval ring of enamel totally enclosing an area of dentine (Fig. 25d). In *Equus*, this column is united by a narrow isthmus with the main prism of dentine forming the body of the tooth.

The cheek-teeth are protruded from the alveoli in step with the wear of the crowns. They are open-rooted in the earlier stages of wear, the four roots closing the pulp cavity only at a late age. The upper set are roughly square in section, the lower narrower and rectangular. Both show a basic selenodont pattern of enamel on the worn chewing-surface, much complicated in the upper by the crimped folds of enamel and in the lower by accessory lobes on the lingual side of the tooth. These last give a transversely somewhat compressed quatrefoil pattern of enamel.

These features of the teeth constitute special adaptations to the way of life of the group. The true horses are steppe animals in the wild state and *Hipparion* was also an inhabitant of grassy plains. Exclusively grazing animals, especially in a dry steppe environment, are subject to severe tooth-wear, not only from the siliceous skeletons of the grasses themselves but also because of the gritty nature of the herbage on dusty plains. To enable the teeth to last out the lifetime of their owner they have developed a crown of great height and the copious cement coating reinforces the enamel and dentine. The crimped enamel pattern of the

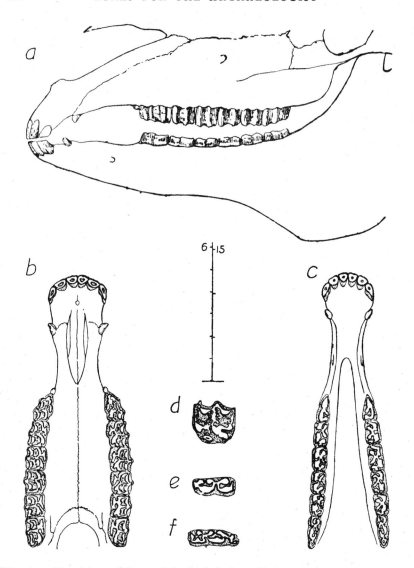

FIG 25.   Dentition of horse (♂), (a) left lateral view and (b, c) the two
          occlusal views. (d, e, f) three occlusal views of teeth of *Hipparion*:
          (d) P⁴, (e) P₄ and (f) M₃, at 2x the same scale.

chewing surface makes a rough sharp file, well designed to crush and
comminute a tough and fibrous diet.

ARTIODACTYLA. Suiformes (pig-like). *Hippopotamus amphibius.* $\frac{2 \cdot 1 \cdot 4 \cdot 3}{2 \cdot 1 \cdot 4 \cdot 3}$.
(Fig. 26). The incisors are large, cylindrical and, in the mandible,
procumbent. They and the canines are open-rooted and continuously
growing. C^1 is short and stout, bearing against the distal wear-facet

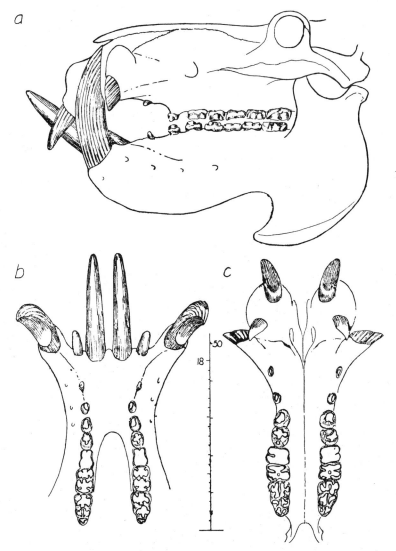

FIG 26. Dentition of *Hippopotamus*, left lateral, lower and upper occlusal views.

of the enormous C_1. In fossil individuals, larger than modern survivors of the species, this tooth may be up to 3 inches in diameter and 20 inches long along the outer curve. It is bent, like the tush of a pig, in the arc of a circle and is sub-triangular in section with longitudinally and diagonally ribbed enamel.

The cheek-teeth are complete, the molars with four high, conical main cusps. When worn, these present a quatrefoil enamel pattern. The premolars are large, but simpler in pattern.

Sus scrofa (both wild and domesticated races). Complete, and there-fore generalized, bunodont dentition: $\frac{3 \cdot 1 \cdot 4 \cdot 3}{3 \cdot 1 \cdot 4 \cdot 3}$. (Fig. 14 p. 77).

The upper incisors are short and stout, with strongly-curved roots. C^1 is short, curving downwards, forwards and upwards. The lower incisors are long and slender, with straight roots, closely set in an almost horizontally-procumbent parallel row. C_1 is long, triangular in section and open-rooted. It curves forwards, outwards and upwards. Its distal surface rubs, with every movement of the jaws, against the recurved mesial surface of the C^1, forming in use an elongated wear-facet which truncates the crown of the tooth very obliquely, maintaining a sharp point and edge to the formidable 'tush'. The adult canines erupt at age 6 months.

Premolars, above and below, are small, narrow and sectorial, save for P4, which is fairly wide and molariform. $M1-3$ increase in length, the crown consisting of four main cusps with a multiplicity of accessory tubercles, the whole wearing to an efficient grinding surface of enamel folds and dentine. The M3's are particularly long, having an extensive tapering talon, or heel, behind the main cusps. The M3's erupt at age 2 years, though the animal continues to grow in stature for another 18 months.

The European wild pig, *Sus scrofa*, may be distinguished by its lower canine tushes from the Asiatic *Sus cristatus*, for, in the former, the tooth has a sharply triangular section with a 'bead' at the bucco-distal angle and the faces of the triangular prism are more or less plane, or even concave. In the latter, however, the faces of the prismatic tooth tend to be convex and the angles rounded, with no suggestion of the 'bead'.

It is considered that our domesticated swine are descended, originally, from the Asiatic species, though doubtless they have been crossed from time to time with wild individuals of *Sus scrofa*. The tushes of domesti-cated beasts, generally smaller, usually tend rather to the *Sus cristatus* form, and the presence of any well-defined 'bead' in the tush points to its having belonged to a wild animal. This feature may be of value in distinguishing a hunted from a bred meat-supply and has a bearing on economics of early human settlements in which pig remains may be found.

The Ruminants. Families Cervidae and Bovidae. Members of these two families, the deer and cattle respectively, are closely related (see the table of the mammals, p. 256) and have, superficially, only very slight differences in dentition. The general pattern is extraordinarily constant in both (Fig. 27).

Deer (Cervidae) (Fig. 27d, e, f). $\frac{0 \cdot 0-1 \cdot 3 \cdot 3}{3 \cdot 1 \cdot 3 \cdot 3}$. The upper incisors are wanting, as is the canine, in the species with which we are here con-cerned, save, perhaps, as an early-shed vestige. The C_1 is incisiform and is closely associated with the row of true incisors, from which it is hardly

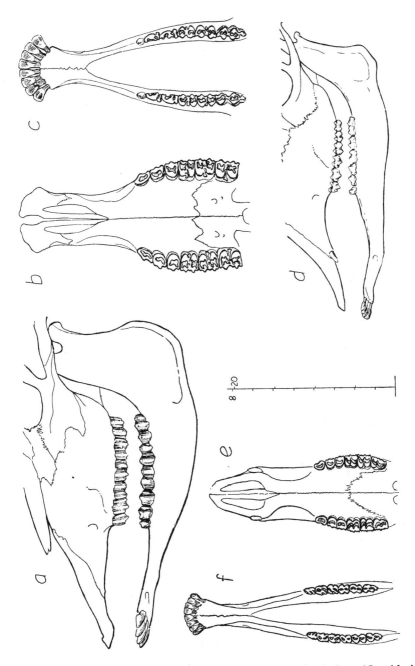

FIG 27. Dentitions of ox (Bovidae) (a, b, c) and of reindeer (Cervidae) (d, e, f). Left lateral and the two occlusal views respectively. Both on the same scale.

to be distinguished. There is a long diastema and the cheek-teeth consist of molariform premolars and molars. These are selenodont, with low crowns, the premolars having a single pair of crescentic cusps, buccal and lingual, the molars two pairs each, M3 having, in addition, a third, distal, heel-like cusp. There is often a small accessory pillar arising from the base of the crown, in the fold between the lingual crescents of the upper molars and in that between the buccal crescents of the lower. The lower cheek-teeth are somewhat narrower than the upper. The upper milk-molars are rather longer mesio-distally and less regular in pattern than the true molars. In the mandible, m_{1-2} closely resemble the premolars which replace them, but m_3 has 3 lobes, resembling in this feature the third permanent molar.

The absence of upper incisors is typical of ruminants. The lower incisors are opposed, in life, by a hard fleshy pad borne on the premaxilla, against which the food, chiefly herbage and foliage, is held by the lower incisors and pulled, rather than cut, off.

Cattle (Bovidae) (Fig. 27a, b, c). The above description of the cervine dentition applies also to cattle, sheep, goats, antelopes and gazelles, the hollow-horned ruminants, save that here the cheek-teeth are often markedly hypsodont and prismatic and, in the case of the cattle, with considerable external cement and a strongly developed accessory basal pillar in the molars. The genera and species differ only in minor details of tooth-pattern and proportions, so that, apart from differences in their size, the groups are hard to distinguish by the teeth alone. Indeed, these slight differences do not seem ever to have been systematically and exhaustively studied, so that, from the point of view of the archaeologist, who seldom has available complete skulls with horn-cores, this is a serious gap in our knowledge.

6

The Axial Skeleton

‣‣‣‣‣‣‣‣‣‣‣‣‣‣‣‣‣‣‣‣‣‣‣‣‣‣‣‣‣‣‣‣‣‣‣‣‣‣‣

THE AXIAL SKELETON consists, with the skull, of the vertebral column, ribs and sternum* (see p. 109 ff).

The vertebral column, or backbone

This consists of a chain of *vertebrae* subdivided into 5 anatomical groups:—the *cervical* (neck), *thoracic* (trunk), *lumbar* (loins), *sacral* (forming the median part of the pelvis or hip-girdle) and *coccygeal* or *caudal* (tail).

The number of vertebrae in each group is variable in different mammalian species, save for the cervicals, which are seven in number, with rare exceptions (e.g., some sloths), whatever the length of the neck. Thus, for example, the giraffe (Fig. 2h) and the elephant (Fig. 4a), alike, have 7 cervical vertebrae, though these are much elongated in the former and exceedingly short and compressed in the latter.

The thoracic vertebrae bear each a pair of *ribs*, which are joined by costal (rib) cartilages with the *sternum* (breast-bone), forming the *thorax*.

The lumbar vertebrae connect the thorax with the hip-girdle.

The sacral vertebrae, more or less fused together to form the *sacrum*, lie between the two halves of the hip-girdle, dorsally, joining it firmly to the vertebral column.

The coccygeal or caudal vertebrae continue the bodily axis into a more or less well-developed tail. In apes and man, where, alone, the external tail is not developed, the vestigial tail is called the *coccyx* ('cock-six').

A typical vertebra (Fig. 28) consists of the following main parts:—

1. The body or *centrum*, a generally short, more or less cylindrical mass of bone, with a thin dense layer of bone-substance externally and a close cancellous (spongy) structure within;

2. An arch, called the *neural* (nerve) *arch*, springing dorsally from each side of the body and enclosing an opening, the *neural canal*, occupied in life by the spinal chord, the nervous axis of the body;

3. A process projecting dorsally in the mid-line from the summit of the neural arch—the *spinous process* or *neural spine*.

4. *Transverse processes*, projecting more or less laterally from each side of the arch;

5. Two pairs of processes bearing articular facets, the *anterior* and *posterior zygapophyses* (yoke-processes), by which each vertebra is linked, respectively, with that preceding and that succeeding it in the column.

* This properly forms part of the shoulder-girdle, not of the axial skeleton, as treated here.

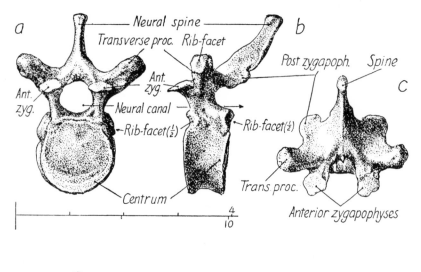

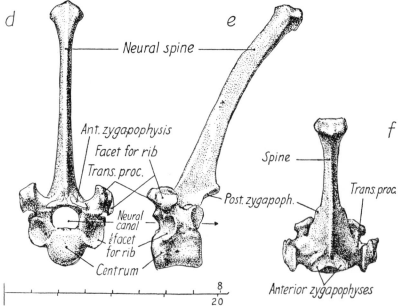

FIG 28.   Thoracic vertebrae of: (a, b, c) man and (d, e, f) horse, to show basic similarity of structure and differences in detail and proportions. Cranial, left lateral and dorsal views.

Between the bodies of adjacent vertebrae there lies, in the fresh specimen, an intervertebral disc of resilient fibrocartilage, and the bodies, arches and neural spines are further connected by strong longitudinal *ligaments* of fibrous tissue. A small amount of elastic movement is thus permitted between adjacent vertebrae, by compression of the disc and tension of the ligaments. As a whole, therefore, the vertebral column is capable of considerable latitude of movement in any plane, while being extremely resistant to longitudinal compression or tension.

The vertebrae are first formed in cartilage, which gradually ossifies during youth, beginning at several distinct centres, whence the ossification spreads until the different parts achieve complete bony union (synostosis) as the adult stature of the individual is attained. In particular, the vertebral centrum, or body, is represented by three such centres—a main block and a pair of somewhat flat, plate-like ossifications representing its articular surfaces. These are finally joined to the body at its cranial and caudal extremities, respectively, only when growth is completed. In youthful mammalian remains these *epiphyses* (additional bodies) are often found still loose and their nature may be puzzling until their true relation to the vertebral bodies is appreciated (Fig. 30). (See also epiphyses of the 'long' bones, pp. 131–2.)

The vertebrae belonging to the five different regions have peculiar features by which they may be distinguished, but the terminal members of each region tend to resemble those of the adjacent region, so that the transition is not abrupt, but more or less gradual.

CERVICAL VERTEBRAE (Fig. 29a). These are, save exceptionally, without movable ribs and are distinguished by their wide, dorso-ventrally compressed bodies and *transverse foramina* (canals) perforating the bases of the transverse processes. The spinous processes tend to be forked, or bifid.

The first two cervicals are modified and bear special names. The first, called the *atlas*, bearing the globe of the (human) head upon its shoulders, like the fabled giant of that name, has two facets or articular fossae to receive the occipital condyles of the skull, which is enabled to move at these articulations in a sagittal plane (nodding motion). The atlas is peculiar in that it lacks a body, consisting only of a more or less elongated ring of bone with transverse processes pierced, as in other cervical vertebrae, by foramina.

The second cervical vertebra, the *axis* (axle) or *epistropheus*, has a projection from its body in a cranial direction, called the *odontoid process* (tooth-like projection) or *dens* (tooth), which enters and articulates with the ventral arch of the atlas, being in life held in contact with a facet there by a transverse ligament. This ligament divides the ventral part of the ring of the atlas from the neural canal. On this projecting axle, the atlas is free to rotate from side to side (motion of shaking the head). Some quadruped atlases and axes are shown in Fig. 32, for comparison with the human bones in Fig. 29a.

The process of ossification of the axis shows that the odontoid process is, indeed, the missing centrum of the atlas, which has become attached to the body of the axis for the performance of its particular function. Articular facets at each side, facing caudally on the atlas and

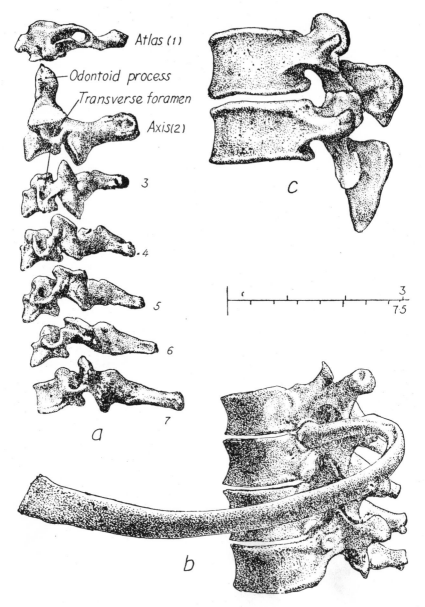

Atlas (1)

Odontoid process

Transverse foramen

Axis (2)

3

4

5

6

7

a

c

b

3
7.5

FIG 29. Human vertebrae: (a) the seven cervicals (separated), (b) four
thoracics showing the articulation of a rib, (c) two lumbars (articulated). All in left lateral view.

cranially on the axis, meet to support the movements of the atlas about
the odontoid process.

The remaining 5 cervical vertebrae are more typical of their kind,
the last one or two showing resemblances to the thoracic series which

succeeds them. In many species (e.g., man) the 7th cervical has a very long spinous process with a club-like extremity, by which it may be distinguished from all the rest.

THORACIC VERTEBRAE (Fig. 29b). These are marked, apart from other features, by the facets for the rib-articulations (see below). Their bodies increase in size caudally and become at first somewhat compressed laterally, then rounder, and, approaching the lumbar region, wider transversely. In many quadrupeds the spines are very long, especially in the anterior members of the series. The spines of most of the thoracic vertebrae incline caudally, while that of one towards the end of the series (anticlinal vertebra) projects at right angles to the profile-line of the vertebral column. The remaining thoracic spinous processes and the succeeding lumbar are inclined cranially towards it.

LUMBAR VERTEBRAE (Fig. 29c). These are without ribs, but the transverse processes are often very long and flattened dorso-ventrally, resembling short ribs. The centra are larger and more massive than in the other regions, the spinous processes short, stout and, as noted above, often inclining cranially.

SACRAL VERTEBRAE (Fig. 31). This is a small group of vertebrae, usually more or less fused together, at least in adulthood, to form a wedge-shaped body, the sacrum, which lies dorsally between the two halves of the pelvis and unites them rigidly.

CAUDAL VERTEBRAE. These are very variable in number, according to the degree of development of the tail. In mammals with long tails the first few have functional zygapophyses, a complete neural canal and prominent transverse processes, but gradually the arch disappears, the various processes are reduced in size and prominence and the vertebrae become mere sub-cylindrical centra without other features. Students trained only in human anatomy may tend to forget the existence of tails in other animals and to be puzzled when faced with loose caudal vertebrae found in archaeological contexts. To the uninitiated they may seem to resemble phalanges and their determination if thus interpreted is likely to be a lengthy business!

A vertebral formula briefly summarizes the numbers of vertebrae found in the different groups. Thus, for man: C7, T12, L5, S5, Cd4— or, simply: 7 . 12 . 5 . 5 . 4 ., the groups being understood.

The ribs

A typical rib (Fig. 29b) from the middle thoracic region has a more or less strongly-curved *shaft*, a *head* at the proximal end bearing a terminal articular facet, and a *tubercle* at a short distance from it, with another articular facet.

The head of the rib articulates at the side of the interspace between the bodies of two adjacent thoracic vertebrae and the tubercle with a facet on the ventral surface of the transverse process of the more caudal of these two vertebrae. In consequence of this oblique attach-

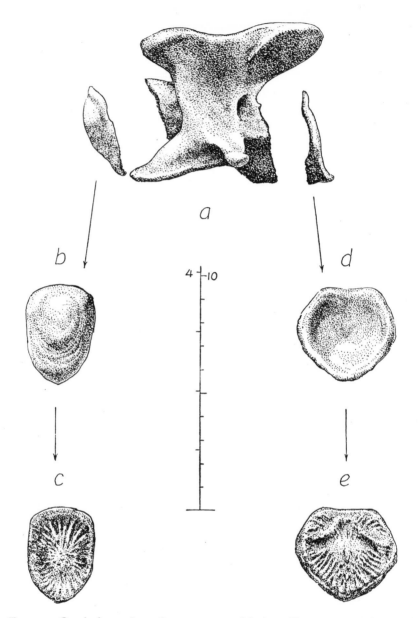

FIG 30.   Cervical vertebra of a young ox, with the still separate epiphyses of
its centrum: (a) left lateral view with the epiphyses detached;
(b, c) cranial and caudal views of the anterior epiphysis; (e, d) the
same views, respectively, of the posterior epiphysis.

ment the shaft of the rib curves ventrally and somewhat caudally. A thoracic vertebra, therefore, exhibits two half-facets on each side, at the extremities of the body, for the heads of two ribs, shared by the preceding and following vertebrae, with a single facet at the extremity of the transverse process for the tubercle of the rib whose head articulates at the more cranial of the two half-facets.

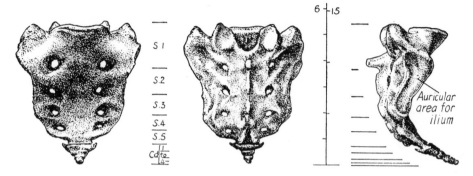

FIG 31.   The human sacrum and coccyx. Five fused sacral and four separate coccygeal (=caudal) vertebrae. (a, b, c) Ventral, dorsal, and right lateral views.

A rib may readily be assigned to its correct side of the body by recognition of the shallow channel for vessels and nerves which lies within its curve, close to its caudal margin.

Ventrally, the distal extremities of most of the ribs are connected more or less directly by *costal cartilages* with the sternum. The cartilages are ossified in some species, when they are described as *sternal ribs*.

The sternum, or breast-bone (Fig. 33e, d)

This is a bony structure occupying the midline of the thorax, ventrally. It is more or less distinctly composed of segments or *sternebrae*. The most cranial of these is often somewhat elaborated and is termed the *presternum* (*manubrium sterni* in human anatomy). The last is called the *xiphisternum* (*xiphoid* (sword-like) *process* in man) and the intervening segments make up the *mesosternum*.

These parts are very variable in shape and development in the different groups and may sometimes be characteristic. Unfortunately, the sternum is not very dense in structure, so that it is infrequently preserved unless an entire skeleton is present, and therefore seldom figures in the collections of more usually disjointed, scattered and broken bones from archaeological sites.

The first few ribs are directly connected with the sternum by their individual costal cartilages, the middle ribs often only indirectly by the junction of their cartilages with those of the former group. The last few ribs may be 'floating', their distal extremities entirely free. In addition to ribs, the presternum gives articulation to the medial ends of the clavicles, where these are present.

The Thorax as a whole. This arrangement of ribs, movably and obliquely articulated with the vertebrae dorsally and with the sternum ventrally, by cartilages or distinct sternal ribs, confers some degree of flexibility on the thoracic cage as a whole. One reason for this, of course, is to enable it to adjust itself to flexions of the vertebral column. In addition the arrangement is necessary for respiration.

When the sternum and distal ends of the connected ribs are pulled cranially by the appropriate muscles, the dorso-ventral diameter of the thorax is increased and air is drawn into the lungs by the decrease of pressure within the cavity (inspiration). Expiration takes place when the muscular pull is relaxed and the structures return to their former positions by elastic recoil and their own weight.

The movements of the ribs and sternum in respiration are assisted in life by the action of the *diaphragm*, a large domed muscle, which is peculiar to the mammals, completely dividing the thoracic from the abdominal cavity.

Special features of the axial skeleton in different mammals

			Vertebral formula		
INSECTIVORA	C	T	L	S	cd
Hedgehog (*Erinaceus*)	7	15	6	3	11
Mole (*Talpa*)	7	13	5	6	11
Shrew (*Sorex*)	7	14	6	?4	?18

The atlas has usually only short transverse processes. The neural spine of the axis is generally large, while those of the remaining vertebrae are inconspicuous. The sternum in the mole has an enormously long, strong, keeled presternum, while the rest of the sternum is narrow. This is doubtless a function of the burrowing habit and powerful fore-quarter musculature.

RODENTIA	C	T	L	S	cd
Simplicidentata	7	13	6	3	17-27
Lagomorpha	7	12	7	4	12

The sternum is generally long and narrow.

The sacrum in rodents generally consists of a single wide vertebra connecting the ilia, the others narrower and ankylosed to it.

In the beaver (*Castor*), the sacral vertebrae have increasingly wide transverse processes which nearly meet the ischia. The 25 caudals are short, broad and depressed, forming the flat, spatulate tail.

PRIMATES	C	T	L	S	cd
Man (*Homo*)	7	12	5	4	4

The human atlas is a mere ring of bone with articular facets above and below and short, blunt transverse processes. The axis has a stout, prominent, odontoid process (Fig. 29). The spines of the cervicals tend to be bifid, save for the last two, in which they are rather club-shaped. C7 has a very prominent spine. In the thoracic series the bodies become shorter and wider, passing into the lumbars, where the body is very large. The spinous processes incline uniformly downwards, becoming short and stout in the lumbars. The sacrum is short, strongly curved and wedge-shaped. The coccygeal vertebrae are mere bony beads.

The thorax in man and apes is wider transversely than dorso-ventrally, so that the ribs are more strongly curved than in quadrupeds, where the dorso-ventral diameter is the greater. This feature distinguishes human from (for instance) ungulate ribs, even in smallish fragments. The costal cartilages are never ossified. The sternum has a wide, separate manubrium, affording articulation to the medial ends of the strong clavicles (Fig. 33c). The mesosternum is short and flat, ossified in a single piece but indistinctly segmented. The xiphoid process is more or less cartilaginous during youth and only becomes ossified in middle age.

CARNIVORA	C	T	L	S	cd
Cat (*Felis*)	7	13	7	3	18-24
Dog (*Canis*)	7	13	7	3	11-21
Bear (*Ursus*)	7	14	6	3	8-10
Otter (*Lutra*)	7	14	6	3	25-26
Badger (*Meles*)	7	15	5	3	18
Stoat (*Mustela*)	7	14	6	3	18
Marten (*Martes*)	7	14	6	3	18

The atlas has deep articular fossae for the occipital condyles and wide, wing-like transverse processes.

The axis has a long, slender, odontoid process and a large neural spine, produced both cranially and caudally (Fig. 32a–d). The spines of the remaining cervicals are small, increasing in length to C7. The transverse processes of the cervicals are large and trifid in appearance.

The long, slender spines of the anterior thoracics slope caudally to T11 (the 'anticlinal' vertebra), the spine of which is upright. The short, stout spinous processes of the posterior thoracics, with those of the lumbars, slope cranially towards it.

The lumbar vertebrae have long, cranially-inclined transverse processes.

The sternum is composed of 8-9 distinct sternebrae, long, narrow and of square section. The manubrium is slightly expanded laterally at its cranial extremity; the xiphisternum is long and slender. Sternal ribs are present. The vertebral ribs are slender, sub-cylindrical and but slightly curved—the first few almost straight.

PROBOSCIDEA	C	T	L	S	cd
	7	19-20	4-3	?4	31

In accord with the shortness of the neck, the cervicals are very short and compressed. The atlas is very like the human atlas in form. The axis has a short odontoid process and a very strong spine. The remaining cervicals have disc-like bodies with comparatively short spines,

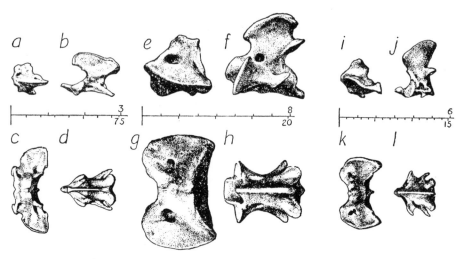

FIG 32. Atlas and axis (cervical vertebrae 1 and 2) of: (a, b, c, d) dog; (e, f, g, h) ox; (i, j, k, l) pig. Left lateral and dorsal views.

save for C7. The thoracics and lumbars are very massive. Those of the extinct *E. antiquus* have spines very upright as viewed from the side, unlike the living species and the extinct mammoth (*E. primigenius*), in which they slope sharply in a caudal direction. The sacrum consists, as in the rodents, of a single vertebra with a varying number of others ankylosed to it. The ribs are rather broad and flat as in other ungulates.

PERISSODACTYLA	C	T	L	S	cd.
Horse (*Equus*)	7	18	6	5	13-20
Rhinoceros	7	19	4		
ARTIODACTYLA	7	12-15	7-4		

The atlas is very long with deep fossae for the occipital condyles. The transverse processes are flattened but not wide, as in the carnivores. The odontoid process of the axis is generally spout-shaped (Fig. 32e, h). In the long-necked species, the bodies of the other cervicals are long and *opisthocoelous* (hollow behind), i.e., the cranial articular surface of the centrum is markedly convex, the caudal correspondingly concave. This is especially the case in the horse and rhinoceros and in the ruminants (Fig. 30a), but the feature is only slightly developed in the pig and hippopotamus, members of the less-specialized Suiformes.

The trunk (thoracic and lumbar) vertebrae are also, generally, somewhat opisthocoelous. The spines of the thoracics are long and laterally compressed, being enormously long in the bison. The lumbar transverse processes are long and dorso-ventrally flattened. The tail is very variable in length and number of vertebrae.

Among the common domestic animals of the Artiodactyl group the vertebrae of sheep and pig are of similar dimensions and are easily confounded. The following special points of distinction are worth noting for the particular archaeological circumstances we have in mind, where it may be necessary to know them apart.

	SHEEP	PIG
Atlas	Caudal margin in dorsal view sinuous	Margin evenly curved
	Caudal margin in ventral view but slightly concave	Margin deeply concave with a median tubercle or spine directed caudally
Axis	Odontoid process like a jug-lip	Process a sub-cylindrical tubercle, more like that of man
	Caudal articular facets high on the spinous process	Facets low
	Transverse processes well-developed	Transverse processes only slight
Other cervicals	Centrum strongly opisthocoelous	Centrum hardly opisthocoelous

In ruminants the sternum consists of 7 segments, the presternum narrow, widening to the square last mesosternal segment. The xiphoid process is thin and flat. In the Suidae, 6 segments only can be distinguished, the presternum narrow and keeled, the mesosternum increasing in width to the last segment. In the horse, the presternum is keeled and projects cranially beyond the 1st rib, becoming wider caudally. In the rhinoceros, it remains narrow throughout.

In all this group the ribs tend to be much flattened, the first few very straight where the thorax is narrow anteriorly. The sternal ribs are short and stout, articulating with the vertebral ribs by a cup-and-ball joint.

This account of the axial skeleton and of the differences respecting it between mammalian species is rather summary and incomplete for two reasons.

First, in the conditions met with by the archaeological osteologist the parts of the axial skeleton found are often very incomplete. This is due, in large part, to the mainly cancellous internal structure of the bones concerned and their generally only very thin investment of dense bone substance. For this reason they are less resistant to decay than, for example, the stout shafts of the long bones. In ungulate vertebrae, also, the prominent spines and other processes are frequently found broken.

Secondly, extraordinarily little attention seems to have been given to determination of species from vertebrae, so that little detailed information is available in the literature to enable characteristic and easily recognized features within the Orders to be quoted. Despite the former consideration, the material is seldom so deficient that no useful conclusions could be reached if the comparative features were better known. There is room for much more work here.

7

Shoulder- and Hip-girdles

+-+

THE SHOULDER- AND HIP-GIRDLES form links between the fore and hind limbs and the axial skeleton and afford firm bases for the articulation of the proximal segments of these.

Shoulder-girdle

This consists, on each side, of a generally somewhat triangular *scapula* (shoulder-blade), with or without a *clavicle* (collar-bone). The latter, when present, articulates at its lateral end with the scapula and, medially, with the presternum, cranially to the first rib (Fig. 33c).

The scapula has a large main articular surface, shaped like a somewhat irregularly-oval shallow dish, at its ventral angle. This is the *glenoid cavity*, which affords articulation, in a ball-and-socket joint, for the head of the humerus (upper arm bone). The function of the scapula is to form a movable, but steady, base for the attachment of the fore-limb. One set of muscles, arising on the scapula itself, has the task of holding the head of the humerus constantly in contact with the glenoid cavity. The muscles which move the scapula, and can fix it in any position within its limits of travel, arise from the axial skeleton and are inserted round the margins of the blade-bone. The movements of the scapula thus widen the range of movement of the fore-limb, while remaining fixed by the opposed tension of the muscles whenever the limb is under load.

In many quadrupeds, the area of the blade is increased by a more or less developed cartilaginous extension of its vertebral border, seen only in fresh or dried specimens (Fig. 35e).

The scapula occupies a dorso-lateral position in relation to the more cranial part of the thorax. A more or less prominent *spine*, or elevated process, divides its dorsal surface into two fossae (*supra-* and *infraspinous* fossae in man, *pre-* and *post-spinous* in quadrupeds). Its thoracic surface is somewhat hollowed (*sub-scapular* fossa). The tendons of the muscles arising from and lying within these fossae converge towards the periphery of the glenoid cavity and are inserted at the tuberosities surrounding the neck of the humeral head. By their tension they maintain this head in close apposition to the cavity.

The distal part of the spine may be prolonged into a more or less prominent, overhanging process, the *acromion*, which, when it is strongly developed, has a part in the protection of the shoulder-joint and affords articulation with the clavicle. The acromion may be extended, more or less at right-angles to the spine, in a caudal direction (*metacromial process*). Another process, the *coracoid*, projects from close to the cranial margin of the glenoid cavity. Like the acromion, this process is generally small, or even degenerate, in specialized quadrupeds. Where it is well developed, its apex gives origin to the flexor muscles of the arm and assists in the protection of the very mobile shoulder-joint.

The clavicle ('little key', from the resemblance of its S-curve in man to an ancient type of key) functions as a strut (compression-member) between the scapula and the presternum, maintaining the shoulder-joint at a constant distance from the midline of the thorax. It is fully developed only in the Primates and in other, more primitive, mammals, where the fore-limb has great latitude of movement, especially in abduction (extended laterally, at right-angles to the M.S.P.). The clavicle resists the medial thrust of the limb and prevents lateral compression of the thorax, and consequent restriction of respiration, when the limb is under load in this attitude. The functional relation of the shoulder-girdle as a whole with the manner of life of the animal will be apparent when we consider its development in the various groups.

Characters of the shoulder-girdle in different mammals

INSECTIVORA. Mole (*Talpa*) (Fig. 33b). The scapula is very long and narrow, rod-like rather than blade-like, with spine and acromion only slightly developed. The clavicle (possibly clavicle and coracoid combined) is almost cubical, so stout and short is it. This is clearly a feature adapted to the action of the enormously powerful fore-limb, used in burrowing.

Shrew (*Sorex*). The scapula is narrow, but more blade-like than in the mole. The slender acromion is bifurcated into an anterior portion supporting the clavicle, and a posteriorly-diverging metacromion. The clavicle is very long and slender.

Hedgehog (*Erinaceus*) (Fig. 33a). The scapula is of normal blade-form, with a well-developed spine and undivided acromion. The clavicle is present, but is small and evidently unimportant in an animal which neither climbs nor digs a burrow.

CHIROPTERA (Bats: Fig. 33d). Scapula large and oval, pre-spinous fossa very small, spine short. There is a large, undivided acromion and a long, curved coracoid. The clavicle is also very long—evidently an important structure in a flying animal.

RODENTIA. The scapula is often long and narrow, of very variable outline. The acromion is long, often with a large metacromial process, as in the hare (*Lepus*) (Fig. 33g), the marmot (*Marmota*) (Fig. 33h) and the porcupine (*Hystrix*) (Fig. 33f), but the beaver (*Castor*) (Fig. 33e) has a very large and strong, but undivided, acromion.

In some species (e.g., hare), the notch between acromion and spine is very deep. In all these the coracoid is no more than a small, blunt

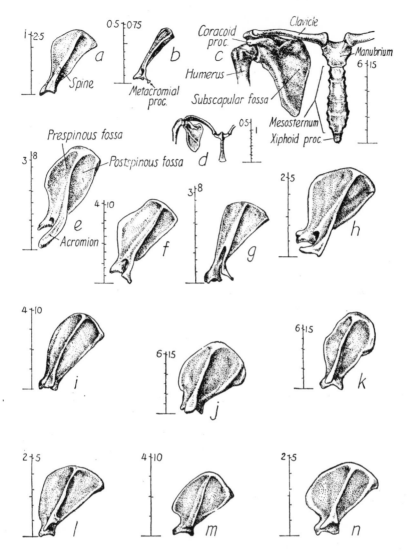

FIG 33. Shoulder-girdles and scapulae: (a) hedgehog, (b) mole, (c) man, (d) pipistrelle bat, (e) beaver, (f) porcupine, (g) hare, (h) marmot, (i) dog, (j) brown bear, (k) hyaena, (l) domestic cat, (m) badger, (n) otter. All are left scapulae in lateral view, save (c) and (d), the right, seen from the ventral side.

process. The clavicle is small, slender and, in some, is absent altogether. PRIMATES. In man (Fig. 33c), the scapula is short and wide, a roughly right-angled triangle with the right-angle truncated by the glenoid cavity and the hypotenuse formed by the vertebral border. The strong, high spine divides its dorsal surface into a small supra-spinous and a large infra-spinous fossa. The acromion is very long and strong, expanded distally and over-hanging the shoulder-joint. The coracoid process is a relatively long, but stout, hook. The clavicle is rather short and stout, s-curved, crossing the shoulder diagonally from back to front, in a medial direction, to meet the manubrium of the sternum. The whole structure of the shoulder-girdle bespeaks a powerful, mobile and adaptable fore-limb. This description applies, with minor differences of form and detail, to the apes and lower Primates. It is significant for the history of man's evolution that these, his closest living relations, are nearly all arboreal in habit.

CARNIVORA. The well-developed spine divides the scapula into practically equal pre- and post-spinous fossae. The acromion is prominent, sometimes with a well-marked metacromial process; the coracoid small. The clavicle, when present (Felidae, Canidae) is rudimentary and functionally useless. It is, surprisingly, absent altogether in so unspecialized a Family, and such capable climbers as the Ursidae (bears).

These features point to a somewhat advanced quadrupedal status in the Order, but without such complete loss of adaptability in the movements of the fore-limb as is seen in the ungulates.

Felidae (Fig. 33l). The scapula is D-shaped; the caudal border rectilinear, the cranial almost semicircular. The spine crosses the D diagonally to its lower corner, making an angle of about 30° with the caudal border. The acromion is fairly strong and there is a short, stout metacromial process. The crest of the spine is somewhat turned over caudally.

Canidae (Fig. 33i). The outline of the scapula is sub-rectangular, save in the fox (*Vulpes*), where it is more rounded, with a marked coracoid notch. The spine runs diagonally. The acromion is more strongly developed than in the cats, but the metacromion is only slightly indicated.

Ursidae (Fig. 33j). The scapula is somewhat D-shaped, but there is more of an angle at the dorsal border at the point where the spine arises. The spine makes an angle of nearly 45° with the caudal border. The acromion is strong, without any indication of a metacromial process.

Mustelidae. The outline of the scapula is very variable. It tends to be short and broad with a very wide glenoid cavity in comparison with its total area.

Badger (*Meles*) (Fig. 33m). Rectangular, with a marked coracoid notch. Acromion weak.

Marten (*Martes*). Almost oval, with small acromion and short, stout metacromial process.

Stoat (*Mustela*). Rather oval, save that the caudal border is straight and appears to be a chord cutting off a segment parallel to the long axis of the oval. Acromion slender but prominent, with a small metacromial process.

Otter (*Lutra*) (Fig. 33n). The outline is similar to that of the badger, but the spine is nearly parallel with the caudal border, instead of diagonal, and the dorsal angle, in consequence, is less pronounced. The acromion and metacromion are more strongly developed than in the badger.

Glutton (*Gulo*). The scapula is very like that of the badger, save that, here, the acromion and metacromion are strong.

Hyaena (Fig. 33k). The scapula is a parallelogram in outline, though with rounded-off angles, the spine forming the long diagonal. The acromion is dog-like rather than cat-like, i.e., without a metacromial process.

PROBOSCIDEA (Fig. 34). The scapula is apparently very variable in form in the different species. In the extinct members this is probably due, in part, to deficient material and imaginative restoration. There is no clavicle.

Elephas meridionalis (Fig. 34a). The scapula is markedly quadrilateral, with almost rectilinear borders. There is a rather small pre-spinous and an enormous post-spinous fossa. The caudal border of the latter part projects in a prominent, but obtuse, angle. The acromion is relatively small, but recognizable, and a very long mid-spinous process overhangs the post-spinous fossa, its slender extremity being directed rather ventrally.

E. antiquus (Fig. 34b). The borders of the scapula tend to be concave. The pre-spinous fossa is narrow, the post-spinous even wider than in *meridionalis* and the angle of its caudal border is somewhat acute. The mid-spinous process arises along the whole crest of the spine, but is relatively short. Its caudally most prominent part is at about mid-spine and forms a very obtuse angle. The acromion is only very slightly developed.

E. primigenius (Fig. 34c). The scapula is triangular, with rounded angles and somewhat concave borders. The pre-spinous fossa is exceedingly narrow, so that the border between the origin of the spine and the most cranial angle, forming a distinct rectilinear side of the quadrilateral in *E. antiquus*, has its contour reduced, in *primigenius*, to a bluntly-rounded border. The two caudal borders of the large post-spinous fossa lie almost at right-angles, though the angle itself, where they meet, is blunt and rounded. The acromion is reasonably well developed. The mid-spinous process has the form already described for *E. meridionalis*.

E. africanus (Fig. 34d). The scapula is similar to that of *meridionalis*, save that the borders are, except the caudo-ventral, convex and the angles not so marked. The pre-spinous fossa is relatively wider than in *meridionalis*. There is a considerable, somewhat knobbed, acromion and the prominent, slender mid-spinous process arises from the ventral third of the spine only.

E. maximus (syn. *indicus*) (Fig. 34e). The whole scapula is much narrowed in its dorsal third, where the pre- and post-spinous fossae

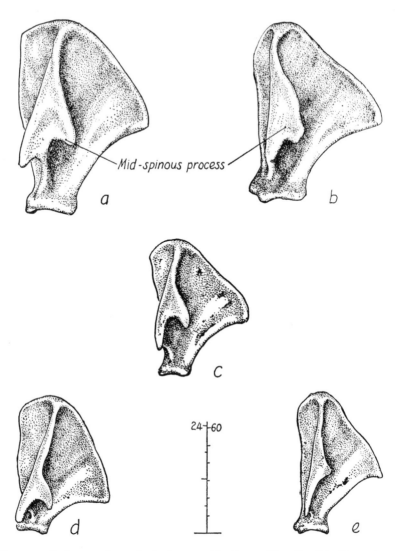

FIG 34.   Left scapulae of elephants: (a) *E. meridionalis*, (b) *E. antiquus*, (c) *E. primigenius*, (d) *E. africanus*, (e) *E. maximus* (Indian). All on the same scale.

are sub-equal. The latter is, however, much prolonged into an acute-angled caudal angle, making the relative overall proportions similar to those described for *E. africanus*. The acromion is vestigial and a short, blunt mid-spinous process arises from the middle third of the crest of the spine.

PERISSODACTYLA. *Rhinoceros* (Fig. 35a). Scapula long and narrow, sub-rectangular, the spine arising in the middle of the short dorsal border and nearly bisecting the blade parallel to the longer sides. The acromion

is practically indistinguishable, but there is a large mid-spinous process, turned caudally and overhanging the post-spinous fossa, which
is the smaller of the two divisions. The coracoid process is a prominent
stout knob. No clavicle.

Horse (*Equus*) (Fig. 35b). The scapula is long and narrow, more
triangular than in the rhinoceroses, with a wide neck. The origin of
the spine divides the dorsal border unequally, about one third of the
area of the blade lying in the pre-spinous fossa, two thirds in the post-
scapular. The acromion is rudimentary, but the coracoid is a prominent rounded knob. The spine ends nearly in the mid-line of the
neck (diff. ruminants). A mid-spinous process is only indicated by a
slight, diffuse retroversion of the edge of the spine. No clavicle.

ARTIODACTYLA. Suiformes. *Hippopotamus* (Fig. 35d). The scapula is
relatively short and wide, irregularly polygonal in outline. The three
major borders are rectilinear, but the two dorsal angles are truncated.
The spine is low and follows an irregular course from its origin, well
inside the dorso-cranial angle, to its indeterminate end at the glenoid
cavity. Its edge is irregularly turned caudally to overhang the post-
scapular fossa, but there is no well-defined mid-spinous process. The
coracoid is a stout, short hook below a well-defined coracoid notch in
the pre-scapular border. There is no acromion.

Pig (*Sus*) (Fig. 35c). The scapula is an isosceles triangle with regular
borders. The origin of the spine divides the dorsal border into one
third (pre-spinous) and two thirds (post-spinous) and ends without
trace of an acromion near the midline of the neck (diff. ruminants).
The crest of the spine is turned, along most of its length, to overhang
the post-spinous fossa, and there is a well-marked mid-spinous process
in its dorsal third. The coracoid process is a mere swelling cranially to
the glenoid cavity. The neck of the scapula is well marked, but there
is no real coracoid notch.

The scapula of a pig is readily distinguished from that of a ruminant
of comparable size (e.g. sheep) by the almost central position of the
spine relative to the neck of the bone and by its thickened borders.
These make the pre- and post-spinous fossae, as well as the sub-
scapular fossa, markedly excavated close to the neck, which is the part
of the blade-bone most often well preserved.

Ruminants (Cervidae, Bovidae) (Fig. 35e, f, g, h). The scapula is extraordinarily alike in all the ruminants, the genera differing only in minor
details. One general description thus serves for all. Exact determination is usually possible only with adequate comparative material.

The blade is almost an isosceles triangle in shape, the dorso-caudal
angle being slightly more acute because a convexity of the cranial
border in its dorsal third brings the dorso-cranial angle close to a blunt
right-angle. The spine arises at the boundary between the cranial
fourth and the caudal three-quarters of the dorsal border and runs in
an almost straight line to the neck of the scapula, where it ends well

short of the glenoid cavity. The crest of the spine is somewhat sinuous, overhanging the post-spinous fossa in its dorsal two-thirds and inclining towards the pre-spinous side in its acromial part. The acromion, at the highest point of the spine, is represented only by a slightly thickened projection, separated by a shallow notch from the termination of the spine at the neck of the blade. The coracoid is a short, somewhat hooked, process, only slightly less rudimentary than in the Perissodactyla.

Even generic morphological distinctions reside in slight differences in curvature of the borders of the blade, in the shape and extent of the sub-acromial notch of the spine and in the form of the glenoid cavity and adjacent coracoid hook. These are almost impossible to describe in words. Some examples are illustrated in Hue (1907) and should also be studied in recent comparative material. Absolute dimensions are at least a negative guide, enabling some genera to be excluded with a fair degree of certainty and making it improbable that the bone in question belongs to some others. The likely attributions are thus reduced to only a few.

A small number of possibly distinctive points may, however, be indicated, though they are not based on study of any large number of specimens and are less likely to be useful in the case of fragmentary material.

Elk (*Alces*). Blade rather wide in proportion to its length, sub-acromial notch fairly deep, acromion scarcely thickened, glenoid cavity almost circular and the antero-lateral lip of the cavity prominent. Coracoid, a prominent knob, not excavated on its thoracic aspect into a hook.

Red deer (*Cervus elaphus*) (Fig. 35e). Caudal border of blade markedly convex in its middle third. Neck of blade slender. Antero-lateral lip of glenoid cavity not prominent but distinct from coracoid in lateral view.

Reindeer (*Rangifer*). Caudal border of blade straight. Neck relatively wider, sagittally, than in red deer. Spine has a strongly undercut sub-acromial notch. Acromion slightly thickened. Glenoid cavity oval. Coracoid very blunt, merging with the anterior lip of the cavity in lateral view, but slightly excavated on its thoracic aspect to form a blunt hook.

Fallow deer (*Dama*). Dorso-caudal angle of blade barely acute, very close to a right-angle. Crest of spine markedly overhangs post-spinous fossa in its middle third. Neck of blade slender. Well-marked sub-acromial notch. Coracoid relatively light and well detached in a hook. Anterior lip of glenoid cavity indistinct, so that the cavity is practically circular. Smaller than red deer.

Roe deer (*Capreolus*). Very small size—less than sheep, but slender in the manner of all deer. Dorso-cranial angle of blade well rounded. Dorso-caudal angle markedly acute (close to 65°). Coracoid slender and well detached from anterior lip, though the latter is not very prominent. Glenoid cavity slightly oval.

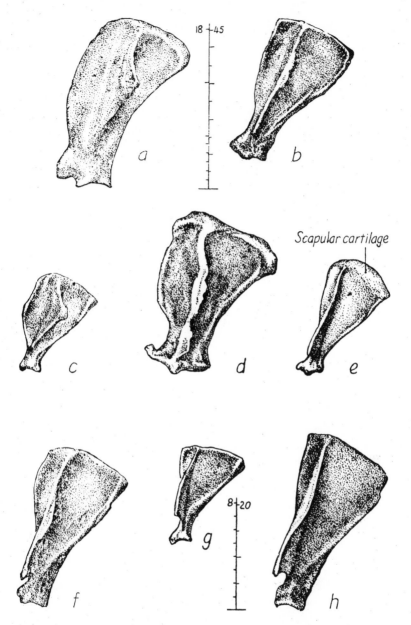

18 ⊢45

Scapular cartilage

8⊢20

FIG 35.   Ungulate scapulae: (a) rhinoceros (*Tichorhinus*), (b) horse, (c) pig, (d) hippopotamus, (e) red deer, (f) ox, (g) sheep, (h) bison. (a, b, d, f, h) upper scale; (c, e, g) lower scale. Left scapulae.

Cattle (*Bos*) (Fig. 35f). Scapula relatively long and narrow, with a stout neck. The dorso-cranial angle is acute, the dorso-caudal obtuse. The crest of the spine is more sinuous than in the deer. The acromion is indistinct and there is no definite sub-acromial notch. The glenoid cavity is somewhat oval and the coracoid, though blunt, arises in clear detachment from its anterior lip.

Bison (Fig. 35h). The scapula is very long and narrow, with a stout neck and sinuous crest to the spine. The length of the blade is associated with the extremely prominent neural spines of the anterior thoracic vertebrae, giving the animal the characteristic hump at the withers. The general outline of the blade is much more rounded than in *Bos,* both dorsal angles being indistinct and the vertebral border convex. The acromion and sub-acromial notch are more distinct than in *Bos.* The glenoid cavity is markedly kidney-shaped and the coracoid, though arising close to its anterior lip, is distinct from it and forms more of a hook than in *Bos.*

Sheep, Goat (*Ovis, Capra*) (Fig. 35g). The scapula has a blade proportionately wider than in *Bos* and a much more slender neck, as in the deer. The course of the crest of the spine is more sinuous, however, than in the latter and the outlines of the blade more severely rectilinear. The acromion is somewhat thickened and the sub-acromial notch perhaps more pronounced in goat than in sheep. The coracoid is large and distinctly hooked, but is scarcely separated from the anterior lip of the glenoid cavity, which, save for the projection of the lip, tends to be only slightly oval or almost circular.

Saiga. All borders of the blade are convex and the spine, for a ruminant, is high. Its crest follows a rather straight course and has no thickening at the acromion nor any sub-acrominal notch. The glenoid cavity is rather long sagittally and narrow, with a prominent anterior lip. The coracoid arises close to it, but is slender and well-detached in a hook.

Chamois (*Rupicapra*). The scapula is very similar in size and lightness of build to that of the roe, but has a very straight caudal border and a more obtuse dorso-caudal angle (70°). The spine is not distinctive, but the glenoid cavity is nearly circular and the coracoid, though somewhat hooked, is scarcely distinguishable from its anterior lip.

Musk-ox (*Ovibos*). The scapula is about twice the size of that of a sheep or a goat but of similar proportions. The dorso-caudal angle is, however, not acute, as in these, but is close to a right-angle. The sinuous spinal crest resembles that of *Bos,* but the acromion is slightly thickened. The coracoid and anterior lip of the glenoid cavity are scarcely separate.

The hip-girdle or pelvis (Fig. 36)

This consists of a bony structure on either side, the *os innominatum* (unnamed bone) or, in man, *os coxae* (hip-bone), meeting its opposite half ventrally and connected therewith dorsally by the sacrum. Strictly

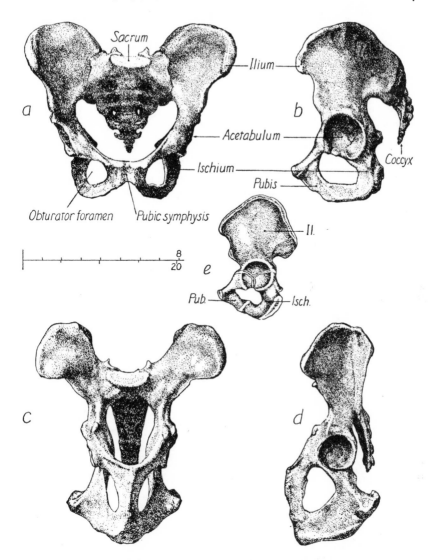

FIG 36. Pelves of (a, b) man (♂), and (c, d) bear (*Ursus arctos*), for comparison. Ventral and left lateral views. (e) An immature human left os innominatum to show the still separate bones and cartilages in the process of ossification.

speaking, therefore, the pelvis includes the sacrum, though the ossa innominata are often loosely referred to as the right and left 'halves' of the pelvis.

The main function of the pelvis is to link the hind limbs to the vertebral column, but, unlike the shoulder-girdle, this basis of attachment is not itself movable in relation to the axial skeleton but is rigidly fixed to it by short, strong ligaments. Further functions are to assist in the support of internal organs and to afford attachments to the muscles moving the hind limb.

Each os innominatum consists of three bones, the *ilium*, *ischium* and *pubis*, separate in youth but becoming fused together as soon as adult stature is attained. These three come together at a tri-radiate junction (Fig. 36e) to form a roughly hemispherical cup, the *acetabulum*, which receives the head of the thigh-bone (femur) to form a universal joint. The ilium connects dorsally with one side of the sacrum, the ischium projects caudally and bends ventrally to meet the pubis, while the two pubes meet ventrally in the midline of the body at the *pubic symphysis*. Ischium and pubis thus enclose on each side a large oval opening, the *obturator foramen*. The complete pelvis forms a more or less long tube, through which, in the female, the foetus passes during parturition.

Though the separate bones of the two ossa innominata are completely ankylosed on each side in early adulthood, the joints between the sacrum and the two ilia (*sacro-iliac* joints) and the joint at the symphysis pubis are not so united until later in life, if at all. The ossa innominata, therefore, generally fall apart on decay of the ligaments and complete pelves are seldom found in the fossil state, at least in man.

Particular features of
the pelvis in different groups of mammals

INSECTIVORA. Pelvis very variable in form. In some genera the pubic symphysis is long and completely ankylosed, in others short, though in contact, and in yet others the pubic bones do not meet at all. The last is the case with the shrews (*Sorex*) and mole (*Talpa*). In the latter, the os innominatum is very long, narrow and straight, as befits a burrower.

RODENTIA (Fig. 37a). The bones are light and slender, the ilium rod-like and scarcely expanded dorsally. The pubes and ischia are large and diverge caudally. The pubic symphysis is long and is usually completely ossified.

PRIMATES. In man (Fig. 36a, b, e), owing to his habitually erect posture, the proportions of the pelvis are very different from those of quadrupeds and, indeed, even from those of his nearest relations, the apes. The os innominatum is very short and broad, the ilium greatly expanded and with a short, wide neck above the acetabulum. Pubis and ischium are short and strongly divergent, the pubic symphysis short and only very rarely ankylosed. The broad and everted ilia form a sort of basin, which plays an important part in supporting internal organs in the erect posture. The opening of the pelvis is somewhat heart-shaped, wider transversely than dorso-ventrally and, owing to the strong curvature of the sacrum, the short tube formed is not cylindrical but bent.

The proportions of the human pelvis are of great value in determining the sex of the individual. The features of importance in this connection are described in Chapter 15 (p. 230). In apes, the os innominatum is much longer, proportionately, than in man, more closely resembling

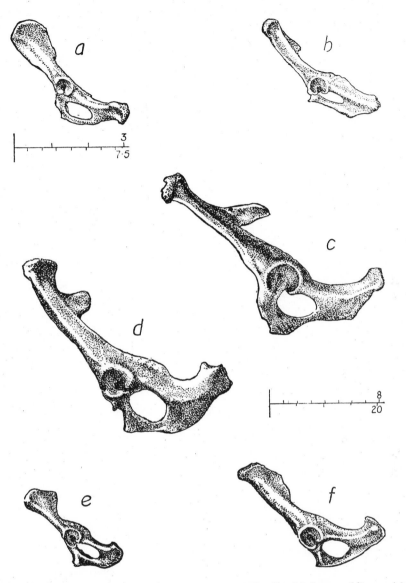

FIG 37. Left innominate bones of (a) hare, (b) pig, (c) horse, (d) ox, (e) sheep, (f) red deer. Left lateral views. All on the same (lower) scale, save (a).

the usual quadruped form. This is especially the case with the ilium, though this bone is broader and more everted than in quadrupeds.

CARNIVORA (Fig. 36c, d). The pelvis is long and narrow, the ischia continuing the line of the ilia and being very nearly as long. The ilium is slender, narrow, and more or less parallel-sided and its ventral surface not everted. The broad ischia are much divergent caudally, with prominent, laterally-directed tuberosities. The symphysis is long and is formed in part by the ischia as well as by the pubes. It is generally ankylosed in the adult animal. In the hyaena the pelvis is much shorter and wider, the ilia being more everted than in other carnivores.

PROBOSCIDEA (Fig. 4a). The pelvis is very wide. The crest of the ilium is enormously expanded dorsally, the whole bone short and fan-shaped; the ischium and pubis relatively short and stout also. The whole appearance of the pelvis is thus much closer to that of man than in most quadrupeds.

PERISSODACTYLA (Fig. 37c). The ilia are very long, broad dorsally but rapidly contracting to a rather long, slender neck above the acetabulum. The ischia are fairly short, as is the pubic symphysis. The obturator foramen is nearly circular. The acetabular notch is rather widely open ventrally.

ARTIODACTYLA (Fig. 37b, d, e, f). Though the whole pelvis is much elongated, the ilia are relatively shorter than in the Perissodactyla, expanded and everted dorsally, but with a neck not so slender. The ischia are long, generally wide and everted caudally, with a well-marked external tuberosity in the middle of the caudal extremity. The symphysis is extremely long, where it is rather short in the Perissodactyla, and the obturator foramen forms an elongated oval. In the Suiformes (Fig. 37b) the acetabular notch is slightly more widely open ventrally, whereas, in all the ruminants, it is more (Bovidae) or less (Cervidae) closed near the ventral margin of the acetabulum by two over-hanging 'lips' of the articular surface (Fig. 37d, e, f). This is a very useful distinctive feature, since the parts of the ilium, ischium and pubis at some distance from the acetabulum are often destroyed in bones from archaeological sites, while the dense acetabulum and its immediate surroundings are more frequently well preserved.

Another feature distinguishing the ruminant os innominatum from that of Suiformes and Perissodactyla is the presence of a deep oval depression on the lateral surface of the ilium, immediately above the acetabulum, the *supra-acetabular fossa*. For the reasons stated above this is also a very useful feature.

As in their other bones, the ossa innominata of the deer (Cervidae) tend to differ in general from those of the Bovidae by their lightness of build and greater elongation, though, in the comparatively heavily built elk (*Alces*), for example, this difference is not so marked, while the feature of slenderness is shared, on the other hand, among the bovids, by the chamois (*Rupicapra*).

8

The Fore-limb

+‒+

'Long' Bones

THE PRINCIPAL BONES of the limbs, the 'long' bones, differ in structure from those of the skull, axial skeleton and girdles.

The term 'long', as applied to a bone, carries no implication as to length, either absolute or relative to the rest of the skeleton. In the anatomical sense it refers to this peculiar structure, which is, indeed, characteristic of the longest bones in the appendicular skeleton.

A 'long' bone (Fig. 38) consists of a shaft (*diaphysis*) and articular ends (*epiphyses*). The latter bear joint-surfaces, covered in the fresh specimen by articular cartilage, at which they meet and move in contact with adjacent bones.

The shaft of a long bone is constructed of compact bone-substance, somewhat cylindrical in section and hollow, the cavity, in the fresh specimen, being filled with bone-marrow. This has special physiological functions in life, in particular the elaboration of the red blood-cells. Mechanically, the hollow shaft has the advantage, over a solid bone, of much greater lightness with only a very small decrease in strength.

The mechanical principles involved can easily be demonstrated by rolling a sheet of paper of ordinary thickness into a fairly tight, hollow cylinder. The paper thus acquires considerable rigidity and resistance to a bending stress, as well as surprisingly great strength to withstand longitudinal compression. Its strength in these respects would not be commensurately increased if it were a solid cylinder, instead of being hollow, since it is the periphery of the section which does most to resist bending stress.

The epiphyses, on the other hand, have the same kind of spongy (cancellous) internal structure covered by only a thin layer of dense bone, which has already been noted in the bones of the axial skeleton. The epiphyses are short and often very stout and, in their position at the ends of a long bone, they are in no danger of fracture from bending stresses. They do, however, have to withstand pressure from adjacent bones, when these are under load, and the localized tension of the muscle-tendons and joint-ligaments attached to them. The cancellous structure confers great tensile and compressive strength while economizing in material and weight.

Growth of long bones

The long bones are pre-formed in cartilage ('gristle'), which begins in early youth to ossify from one centre for the shaft and others for the terminal epiphyses. These separate bony masses are not firmly united until the adult dimensions of the bone have been attained. The shaft increases in length by the progressive ossification of the layers of cartilage interposed between it and the epiphyses (epiphyseal cartilages) while these constantly grow in advance of the process of ossification until the bone reaches its full size. Growth of the cartilage then stops,

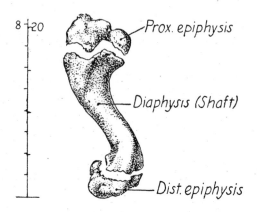

FIG 38.   Humerus of a young pig, to show the still loose epiphyses of the head and tuberosities, and of the distal end, separated from the shaft.

but ossification continues until the epiphyses become united with the shaft by bony fusion (ankylosis). The more prominent processes for the attachment of muscle-tendons often have separate epiphyses. Such are the tuberosities of the humerus (p. 133) and the trochanters of the femur (p. 157), which also have to grow in proportion as the main bone increases in size.

The progress of these changes is of value in determining the age of youthful individuals from the long bones. Fuller details will be found on pp. 226, 229.

All the bones of the limbs and extremities are 'long' bones, as defined, save for two groups of bones, at the wrist (carpus, p. 146) and ankle (tarsus, p. 170) respectively, and for the sesamoid bones (p. 172).

The fore-limb

The fore-limb, apart from its extremity (*manus*, p. 146 ff) consists of two segments ('joints'), the proximal segment (upper arm), represented by the *humerus*, and the distal (forearm), represented by two bones, the *ulna* and the *radius* (Fig. 39).

The humerus has a *head* of more or less spherical form, by which it articulates freely in a ball-and-socket joint with the glenoid cavity of the scapula. The head of the humerus projects somewhat dorsally and caudally from the main axis of the shaft of the bone and is borne on a rather ill-defined *neck*. Two *tuberosities*, the greater, or lateral, and the lesser, or medial, stand at the base of the neck on the anterior aspect of the bone. They afford attachment for the muscles originating on the scapula which keep the head of the humerus in contact with the glenoid cavity. The tuberosities are separated by a *bicipital groove*, which, in life, accommodates the tendon of the long head of the biceps muscle.

The shaft of the humerus is more or less cylindrical, but may have a prominent *deltoid ridge* crossing its anterior aspect diagonally, medially and distally.

The distal articular end of the humerus meets the ulna and radius in the elbow-joint. It is marked principally by a sub-cylindrical pulley-shaped articular surface, the *trochlea,* and, in species with a separately movable radius, a small rounded knob lateral to the trochlea, the *capitulum*. The distal end of the humerus is often much elongated transversely into a *lateral* and a *medial epicondyle*. The latter is usually the more prominent. Immediately above the trochlea, before and behind, are a pair of fossae which respectively accommodate the coronoid process of the ulna in full flexion (*coronoid fossa*) and the olecranon process of the ulna in full extension (*olecranon fossa*) of the forearm. The latter is much the deeper. The floors of these two fossae are usually separated only by a thin septum (partition) of bone, which, in some species, is actually perforated (*supra-trochlear foramen*).

Where the medial epicondyle is supported by a prominent ridge running up on to the shaft of the humerus, this ridge is often grooved or perforated close above the epicondyle to transmit the brachial artery and nerve (*entepicondylar foramen*) (see Fig. 40h[1]). The presence or absence of this foramen is of systematic importance. The lateral epicondyle may also, in some species, run proximally into a pronounced ridge, the *supinator ridge* (Fig. 40f).

The ulna meets the humerus in its deep *trochlear notch*, which receives the trochlea of the humerus in a hinge-joint. The notch is delimited in front by the *coronoid process* and behind by the *olecranon process*. At the extremity of the latter is inserted the tendon of the triceps muscle, the principal extensor of the forearm. Its development is, therefore, a measure of the power of that muscle. While the ulna thus always plays the major part in forming the elbow-joint, its shaft and distal epiphysis are often much reduced in size and independence, particularly in the more highly-specialized quadrupeds.

The radius, in species having a separately-movable radius, lies alongside the ulna on its lateral side. The *head* of the radius, in these species, is somewhat cylindrical, bearing with its circular end on the capitulum of the humerus and being more or less free to rotate about its own axis against a small lateral hollow facet on the ulna (*radial notch*), with which, in life, it is maintained in contact by an annular ligament encircling the head. In most quadrupeds, however, the radius has become the principal

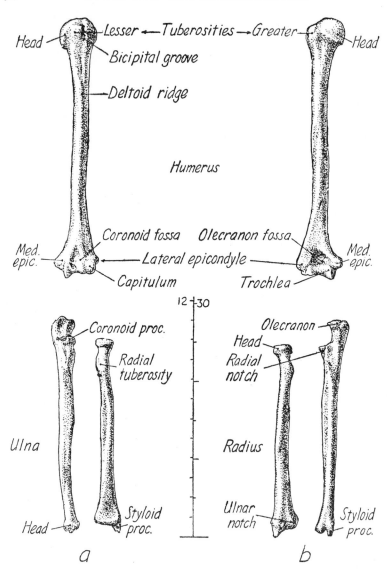

FIG 39. Left arm-bones of man, anterior and posterior views. Separated to show named parts.

bone of the forearm and is more or less immovably fixed by ligaments, or even by ankylosis, to the ulna. In so doing, the radius has come to lie in front of the ulna instead of beside it, playing a somewhat more important role than before in forming the elbow-joint and supporting nearly the whole load borne by the limb. It thus almost entirely supersedes the ulna in its distal contact with the bones of the carpus (wrist). The relative development of ulna and radius is therefore a point of importance in determining the degree of specialization attained by the animal owning them, and, hence, in helping to assign the bones to a particular species or larger group.

Special features of the
fore-limb bones in the different groups

INSECTIVORA. The humerus is generally relatively long and slender but the neck of its head is indistinct. The tuberosities are large and project above the articular surface of the head. The distal part of the shaft curves anteriorly rather sharply. The deltoid ridge is long and prominent and the olecranon fossa deep. Ulna and radius are separate, the former well-developed, but little movement between them is possible.

Hedgehog (*Erinaceus*) (Fig. 40a). Supra-trochlear foramen present and large. Entepicondylar foramen lacking. Ulna much stronger than radius.

Mole (*Talpa*) (Fig. 40b). The humerus is exceedingly short and stout with an enormous distal articulation. A large saddle-shaped proximal articulation with the clavicle is present, as well as a narrow, oval head articulating at the glenoid cavity. Both epicondyles have slender, proximally directed processes. There is an entepicondylar foramen. Ulna and radius are relatively long, equally developed, separate, but of restricted movement between themselves. The peculiarities of this fore-limb are specializations to support the very powerful digging muscles.

Shrew (*Sorex*) (Fig. 40c). All fore-limb bones slender, ulna and radius equally developed.

CHIROPTERA (Fig. 40e). All fore-limb bones are slender, the humerus very long, the radius more than half as long again. There is no entepicondylar foramen. The radius is by far the more important of the forearm pair and the ulna is ankylosed to it.

RODENTIA. The fore-limb bones are very variable—humerus generally slender and straight, with but slightly-developed muscular processes, a supra-trochlear perforation but no entepicondylar foramen. The ulna and radius are separate, with a variable amount of movement between them possible in various species. Extremes, for our purposes, are represented by the hare (*Lepus*) and beaver (*Castor*) (Fig. 40d). The former has a smooth, slender, rather curved humerus with a narrow trochlea. The ulna is stouter than the radius, which is closely applied to it and relatively immovable. In the beaver, both deltoid and supinator ridges are prominent and the medial epicondyle is especially strongly developed. The former is a notable runner, the latter animal less specialized and far more adaptable in movement.

PRIMATES. In man and other higher primates the fore-limb (arm) is especially characteristic. The humerus is extremely long, slender and straight, with but slightly prominent muscular attachments. The head, in particular, is almost hemispherical in shape, affording great latitude

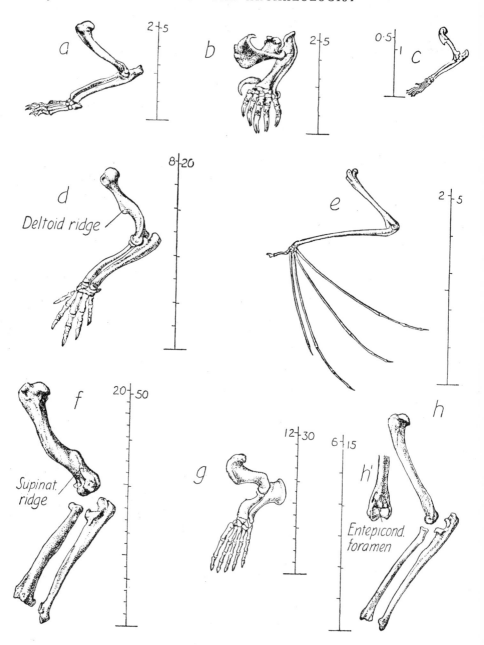

FIG 40.   Bones of the left fore-limb and manus in some mammalian groups:
(a) hedgehog, (b) mole, (c) shrew (Insectivores), (d) beaver (Rodent),
(e) bat (Chiropter), (f) bear and (h) cat, fissipede Carnivores,
(h¹) anterior view of humerus to show entepicondylar foramen,
(g) seal (pinnipede Carnivore). Lateral view in all cases.

of movement in all directions, and this is distinctive. However extensive the articular surface of the humeral head in quadrupeds, it is never so strongly curved in every direction as to be quite hemispherical, even in the Carnivora. Owing to the prominent head and the relative slightness of the tuberosities, these latter never extend proximally beyond the articular surface of the head, as is commonly the case in quadrupeds. At the distal end of the humerus, the trochlea is flanked laterally by a distinct and prominent capitulum for the articulation of the head of the radius. The medial epicondyle is specially prominent, since it gives origin to the strong common flexor tendon of the hand- and finger-muscles, necessary for a firm grip in climbing and manipulating.

The coronoid fossa is more marked, the olecranon fossa less so, than in quadrupeds, though the latter remains the deeper of the two in the absolute sense. There is neither a supra-trochlear foramen, nor an entepicondylar foramen.

The ulna and radius are of equal development, separate and freely movable the one on the other. The ulna plays the larger part in forming the elbow-joint, with a deep trochlear notch and a prominent coronoid process. The olecranon process, however, though stout, is very short, and the triceps muscle, which extends the forearm at the elbow, has, in man, a leverage of no more than 1 inch from the centre of the elbow-joint. This is markedly distinct from the condition seen in quadrupeds, where the olecranon is relatively long. The mechanical reason for this is that, in quadrupeds, the triceps tendon is under constant tension while the animal is standing in order to maintain the extension of the partly flexed forearm. In man and the apes, where the fore-limb, when used for progression (as in climbing) is a tension- rather than a compression-member, the strong extensors of the quadrupeds are replaced by power-ful flexors of the forearm, in particular, the biceps and brachialis muscles. Thus the long olecranon process is unnecessary. The relative weakness of the power of extension of the arm in man is shown by the fact that it is regarded as something of a feat of strength to raise the body more than a few times in succession by extension of the arms alone in the 'on-the-hands-down' position beloved by P.T. instructors! The distal end of the ulna forms a sub-cylindrical rounded head, with a medially-situated *styloid process*.

The radius lies alongside the ulna, laterally to it, and articulates with it at a shallow radial notch. The head of the radius is almost cylindrical with a slightly depressed circular terminal facet for articulation with the capitulum of the humerus. In the Primates this small facet is the sole point of contact of the radius with the humerus. In most quadrupeds the radius has a considerable area of contact with the trochlea of the humerus also.

At a short distance distally from its head, the radius bears a medially prominent *radial tuberosity*, at which is inserted the tendon of the biceps muscle. This flexor, in contrast with the triceps extensor, has a leverage of between 2½ and 3 inches from the centre of the trochlea, a very considerable mechanical advantage. From the radial tuberosity, distally, the shaft of the radius is bowed laterally and widens towards its distal epiphysis. The distal articular surface of the radius forms a nearly rectangular hollow and articulates with the greater part of the carpus. A medial *ulnar notch* affords articulation to the head (distal extremity) of the ulna.

Movements of pronation and supination. A free movement between ulna and radius is necessary to the arboreal and manipulative hand and is worth some detailed consideration.

While the ulna forms the chief part of the elbow-joint, it is the radius which carries the greater part of the hand. Now the radius is free at its proximal end to rotate about its own axis at the radial notch of the ulna, which is fixed by its trochlear notch in a one-plane hinge-joint with the humerus. In rotating, the distal end of the radius describes an arc about the axis of the head of the ulna. Thus, with the forearm horizontal, when the head of the radius makes half a turn medially, its shaft crosses over that of the ulna to bring the distal end of the radius to the medial side of the head of the ulna, thus turning the hand palm downwards (*pronation*). The reverse movement, returning the shaft of the radius to lie parallel with and laterally to the ulna, is termed *supination* (palm upwards).

Without this freedom—superfluous in a quadruped fore-limb devoted solely to terrestrial progression—many manipulative movements (e.g. the use of a screwdriver) would be practically impossible. In an ape, arboreal agility, involving grasping branches at all angles, would also be severely restricted without it.

Man, though doubtless of arboreal ancestry, has long forsaken the trees, as a normal habitat, for the ground, becoming somewhat adapted, as regards the lower extremities (see p. 173) to terrestrial progression. He has, however, retained the upright posture and free hand. It is to be expected, therefore, that there would be notable differences in the development of the fore-limb as between man and the apes. This is, in fact, the case. Our cousins, the apes, which have remained arboreal in habit, and especially those, like the gibbons, which progress chiefly by brachiation (swinging by the arms), have enormously strong, elongated fore-limbs and legs very short in comparison with those of man. Since the power behind the movements of pronation and supination depends, to some extent, on the distance separating the shafts of the ulna and radius these bones are more bowed, as well as being relatively longer and stronger, in apes than in man.

CARNIVORA. The flesh-eaters are, on the whole, quadrupeds of more specialized habit than the foregoing Orders. Only two in our list (bear and badger), are plantigrade and somewhat more generalized than the rest. It is to be expected, therefore, that the independence and freedom of movement of the fore-limbs should be to some extent restricted in comparison with those of the more adaptable primates, climbers and burrowers. The Pinnipedia (the sub-Order including seals, walrus, etc. (Fig. 4og)) represent an extreme degree of specialization, with their paddle-shaped flippers and the very short limbs of which these form the extremities, but most carnivores are more adaptable.

The humerus is generally less shortened and stout than in more specialized terrestrial quadrupeds, such as the ungulates. The head of the humerus is less hemispherical than in the Primates and the tuberosities project well above its articular surface. The shaft is strongly curved anteriorly and has a prominent deltoid ridge. The Felidae (cats) (Fig. 4oh) and most of the Mustelidae (marten family) have an entepicondylar foramen, but this is absent in the Ursidae (bears) (Fig. 4of), Canidae (dogs) and Hyaenidae (hyaenas). A large supra-trochlear foramen occurs in the Canidae.

The still entirely separate ulna and radius tend to be somewhat longer in proportion than in the more primitive insectivores, rodents and primates. Though independent, the ulna and radius in most carnivores are rather closely fitted to one another and have, consequently, lost their mobility to a large extent. Only in some climbers (e.g. cats) are any considerable movements of pronation and supination possible. A cat turns up the pad of a forepaw in washing its face; a dog cannot do this. There is, therefore, no distinct capitulum of the humerus for the articulation of the head of the radius in most carnivores.

The radius lies more in front of the ulna, forming a larger part of the elbow-joint than in man. The ulna has a long, transversely-compressed olecranon process—a sure indication of quadruped status, for the mechanical reasons referred to above (p. 137). The long olecranon increases the leverage of the extensor muscles and thus lightens their load.

In all carnivores the humerus is relatively long in comparison with the ulna and radius, though proportions relative to the body as a whole vary very much. Thus, dogs and foxes have long fore-legs, badgers and the other Mustelidae short. In the seals (Fig. 4og) the fore-limb bones are exceedingly short and strong, the humerus strongly curved, the ulna very stout proximally and the radius, conversely, at its distal end.

The ungulates (hoofed mammals), including the Orders Proboscidea, Perissodactyla and Artiodactyla, are all somewhat specialized quadrupeds, in which the humerus tends to be short and stout and the forearm bones relatively much longer than in the carnivores. This is, however, not the case in the Proboscidea, a relatively primitive Order in respect of the development of the limbs, nor in the short-legged Suiformes, among the Artiodactyla.

The humerus is generally very straight and flat on its medial side, without any marked medial epicondyle such as is seen in man, for example. The trochlea tends to be wide and laterally displaced relative to the line of the shaft.

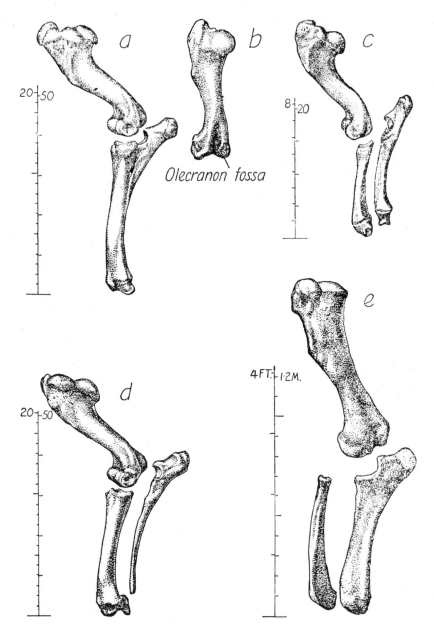

20—50

8—20

Olecranon fossa

4 FT.—1·2 M.

20—50

FIG 41.   The left fore-limb bones in typical ungulates. (a, b) horse, (c) young pig, (d) ox, (e) elephant. All in left lateral view, save (b) posterior view.

The ulna varies very much in its relative development compared with the radius.

PROBOSCIDEA. Elephant (*Elephas*) (Fig. 41e). In this group the humerus is very long, straight and relatively slender, in comparison with more specialized terrestrial quadrupeds. It has a powerfully-developed supinator ridge running down to the lateral epicondyle. The head of the bone is large and prominent, without any well-defined neck, and the greater tuberosity scarcely overtops it. As viewed from behind, the olecranon fossa is seen to be long and narrow, with its greatest length in line with the shaft. The ridges of the trochlea, in anterior view, are very oblique to its transverse axis.

The ulna and radius are quite separate, but fixed in pronation. The former has not only the chief part in forming the elbow-joint but its distal end is also larger than that of the radius, an unusual condition peculiar to this genus. For a quadruped, the olecranon process is unusually short and stout. This is possible in so large and heavy an animal only because the elbow-joint is fully extended when the beast is standing at rest, so that the upper-arm and forearm bones are in the same straight line, or even lock in slight over-extension. In this attitude the triceps tendon, inserted at the olecranon, is not under tension and requires less leverage at the olecranon than in most quadrupeds, where the elbow is somewhat flexed in the attitude of standing at rest.

The humerus of the Upnor *E. antiquus* in the British Museum (Natural History) is 4 feet 1 inch long, compared with 3 feet 1 inch for the humerus of the largest Indian elephant in the same collection. The ulna measures 3 feet 9 inches. The dimensions, alone, of such bones, afford a sufficient identification!

PERISSODACTYLA. *Rhinoceros* (Fig. 42b). The humerus is very short and stout, with a much twisted appearance owing to the presence of a strong supinator ridge crossing the posterior aspect of the shaft, obliquely distally and laterally. The lateral margin of the olecranon fossa follows the line of this ridge. The tuberosities are very large, standing high above the articular head, and the greater overhanging the bicipital groove. There is a very prominent deltoid ridge of which the crest is turned over posteriorly.

The ulna is a separate bone with a well-developed distal epiphysis, but the massive radius is closely applied to it and occupies the whole width of the trochlea. The olecranon is both long and strong. Both bones are very stout.

Horse (*Equus*) (Fig. 41a, b). The humerus is much more slender than that of the rhinoceros, as befits an animal of lighter build, but is markedly stout and rugged in comparison with that of an ox of similar stature. The tuberosities are large and high and the deltoid ridge marked, but the supinator ridge, though stout, is not unduly prominent. The trochlea is thicker and its profile in distal aspect simpler and less sharply sculptured than that of an ox.

The ulna shows extreme reduction, tapering off to a point and being fused, even in youth, with the radius in mid-shaft. Only a mere tooth-pick vestige persists distally in exceptionally well-preserved specimens and even this is firmly ankylosed with the radius. The olecranon is long and narrow transversely, but deep sagittally, markedly deeper than in the ox. The sole function of the ulna in a horse is to provide the poster-ior part of the olecranon notch and a strong lever for the attachment of the extensors of the forearm. It is the radius which carries all the weight transmitted by the humerus to the manus. This is a strong, relatively short, heavy bone, its shaft rather D-shaped in mid-section, the con-vexity to the front. The distal end of the radius, connecting with the whole of the remaining carpals, has a multi-faceted, rather complicated epiphysis, easily distinguished from that of the ox, which has even more numerous articular facets. In fossil and sub-fossil specimens the proxi-mal remnant of the ulna is most usually detached from the radius by a fracture just above the point where its thin, tapering shaft is fused with the radius. The separate ulna is then recognized and determined by the characteristic depth of the olecranon process and the radius by the remnant of the ulnar shaft firmly fused to the mid-point of its own.

This picture of extreme specialization in the horse and reduction of bone to the bare essentials of a one-plane lever is repeated in the hind limb (p. 163 ff) and in both extremities (pp. 153, 176).

ARTIODACTYLA. This group is, in general, distinguished from the Perissodactyla by the lighter build of the fore-limb bones, the less rugged muscular impressions and the much slighter development of the del-toid ridge. The ulna, though much reduced in many species, is always present for its entire length and is fused with the radius, if at all, only in aged individuals.

The sub-Order Suiformes, including pigs and hippopotami, are shorter-legged, of heavier build and less specialized in their limb-bones than the ruminants.

Pig (*Sus*) (Fig. 41c). The humerus is short and rather stout, especially in domesticated races. Its head is small, the tuberosities very high and overhanging the bicipital groove. The deltoid ridge is fairly prominent and a well-marked supinator ridge runs out to the lateral epicondyle. The olecranon fossa is short, oval above and the trochlea narrow. Owing to the shortness of the shaft in the domesticated pigs, the humerus has the appearance of possessing a marked S-twist, which distinguishes it at once from that of a ruminant (e.g. sheep) of com-parable size.

The ulna and radius are separate, complete and equally developed, but immovably applied to each other. The ulna is short and stout with a very long olecranon, close to one-third the total length of the bone when it is measured to the coronoid process. The shortness accentuates the sharpness of the bend, hollow posteriorly, which it has in common with other ungulate ulnae. The articular surface at the trochlear notch is very narrow transversely.

The radius shares the bend of the ulna, since the shafts are parallel and in contact. It lies well in front of the ulna, proximally, extending across the whole of the trochlea. The entirety and absence of any reduction of the ulna distinguishes it readily from that of any ruminant.

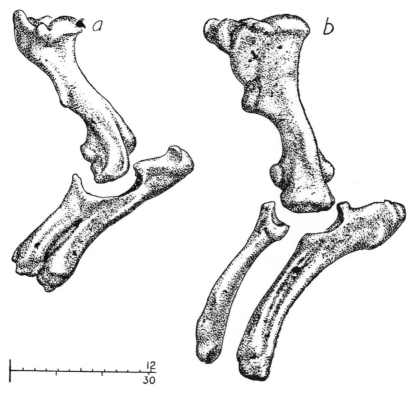

FIG 42. Left fore-limb bones of: (a) hippopotamus, and (b) rhinoceros. Left lateral views. Both on same scale.

The 'twistiness' of pig long bones, hard to describe exactly, but highly characteristic, is shared by the forearm bones. In wild pigs the limb bones are longer and more slender, so that this feature is less accentuated.

Hippopotamus (Fig. 42a). Owing to the large size of the animal and the shortness of the limbs, the humerus is very stout indeed for an artiodactyl and could easily be mistaken for that of a rhinoceros, since it has also rather marked deltoid and supinator ridges. On close comparison, it is, however, relatively more slender in the shaft, the tuberosities even more prominent and the trochlea is clearly more like a double-sheave pulley-block than the single-sheave form of the trochlea in the rhinoceros. The deltoid ridge rises into a prominence rather triangular, seen in sagittal profile, than square, as in *Rhinoceros*.

The ulna and radius are extraordinarily short and stout, being almost rectangular in profile, while those of *Rhinoceros* are longer and elegantly waisted in mid-shaft. Owing to its shortness, the ulnar shaft has the same marked, posteriorly concave curve as that of the pig and a long, relatively slender olecranon, where, in *Rhinoceros*, the process is short and very deep in a sagittal plane. As in the pigs, the ulna and radius are fully formed and quite separate in youth, though, because of their form and curvature, immovable in relation to one another.

The sub-Order Ruminantia (Fig. 41d) includes animals (e.g. cattle, deer) often of considerable size, but longer-legged and of lighter, more speedy build than the Suiformes.

The humerus is invariably short and often very stout, the ulna and radius, in comparison, long. The latter takes over from the ulna the main weight-bearing function. The ulna has a long, strong olecranon, less deep sagittally than that of the horse, for instance, and forms the posterior part of the notch for the trochlea of the humerus. Its shaft, however, though present in its entire length, is generally reduced to a mere splint, thin and blade-like transversely. This is closely applied to the shaft of the radius for the middle third of its length and is even ankylosed with it in some old individuals, as is also the distal epiphysis with that of the radius.

The radius is a strong, gently-curved bone of somewhat D-shaped section, the convexity to the front. It lies, at its proximal end, directly in front of the ulna, the epiphysis bearing on the whole width of the trochlea of the humerus. The fore-limb being fixed in pronation, the distal end of the radius lies somewhat medial to that of the ulna, of which the epiphysis meets only the lateral and posterior part of the carpus. The flattened posterior surface of the radius has a roughened area immediately adjacent to the proximal epiphysis, where it is closely fixed by ligaments in front of the trochlear notch. Close to the lateral margin of the radial shaft and extending over about the middle third of its length is a long, narrow depressed 'scar' with a roughened surface at which the shaft of the ulna is similarly attached, or even occasionally ankylosed in old individuals. The distal epiphysis is wide transversely and has a somewhat complicated articular surface which meets the proximal row of irregularly shaped carpal bones.

This general description serves for all the genera of the sub-Order. Differences in the fore-limb bones, even between families, are confined to proportions and details of the articular surfaces. Thus, the more long-limbed and lightly-built deer (Cervidae) are usually distinguishable from the cattle, sheep, antelopes, etc. by the relatively greater length and gracility of the bones, but ready distinctions between genera of the same family rest more on the absolute dimensions than on morphological details. There can be little confusion, in point of size, on the one hand, between red deer, fallow deer and roe, or between ox, musk-ox and goat on the other, but when it comes to deciding between elk and giant deer among the Cervidae, or between ox and bison or sheep and goat in the Bovidae, the difficulties are much greater and can only be resolved, if at all, by close study of the specimens and comparison with an extensive material, such as is only likely to be found in a national collection. This is, therefore, a matter for the specialist, though the variety of possibilities is not likely to be large. In fact, in any particular case the choice can be cut down, generally, to a single pair of alternatives. It may safely be taken that, in the present state of our knowledge, even the specialists will not often hazard a determination between *Bos* and *Bison* or between *Capra* and *Ovis* from the long bones only, though some authors have published descriptions of features claimed to be distinctive.

Among these, one of the best is a well-illustrated paper by J. Boessneck *in* Brothwell & Higgs (eds.), 2nd ed. 1969, pp. 331-358. He takes the domestic sheep, *Ovis aries* Linn., and goat, *Capra hircus* Linn., considering in turn the main regions of the skeleton and pointing out such differences in individual bones as he considers reasonably consistent over the fairly large material examined. He concludes by saying: 'Distinguishing between sheep and goat bones is often not easy, even with the help of the features mentioned above, especially when the bones in question are fragmentary food-remains. With some practice, however, at least a considerable part can be determined.'

This paper gives references to other work on sheep/goat distinctions.

S. Payne, *in* Ucko & Dimbleby (eds.), 1969, pp. 295-305, considers only the metacarpals and gives scatter-diagrams of chosen measurements to illustrate his results.

9

The Fore-extremity (manus)

As with the teeth, in many mammals of the more specialized Orders some of the basic bony units of the fore-extremity have degenerated or are altogether missing. These reductions are often very characteristic and are, therefore, of importance in classification. In order to appreciate them properly, it is first necessary to be acquainted with the full mammalian equipment.

The bones of the manus fall into three divisions:—

1. The *carpus*, a group of up to 8 irregularly-shaped small bones, forming, within itself, a firm but slightly elastic link, proximally with the ulna and radius and distally with the metacarpus.

2. The *metacarpus*, a set of 5 long bones, which meet the carpus in joints having little latitude of movement, but which afford, at their distal ends, very mobile hinge-joints for the bases of the *digits* (fingers).

3. The *phalanges,* the bones of the 5 digits, 3 to each, save the first digit, which has only 2.

THE CARPUS. This has a full complement, in the mammals, of 8 bones. The nomenclature of the carpal bones is confusing to the beginner because, as so often in osteological terminology, the usual names are those first given to the bones of the human wrist and later transferred to their homologues in the manus of the lower mammals. The names are, to some extent, descriptive of the form and development of the bones in man, so that they do not necessarily correspond at all closely to the shapes found in other mammals.

For the archaeologist the carpal bones are generally of no great importance. Owing to their usually small size and irregular shape, they are frequently but poorly preserved and may easily be overlooked by excavators since, in the earth, they are not readily recognizable as bones.

A brief account of them is nevertheless included here, for the sake of completeness. Fig. 43 shows their arrangement in some less specialized mammals.

Flower (1876) lists the following names and synonyms for the carpal bones:

Radiale	=Scaphoid		=*Naviculare*
Intermedium	=Lunar	prox. row	=*Semilunare, Lunatum*
Ulnare	=Cuneiform		=*Triquetrum, Pyramidale*
Centrale	=Central		=*Intermedium* (Cuvier)

Carpale 1	=Trapezium			=*Multangulum majus*
Carpale 2	=Trapezoid	dist.		=*Multangulum minus*
Carpale 3	=Magnum	row		=*Capitatum*
Carpale 4 } Carpale 5 }	=Unciform			=*Hamatum, Uncinatum*

The first column contains the terms which are most useful to the comparative zoologist, for they are applicable to amphibia, reptiles and birds as well as to the mammals. The second list is that most generally in use by British anatomists at the time of writing of Flower's work. Gray's 'Anatomy', however, in the 29th edition (1946), favours for man the use of an anglicized form of the Latin names in the third column, but prefers 'scaphoid' (boat-shaped) to 'navicular' (presumably because a bone of the tarsus—ankle—already bears that name) and 'trapezium' and 'trapezoid' to 'multangulum majus' and 'multangulum minus' (presumably for the sake of brevity). The middle column at least has the sanctity of usage over many years.

The basic arrangement of the 8 carpal bones in a generalized mammal is in two main transverse rows, with one bone occupying a central position among them. The above list presents them reading from the medial side of the dorsal (volar) aspect of the manus, the first row consisting of 3 bones, the central, and the distal row of 4 bones. To these must sometimes be added a radial and an ulnar sesamoid bone (ossification in a tendon—see p. 172) of which the latter is most often highly developed and has an individual name, the *pisiform* (pea-shaped). Carpals 4 and 5 in lower animals are invariably fused in the mammals. THE METACARPUS. This is the most important division of the manus, for our purposes. In the less specialized Orders there are 5 metacarpal bones, numbered I to V from the radial side. These articulate proximally with the distal row of carpals, of which the most lateral is occupied by two metacarpals, IV and V. A metacarpal or metatarsal (p. 171) may be recognized by its multi-faceted proximal articulation and its smooth hinge-like surface for the distal articulation of the digit.

Each of the metacarpals articulates distally with a digit. The metacarpals are, technically, 'long' bones and, in some specialized quadrupeds they are long indeed and even as stout as the radius. Metacarpals are commonly wider transversely and less deep sagittally than the corresponding metatarsals.

THE PHALANGES. The digits of the manus are 5 in number in the more generalized mammals, though in the majority of species with which we are concerned some are reduced in importance or even absent altogether.

Digit I, the *pollex*, corresponding with the thumb in man, never has more than 2 phalanges, but the rest, where not degenerate, have 3 each. The phalanges are called 1st, 2nd, and 3rd, or *proximal, intermediate* and *ungual* (nail). The first articulates with the corresponding metacarpal, the last is often somewhat modified as the bony core of a

horny claw or hoof. The number of functional digits and their arrangement relative to the main axis of the fore-limb are important systematic
features.

Bones of the manus
in different mammalian groups

INSECTIVORA. There are usually only 7 carpal bones. Scaphoid and lunar
are generally separate but are fused in the hedgehog (*Erinaceus*). The
central is missing in the shrews (*Sorex* spp.) The manus is usually of
moderate size, with small, slightly curved conical ungual phalanges to
carry the unspecialized claws (Fig. 40a, c). In the mole (*Talpa*) (Fig.
40b), however, the manus is relatively enormous, being the main
equipment of a specialized digger. There are present, in addition to all
8 bones of the carpus, a large ulnar sesamoid and a still larger sickle-
shaped radial sesamoid. The metacarpals and phalanges are extremely
short and stout, save for the ungual phalanges, which bear long curved
claws. The digits are almost of equal development.

CHIROPTERA (Fig. 40e). The manus of a bat is modified in an extraordinary manner to support an extensive wing-membrane. The proximal
carpals may all be fused into one. The short pollex, only, is not concerned in supporting the wing and has a claw. All the other digits have
phalanges extremely slender and elongated, forming stiffeners and
'ribs' for the umbrella-like wing.

RODENTIA (Fig. 40d). The carpals are generally 7 in number, as in most
plantigrades, the scaphoid and lunar often being united. This is the case
in beaver (*Castor*), squirrel (*Sciurus*), marmot (*Arctomys*) and the true
mice (*Mus* spp). The hare (*Lepus*) and beaver have a central carpal,
absent in most other genera. The beaver has also a particularly well-
developed radial sesamoid, which is often present, but not so strongly
marked, in other rodents. All, for our purposes, have 5 digits. The
metacarpals are short and the arm-bones long, showing a generalized
evolutionary status.

PRIMATES. Man (Fig. 43a) has 8 carpals, including a well-developed
pisiform, but the *os centrale* is absent. The magnum is the largest of the
carpal bones, though, despite the name, in most other mammals it is
far from being the largest. In man, orang and chimpanzee the carpus
articulates only with the radius, the ulna forming the centre about
which the manus rotates freely in the movements of pronation and
supination. Metacarpal I (thumb) is short and stout, and has greater
freedom of movement at its articulation with the carpus than the rest.
This articulation is in a different plane from those of the other metacarpals, the palmar surface of the bone facing *across* the palm. The other
metacarpals are almost equally developed, longer and more slender
than Metacarpal I. Their distal heads are large, with an extensive, sub-
spherical articular surface. This confers great mobility on the fingers,
which are thus enabled to adapt their grip to irregular objects.

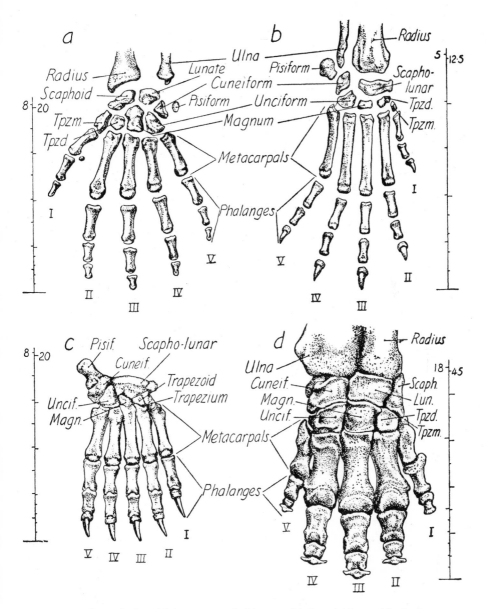

FIG 43.   Dorsal view of the manus of: (a) man, (b) dog, (c) bear, (d) elephant.
The right extremity in all cases save (a). The bones are separated in
(a) and (b) for clearer illustration.

The phalanges of the hand tend to be somewhat flattened on their
palmar surfaces. The ungual phalanges are small, tapering and somewhat
flattened in a palmar plane at their extremities.

The hand of man is an exceedingly mobile and adaptable organ.

Among the Primates, only man can oppose his thumb to the tip of each finger or cross it over his palm to the ulnar side.

In lower primates the manus is longer and narrower than in man, less freely mobile and the thumb less well developed—in some, indeed, only rudimentary.

The Primates alone have true finger-nails and even among the lower members of the Order (e.g. marmoset (*Hapale*)) claws are developed. CARNIVORA (Fig. 43b, c). In the carpus the scaphoid and lunar are fused into a single bone, the scapho-lunar, which also includes the centrale. A large pisiform is present and generally a small radial sesamoid also.

The metacarpal equipment is usually complete, but in *Hyaena* m/c I is missing and is very degenerate in the Canidae. In the Ursidae, however, as might be expected from their lack of specialization in other ways, the pollex is about equally developed with the other digits. Its metacarpal is articulated in the same plane as the rest, so that the pollex is not more mobile than the other digits or opposable to them, as in man.

In the Pinnipedia (seals etc.) (Fig. 40g) the manus forms a flipper and the pollex is the longest of the 5 well-developed digits.

The phalanges of carnivores are more 'waisted' than those of man, the proximal articular facet more deeply hollowed and the distal with a more marked median ridge. The ungual phalanges, carrying strong claws, have a thin lamina of bone reflected anteriorly over the base of the horny claw, which thus grows out of a sort of sheath. The cats (Felidae) have retractile claws which are withdrawn by over-extension of the ungual phalanx.

PROBOSCIDEA. *Elephas* (Fig. 43d). The manus is extremely short and stout, with 8 massive carpals, including a pisiform. The centrale is absent. The trapezium projects distally beyond the rest of the carpus as a whole. The 5 digits, being symmetrically developed about III, the longest and strongest, the axis of the manus runs from the radius, through lunar and magnum to m/c III. Metacarpal IV is the next in order of development and its axis runs from the ulna through cuneiform and uncinate. Metacarpals II, V and I are somewhat less strong, in that order. The metacarpals are short and heavy, the phalanges extremely short, tapering steeply to the relatively small unguals.

The elephant has no true hoofs and is intermediate in the posture of the manus between the digitigrade carnivores and the unguligrade Perissodactyla and Artiodactyla. So great a weight of body could scarcely be borne on the phalanges alone, especially over soft ground, were it not for a great fleshy palmar pad which distributes the weight over a large area and enables both the carpus and metacarpus to take their share. The digits are, thus, not externally detached from the manus as a whole, giving the characteristic pillar-like appearance to it.

The true ungulates are somewhat specialized terrestrial quadrupeds, browsers and grazers, relying for the most part on speedy flight or agility over rough ground for protection against their many enemies.

Some few of the more primitive, heavily built and shorter limbed, rely on a thick skin for passive defence and are, further, provided with formidable defensive weapons, nasal horns or canine tusks, if more active resistance should be necessary. They are, without exception, unguligrade, the terminal phalanges of both manus and pes being encased in horny hooves. The pollex (digit I) is missing in all and most show further reductions in the number of toes. There is no os centrale and the scaphoid and lunar are always separate.

Two lines of evolution have been pursued, distinct from the Eocene on, by two groups of ungulates, placed, in Simpson's classification (Appendix B) in the super-orders Mesaxonia and Paraxonia. The former have the axis of the manus and pes passing through the middle digit (III) of the primitive 5 (Fig. 44a, b) and in the latter the axis falls between the two equally-developed digits III and IV (Fig. 44c, d, e). The further reduction or losses of digits, which have occurred in the two groups in the course of evolution, have taken place more or less symmetrically about these two different axes.

PERISSODACTYLA. Symmetry of the manus about a central axis requires an *odd* number of digits, 1, 3 or 5. Since no true ungulate has a pollex, the functional toes in this group are, therefore 3 or 1 in number. It is necessary to add the word 'functional' because one member of the group, the tapir, though formally perissodactyl in the symmetry of the manus, does possess a somewhat degenerate fourth digit (V) which, however, does not reach the ground in walking. The groups of concern to the European prehistorian comprise only the rhinoceroses (Rhinocerotidae) and horses (Equidae).

Rhinocerotidae (Fig. 44a). In the carpus, scaphoid and lunar articulate with the radius, the cuneiform with the ulna. The distal row is also nearly symmetrical about the magnum, the trapezium (for the missing m/c I) being a mere vestige. There is a very small pisiform. Of the 3 metacarpals, III, based on the magnum, is the largest and longest, II and IV being less developed and about equal in size. All three bones are of moderate length and extremely stout. A minute vestige of m/c V articulates laterally with the uncinate.

The phalanges of all three digits are very short and wide, half as wide again as they are long, but flattened in their palmar planes. The unguals form vertically compressed hoof-cores, which, unlike those of the elephant, are somewhat detached from the manus as a whole.

Equidae. Three-toed horse (*Hipparion*). This extinct genus just survives into human times and is of interest, furthermore, for comparison with the living horses.

The third metacarpal bears the main digit with its hoof and carried the whole weight of the animal on hard ground. The somewhat degenerate m/c's II and IV lie closely alongside it, rather to its palmar side. These bore distally small but complete, transversely compressed, digits with well-formed asymmetrical hoof-cores, which, however, did not

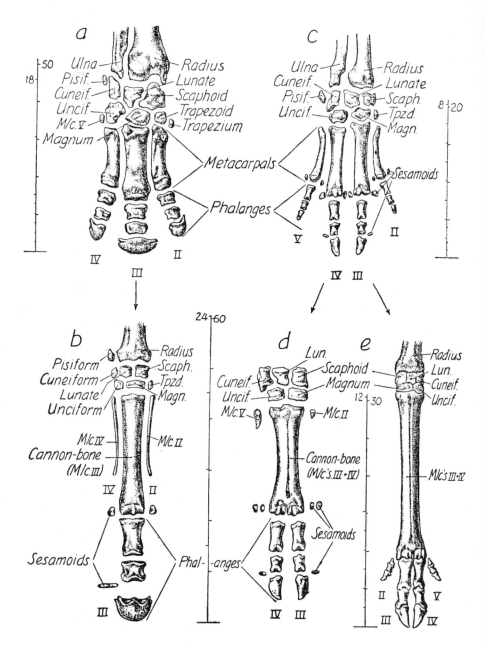

FIG 44. The dorsal view of the manus in various ungulates: (a) rhinoceros, (b) horse (Perissodactyls); (c) domestic pig, (d) domestic ox, (e) red deer (Artiodactyls). (b) and (d) on the same scale. The right manus in each case, save (e), in which the left is illustrated.

normally reach the ground. (See illustration of the pes, Fig. 50d.) They were, perhaps, of use to the animal, like the short digits of the pigs (p. 154), when moving over soft or boggy ground, helping to distribute the weight and preventing the main, rather narrow, hoof from sinking too deeply.

Horse (*Equus*) (including asses, onager, zebras) (Fig. 44b). The genus represents the utmost extremity in reduction of the fore-limb and manus. The radius carries the entire carpus. As in the rhinoceros, the scaphoid and lunar are the main bones of the proximal row of carpals, the cuneiform being small. In the distal row, the much shortened but very wide magnum articulates with them, flanked by a small trapezoid and uncinate. The trapezium has disappeared altogether.

Metacarpal III ('cannon-bone') is a strong but much elongated and gracefully proportioned bone. Close beside and behind it lie a pair of 'splint-bones', the degenerate m/c's II and IV, which taper off to a point near the middle of the length of m/c III. The former articulates proximally with the trapezoid, the latter with the uncinate, but their distal epiphyses and the corresponding digits are wanting and there is no obvious surface indication of their presence.

The distal articulation of the cannon-bone is a strict hinge-joint, with a median ridge which allows no side-play at all to the digit. This is clearly necessary in the sole support of the limb. The proximal phalanx is fairly long, wide and somewhat flattened on its palmar surface. The intermediate phalanx is very short, wide and compressed and articulates distally with a wide, strong ungual phalanx, forming the core of the typical equine hoof. There is a very short, wide transversely, almost rod-like, sesamoid behind the joint between the second and the ungual phalanx.

The manus of the horses is thus extremely simplified and much elongated, the conjoined humerus and radius standing in a ratio to it of only about 3:2 in length. The very long lever thus provided is a special adaptation for speed, the only resort of a genus menaced, in its natural surroundings, by numerous carnivorous enemies, with man, in prehistoric times, not the least predatory of them.

ARTIODACTYLA (Fig. 44c, d, e). This is the even-toed (2 or 4 digits) Order of ungulates. The axis of symmetry of the manus lies between the strong digits III and IV, and digits II and V, if present, are less strongly developed. In the more highly specialized ruminants these are only vestigial.

The carpus consists of the same equipment of ossicles as that of the Perissodactyla, but a medial displacement of the distal row makes each distal member alternate more clearly with the proximal and articulate over some area with two of them.

Sub-Order Suiformes. *Hippopotamus* and pig (*Sus*) (Fig. 44c). In the former, a trapezium is still present in the carpus. It is absent in the latter. All 4 metacarpals are present and separate, II and V only slightly less strong than III and IV in the hippopotamus, markedly reduced in the pig, especially at the proximal articulations, where they are displaced, with the corresponding carpals, to lie somewhat behind the main pair.

The phalanges of the main digits are short and stout, only slightly 'waisted' and somewhat asymmetrical. This is especially true of the ungual phalanges, which form distinctly left and right halves of the small cloven hoof in the pig. In the hippo, the unguals are more nail-like and less asymmetrical.

The second and fifth digits in the pig are short, slight and the phalanges clearly degenerate. The unguals are simple, sub-conical ossicles. Functionally, these surviving toes are of use to the pig, acting in the same way as the sprag of a punt-pole, preventing the limb sinking too deeply into soft ground.

Sub-Order Ruminantia. Cervidae, Bovidae (Fig. 44e and d, respectively). In most of the members of these families the lateral digits are very degenerate. In the deer there remain two small splint-like vestiges of m/c's II and V, still articulated with the carpus, of which the shafts have almost atrophied. Distally, the phalanges of the corresponding digits are complete, but do not reach the ground and have no bony connection with any other part of the manus. In the cattle these last distal vestiges have disappeared and all that remains of the lateral digits is a pair of small, short nodules representing the 2nd and 5th metacarpals. The functional metacarpus consists of a 'cannon-bone', clearly double-barrelled, formed by the almost complete fusion of the two main, much elongated, metacarpals III and IV. A more or less deep furrow, front and back, shows the line of fusion. In section, the marrow-cavities of the two bones are often still at least partly separated by a thin septum of bone. The distal articulations are always separate, each boldly sculptured and with a median ridge, making a pulley-like articular surface for the proximal phalanx. This phalanx is fairly long, but, in the larger ruminants, very thick and strong also. The second phalanx is always much shorter, though almost as thick. The terminal (ungual) phalanges form an almost perfectly symmetrical pair, each the mirror-image of the other, flattened axially, to form the halves of the cloven hoof (larger in proportion than in the pig), which is characteristic of the Ruminant sub-Order. The proportions and details of the metacarpal cannon-bones enable some lower groups within the sub-Order to be easily distinguished.

Cervidae. The metacarpals of the deer are distinguished, in general, from those of the oxen, sheep, etc. by their great length and slight build. Even those of the rather more heavily-built elk (*Alces*) are comparatively slender for their size. All deer cannon-bones are more or less channelled along the proximal part of their length on the palmar surface. This is not so pronounced in the metacarpals as in the metatarsals (p. 179).

Once recognized as cervine, some species can directly be eliminated from the identification in a particular case, on the ground of size alone.

From the examples figured by Hue (1907), some overall lengths of the metacarpal cannon-bone for the different species likely to occur in European contexts are as follows:—

Elk (*Alces*) .. .. 322 mm.
Red deer (*Cervus elaphus*) .. .. 300 mm.
Reindeer (*Rangifer*) .. .. .. 183 mm.
Fallow deer (*Dama*) .. .. 167 mm.
Roe deer (*Capreolus*) .. .. 162 mm.

Among these, the only pair likely to be confused are the last two, when the more slender proportions of the very lightly built roe should enable it to be distinguished. Refer, nevertheless, to the limitations of such figures, noted below.

Bovidae. This family is shorter-legged and more heavily built. The metacarpal cannon-bone never has the posterior longitudinal channel noted in the deer and is altogether more stocky in proportions. This feature of weight and thickness is most strongly shown in the metacarpals of male bison, which tend to be very heavy in the fore-quarters and may have large horns. Despite the elongation of the cannon-bone common to the whole family, the breadth and strength of this bone in the bison is very striking. Absolute measurements, taken from Hue's illustrations, are as follows:—

Domestic ox (*Bos taurus*) .. .. 260 mm.
American bison (*Bison bison*) .. 198 mm.
Musk-ox (*Ovibos*) .. .. .. 186 mm.
Domestic sheep (*Ovis aries*) .. .. 146 mm.
Mouflon (*Ovis musimon*) .. .. 142 mm.
Domestic goat (*Capra hircus*) .. 130 mm.
Ibex (*Capra ibex*) .. .. .. 126 mm.
Saiga antelope (*Saiga tartarica*) .. 152 mm.
Chamois (*Rupicapra*) .. .. 135 mm.

For completeness the following have been measured from actual bones:

Urochs (*Bos primigenius*) (♀) 270
Celtic ox ('*Bos longifrons*') 161—189 (range of several)

Such measurements are only offered as a rough guide to the absolute dimensions of the different species. They must not be taken to represent averages, since they are taken from individuals which may have been selected for illustration for some other character than as representing average dimensions. There are, of course, often wide variations in size also between the sexes and between comparable individuals of different geographical races. With domestication, the range of such variations is naturally greatly increased, through man's conscious or unconscious selection of breeders from stock which best met his needs.

Even the larger wild Bovidae (e.g., *Bison priscus* and *Bos primigenius*) cannot certainly be distinguished by eye from the cannon-bones alone. A good guess may be made with practice in the more extreme cases, however. Efforts have recently been made designed to effect a certain identification by exact measurements of entire specimens and the derivation from them of indices which may be characteristic of the two species. Such operations fall outside the field of the archaeological student of bones and should be left to specialists.

In fact, nothing can, as yet, replace a large recent and fossil comparative material in these difficult cases. Only a few works of fairly restricted scope have yet touched the large field of the metrical and statistical study of animal (as opposed to human) bones. There is here almost unlimited scope for further research.

The phalanges of the manus, like the cannon-bones, are extremely difficult to interpret, within the ruminant group, save on the basis of size. It is even hard to distinguish phalanges of the pes from those of the manus and to assign them to the correct side of the body and of the limb itself. In view of the expertise required and the need for an adequate body of comparative material from all the possible species, no attempt will be made here to offer distinctive criteria. No difficulty will be experienced in differentiating between (say) *Bos* and *Cervus*, but to determine *Bison* in the presence of a *Bos* of comparable size is a task before which most specialists would confess themselves at a loss.

10

The Hind-limb

LIKE THE FORE-LIMB, this (Fig. 45) consists of two segments: the
thigh, represented by the *femur*, and the leg, comprising two bones, the
tibia and the *fibula*. To these must be added a large sesamoid bone
(p. 172), the *patella* or knee-cap.

The femur is generally the largest long bone in the body. Its shaft is
more or less cylindrical in section and somewhat curved longitudinally
in a sagittal plane, with the convexity to the front. The femur has a
head of roughly hemispherical form, which articulates in a ball-and-
socket joint with the os innominatum at the acetabulum. The head is
set on a *neck*, which is longer and more distinct than the neck of the
humerus. The axis of the head and neck makes an angle, more or less
obtuse according to species, with that of the shaft. The head of the
femur generally shows a pit in the centre of its articular surface for the
attachment of a round ligament, by which, in life, it is fastened to the
floor of the acetabulum.

At the base of the neck and laterally to it stands a large process for
the attachment of muscles, the *great trochanter*. In many species this
stands higher than the summit of the head. At the base of the great
trochanter, medially and posteriorly, is a deep oval pit, the *digital fossa*.
To the medial side of the shaft, below the neck and somewhat posterior
to it, is another prominence, the *lesser trochanter*, joined to the greater
by an oblique *trochanteric crest*, which forms the posterior margin of the
digital fossa.

In some species there is, in addition, a *third trochanter* (Fig. 47a).
This forms a salient ridge produced into a thin outstanding plate, a
little distal to the great trochanter, on the lateral side of the femoral
shaft. The edge of this plate is generally turned over anteriorly. Its
presence and development is a feature of systematic importance.

The shaft of the femur thickens towards the distal epiphysis, which
presents two prominent, knuckle-shaped articular surfaces, the *medial*
and *lateral femoral condyles*, separated behind by a deep *inter-condylar
notch* or *fossa*. Anteriorly, the articular surfaces of the condyles meet in a
smooth, wide articular surface, somewhat concave transversely, often
more or less elongated in the axis of the bone, the *patellar area* or
femoral trochlea. This is short in man, very much more elongated and
extensive in most quadrupeds.

The tibia is the shin-bone, the principal bone of the leg, articulating
with the femur at the knee-joint. The wide proximal articular surface

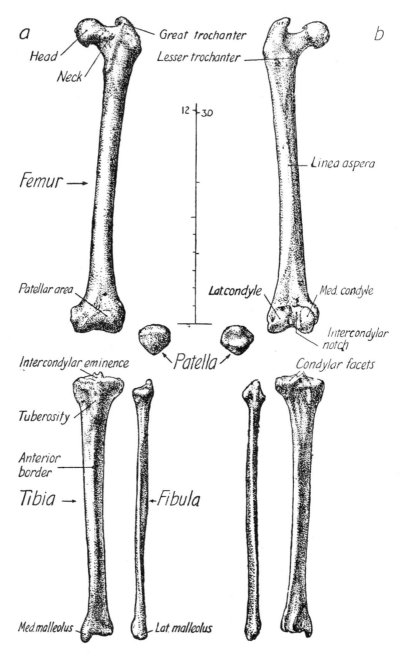

FIG 45.   Left leg bones of man, anterior (a) and posterior (b) views. Separated to show named parts.

consists of a pair of somewhat oval, concave *condylar facets* to receive the condyles of the femur, separated by a roughened *inter-condylar area*, at which are attached, in the fresh specimen, the cruciate ligaments, which play a large part in maintaining the apposition of the bones while permitting free movement in one plane. The edges of the condylar facets, bordering this area, are raised into more or less prominent crests, which fit into the inter-condylar fossa of the femur. In front of the articular areas, and somewhat below them, the shaft of the bone bears a prominent *tubercle*, produced distally into a rather sharp-edged ridge, the *anterior border* of the shaft. The tubercle affords attachment for the patellar ligament, transmitting to the tibia, across the front of the knee-joint, the pull of the extensor muscles of the leg, which occupy the front of the thigh.

The shaft of the tibia is triangular in section, at least in its upper third, in consequence of the sharp anterior border and the flatness of its posterior surface. The anterior border runs somewhat medially from the base of the tubercle. The shaft tapers distally and then widens again to form the rather square articulation for the proximal bone of the tarsus, the astragalus. A process of the tibia, the *medial malleolus*, extending distally beyond the articulation, guards the medial side of the ankle-joint by articulating with the side of the astragalus.

The fibula is a slender bone, lying laterally to the tibia, of which the expanded proximal end articulates with the side of the tibia just below the edge of the platform presented by the lateral condylar facet of the tibia. The fibula, unlike the radius, thus has no contact with the proximal segment of the limb and forms no part of the knee-joint. Distally, its other expanded end articulates both with the lateral side of the tibia at the ankle and, beyond the articulation of the tibia, with the lateral side of the astragalus, forming a *lateral malleolus*. The two malleoli thus embrace the ankle-joint on both sides and prevent displacement of the astragalus.

The fibula has no freedom of movement in relation to the tibia. Rotation (toe in, toe out) of the human leg takes place at the head of the femur, involving the whole leg. The fibula is obviously a somewhat degenerate bone, even in the more generalized mammals, where it is fairly well developed. In many species it is more or less fused with the tibia, both proximally and distally, and is reduced to a mere vestige in the most specialized terrestrial quadrupeds.

The patella (kneecap) (Fig. 51) is the largest sesamoid bone in the body. Were it not for the patella, when the leg is flexed on the thigh at the knee-joint not only would the extensor-tendon bear with some friction on the front of the femur but the important ligaments which maintain the joint would be exposed anteriorly to damage. The dual function of the patella is thus to reduce friction and to protect the knee from the front.

The patella is a local ossification developed in the thickness of the extensor tendon. On the front of the thigh, the powerful extensor muscles converge to a thick common tendon which passes over the front of the knee and is inserted, beyond it, at the tubercle of the tibia. This tendon, being itself inextensible, has no motion relative to the tibia in the movement of flexion at the knee, but where it crosses the end of the femur the patella is formed in its thickness and bears on the wide, transversely-concave facet, there developed for its reception. The tendon itself is thus held off and prevented from rubbing on the femur both when the extensors relax in flexion and when they pull in extending the leg. The patella is somewhat convex anteriorly and its smooth, transversely-convex articular surface fits, like a V-belt over a pulley, on the patellar area of the femur. The bone is very rough both proximally and distally, where the extensor tendon and its distal continuation, the patellar ligament, are, respectively, attached. In man (Fig. 51a, b), the patella is of a thickish lentoid form, whence comes its other Latin name 'rotula' (little wheel). In most quadrupeds (Fig. 51c, d, e, f) it has rather the shape of an inverted pear, much thicker above and tapering below.

Particular features of the
hind-limb bones in different mammalian groups

INSECTIVORA (Fig. 46b, c). The femur has a rudiment of a third trochanter in the hedgehog (*Erinaceus*) (Fig. 46c), among those forming our short list. In all the fibula is fused with the tibia in mid-shaft.

CHIROPTERA. The hind limb is relatively unimportant in the bats. The femur is long and slender, the tibia and fibula even more so, distinct and well separated. A bat can only shuffle along on the flat and uses the hind-limbs chiefly as stretchers of the wing-membrane and as links with the hind extremity, by which it suspends itself when at rest.

RODENTIA. The femur is inconstant in form and development, but generally has a distinct neck and small head. The squirrel (*Sciurus*) and hare (*Lepus*) have long slender femora with a third trochanter immediately below the greater; in the beaver (*Castor*) (Fig. 46d), on the other hand, the femur is very short and stout and the third trochanter stands out in mid shaft. In the marmot (*Arctomys*) the third trochanter forms only a slight ridge, close below the greater. Some rodents, the porcupine (*Hystrix*), for example, have no sign of a third trochanter. The great trochanter is generally very large and stands well above the level of the head of the femur.

The tibia and fibula are equally variable, separate in the porcupine, beaver and marmot; the distal part of the fibula fused with the tibia in the hare, rats and mice (Murinae) and voles (Arvicolinae).

PRIMATES. In man (Fig. 45a, b) the femur is the longest and strongest long bone in the body. For its length it is very slender in comparison with those of quadrupeds and strikingly straight. The cylindrical shaft

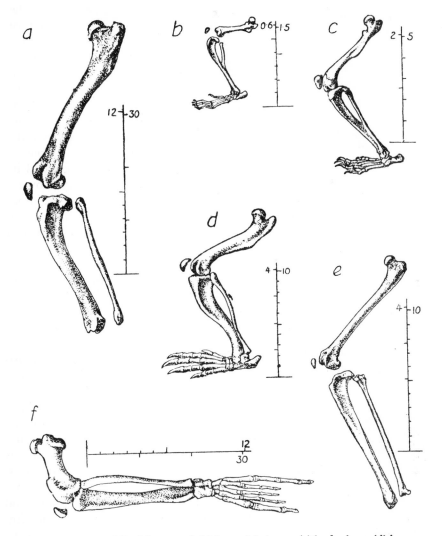

FIG 46. Left hind-limb bones of: (a) bear, (b) shrew, (c) hedgehog, (d) beaver (all plantigrades), (e) cat (digitigrade), (f) seal, in which the hind limbs only function as a rudder.

is somewhat bowed sagittally, with the convexity to the front. The articular surface of the head is rather more than hemispherical and it is set on a long, well-defined neck, forming an angle of about 120° with the shaft—rather more than in most quadrupeds. The greater trochanter is stout, but not prominent, either laterally or in height, for it is far surpassed by the head. The lesser trochanter forms a rounded knob at the posterior part of the base of the neck and is connected with the base of the greater by a marked trochanteric crest. There is no third trochanter, but only a linear roughened area anterior to and below the great trochanter, for the insertion of the tendon of the gluteus maximus muscle. The posterior surface of the shaft is marked by a long, elevated roughened line, the *linea aspera*, at which the fan-shaped great adductor muscle of the thigh is inserted. Owing to the globular head and long neck, the femur has more latitude of movement in man than in quadrupeds. In particular, the thigh may be considerably *abducted* (legs straddled). The contrary movement of *adduction* (bringing the thighs together, as in gripping the saddle on horseback) requires the development of strong muscles and prominent attachments for them—whence the characteristic linea aspera in man and other Primate climbers. The condyles are large and the inter-condylar notch wide. The patellar area is wide, short and not prominent. The medial epicondyle is more strongly developed than the lateral.

The human tibia, like the other limb-bones, is long (but not as long as the femur), slender and straight. The articular areas for the femoral condyles are oval and flat, the inter-condylar crest not prominent. The shaft is markedly triangular in section, not only proximally, but for the greater part of its length. The tubercle is stout, but not unduly prominent. The shaft widens to the shallow, square distal articulation for the astragalus and has a well-marked malleolus articulating with the medial side of that bone.

The fibula is distinct and entire, very long and slender and well separated from the shaft of the tibia. Its proximal end is somewhat clubbed, articulating with the tibia laterally and below the level of the lateral condylar facet. Its distal end is of a rather thick, rounded spatular shape, forming the lateral malleolus for the ankle-joint. The shaft of the fibula is sub-circular in section towards the ends, but quadrilateral towards its middle, owing to the development of some sharp edges and borders for the attachment of muscles.

The patella is of a wide, rather lenticular, form, thinner and wider than in quadrupeds, with very rough surfaces proximally and distally for the attachment of the muscle-tendon and the patellar ligament, respectively.

The thigh and leg bones of the other Primates scarcely concern us. They are, on the whole, stouter in proportion and less straight than in man, the apes and monkeys being climbers and not walkers. In other respects they are very like the human bones. The femur and tibia of Neanderthal man (*Homo neanderthalensis*) were of heavier build and more strongly curved than those of modern man, distinctively human, yet in these features rather more ape-like than in living races of man.

CARNIVORA. In general, the femur (Fig. 46a, e) approaches the human form, being relatively long, slender and straight in the digitigrades (Canidae, Felidae, Hyaenidae), shorter and stouter in the plantigrades (Ursidae, Mustelidae). The great trochanter is seldom higher than the head, save in some cats (Felidae). There is no real third trochanter, though the bears have a somewhat prominent ridge laterally, below the great trochanter.

The tibia and fibula are distinct, the latter slender but generally well separated, save in the dogs (Canidae), which have the lower half of the fibula lying closely alongside the tibia. The tubercle of the tibia in all these quadrupeds is very large, as is the anterior border running down from its base.

In the seals (Pinnipedia) (Fig. 46f) the femur is very short and thick, with scarcely any neck. Tibia and fibula are of almost equal development and generally fused together proximally.

PROBOSCIDEA (Fig. 47e). The femur is very long in proportion to the rest of the limb in the elephants. The bone is straight, with a hemispherical head on a well-marked neck. The head lacks a round ligament, so there is no fossa in the middle of its articular surface. The medial epicondyle forms a prominent shoulder above the distal epiphysis. The tibia is very stout and, in comparison, short, the fibula slender and distinct, but not widely separated from it. Measurements of two individuals belonging to extinct species are as follows:—

	Femur	Tibia
Elephas antiquus (Upnor)	5' 4½" (1·64 m.)	3' 0½" (0·93 m.)
E. primigenius (Adams, Leningrad)	3' 10½" (1·18 m.)	2' 4" (0·71 m.)

PERISSODACTYLA. Rhinocerotidae (Fig. 48b). The femur is exceedingly short and stout, with a short, powerfully developed greater trochanter, a lesser trochanter reduced to a rough ridge and a large third trochanter, laterally in mid-shaft. The head is large and its neck thick and indistinct. Both epicondyles are fairly prominent. There is a deep, roughened fossa on the posterior surface of the shaft, above the lateral condyle. The condyles are large and the inter-condylar notch very deep. The medial border of the patellar area is very prominent indeed.

The tibia and fibula are short and heavy, even the latter being relatively massive and broad distally.

Equidae. In the horses (Fig. 47a, b), the femur is very strong, short in relation to the limb as a whole and with marked muscular impressions. The head is low and broad, without a distinct neck, but the greater trochanter is enormous, far overtopping the head. As if this were not enough, it has a secondary prominence laterally, arising from its base. The lesser trochanter consists of a low, rough ridge along the medial side of the bone, below the head. A fairly prominent third trochanter is present, not so enormously developed as in the Rhinocerotidae but nevertheless very strong. This, alone, distinguishes the equine femur from those of ruminants of comparable size and build. There is a long, narrow, shallow fossa, the lateral supra-condylar fossa, the floor of which is roughened, on the posterior aspect of the shaft, above the lateral condyle.

The borders of the patellar area are very high and rounded. The

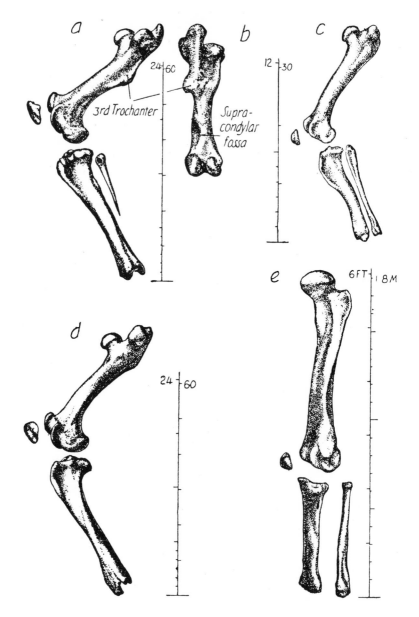

FIG 47. Left hind-limb bones in ungulates. Left lateral view save (b), posterior. (a), (b) horse, note the third trochanter, (c) pig, (d) ox, (e) elephant. The fibulae have been removed caudally for greater clearness.

whole bone has a very stout and rugged appearance, which is distinctive in comparison with the femora of ruminants.

The tibia is also a very strong, heavy bone. The two condylar facets of its proximal end are extensive and, in sagittal view, slope rather steeply up to form a very prominent median crest, the summit of which is divided into two by the rough inter-condylar area. This distinguishes an equine from a ruminant tibia, in which the slope and the crest are not so marked. The tibia has the characteristic triangular section above, with a prominent anterior crest descending somewhat medially from the tubercle, and a transversely flattened posterior surface. Four or more rather rough raised lines cross this surface from above downwards, somewhat diagonally in a medial direction. Their prominence is more marked in the horses than in the ruminants. In posterior view, the shaft is very straight and tapers little towards its distal end. The distal articular surface for the astragalus consists of a pair of deep parallel grooves, set at approximately 45° antero-medially across the sagittal axis of the tibia, as fixed by the anterior crest. This is in marked distinction from the same articulation of the ruminant tibia, where the direction of the corresponding (much shallower) grooves is approximately sagittal. The difference is shown in the characteristic sagittal attitude of the pes in the horses, as compared with the 'splay-footed' position of the ruminants, whereby the heels ('hocks') are brought closer together when standing than the hinder hooves. A horse which habitually shows any trace of the latter attitude is said to be 'cow-hocked'—a term of opprobrium among the equine fancy! The tibia of an ass (*Equus asinus*) is, in proportion to its size, more slender and its shaft more tapering distally than that of a horse (*E. caballus*). The shaft is also somewhat bowed, with the convexity in a medial direction.

The fibula in horses is much reduced. Proximally it consists of a 'splint' with a rounded head, of which the shaft tapers to a sharp point near the middle of the length of the tibia. Distally it is represented by the lateral malleolus, protecting the ankle-joint, which is early ankylosed with the distal epiphysis of the tibia.

This bone thus forms a ready-made bone awl or piercer, with a conveniently knobbed handle. It was often so used, without adaptation, by early man. The discovery of an equine fibula in a geological deposit does not, therefore, prove the contemporary presence of man. This is an error into which the uninstructed archaeologist may easily fall, under the impression that the find is an artificially-pointed bone.

ARTIODACTYLA. Suiformes (Fig. 47c, 48a). As with respect to other parts of their skeletons, the members of this less specialized group of even-toed ungulates have hind-limb bones which differ characteristically from those of the ruminants.

The femur has a rather small, nearly hemispherical, head, set on a distinct, longish neck. The great trochanter is large and laterally prominent, but stands by no means as high as in the horses or in the ruminants. In general it barely exceeds the head in height. The lesser trochanter forms a stout knob of approximately the human shape. In both hippopotami and domesticated pigs (*Sus scrofa*) the shaft is rather short, but not as stout, proportionately, as in the Perissodactyla. There is no third trochanter. In the wild pigs the femur is longer and more slender, in view of the longer limbs and lighter, more athletic, build. In all, the shaft of the femur is much bowed sagittally with an anterior convexity. There is an extensive, but shallow, supra-condylar fossa. The condyles are large, but the patellar articular area is not so high, so extensive or so boldly sculptured as in more specialized ungulates. The lateral epicondyle is very prominent in the hippopotamus, the medial prominent, but less so, in the pigs.

The tibia in *Hippopotamus* (Fig. 48a) is very short and stout, as befits the great weight it has to bear. The anterior crest extends over two-thirds of the shaft. The fibula is widely separated from it, entirely distinct and rather slender in proportion proximally—much more so than in *Rhinoceros*, of similar build and proportions. Distally, it is greatly expanded laterally to form the lateral malleolus of the ankle. Being unspecialized, the fibula thus plays its full part in the ankle-joint.

In wild pigs the tibia is much longer and relatively more slender than in the hippopotamus, but not to the same extent as the tibia of a ruminant of comparable size. In domesticated races it is very short and stocky. The tubercle is much less prominent than in ruminants and the anterior crest, descending from it, runs over only about one-third, or less, of the shaft of the bone. The distal articulation for the astragalus is rather shallow, the parallel grooves directed sagittally, as in all Artiodactyls.

The fibula is, in proportion, a considerable bone, with a shaft at least one-third as thick as that of the tibia. Its distal extremity is not so expanded as that of a hippopotamus, though it does its proper share in maintaining the stability of the ankle-joint.

Chaucer, an accomplished student of the natural sciences of his time and close observer of human foibles, as well as a poet, makes his Pardoner carry about on his avocations a casket of 'pigges' bones', purporting to be the relics of some saint or martyr. It must be supposed that most of the sinners whom this colourful character assoiled—for a cash consideration—would be readily deceived by the substitution. Not so the author of *The Canterbury Tales*. Nevertheless, of all the domestic animal material available to a mediaeval charlatan, the bones of a pig would most closely resemble genuine human remains, and this technical detail did not escape the genial narrator.

Though not closely related zoologically, man and pig are both unspecialized members of their respective Orders and share a similarity in many features of their skeletons with their generalized common mammalian ancestor.

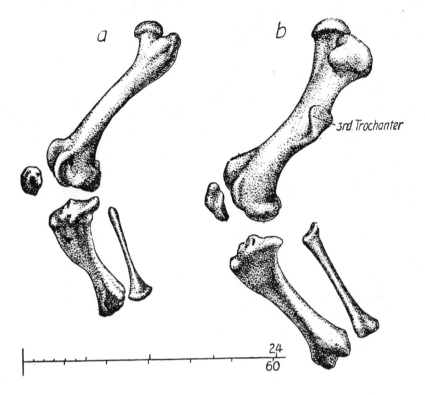

FIG. 48 Left hind-limb bones of: (a) hippopotamus, and (b) rhinoceros.
Left lateral views. The fibulae are displaced caudally. Both on the
same scale. Note the third trochanter in the rhinoceros, as in
the horse (Fig 47).

Ruminants (Fig. 47d). The hind-limb bones of all the Cervidae and
Bovidae are strikingly alike, save in the proportions consonant with
their differing stature and build. Those of large, heavy species, such as
giant deer (*Megaceros*) and elk (*Alces*), among the deer, and cattle (*Bos*)
and bison (*Bison*) among the Bovidae, are proportionately long and
something more than proportionately stout. This is in accordance with
the mechanical principle that doubling the linear dimensions of a solid,
such as the mammalian body, squares its surface and cubes its volume.
Since the weight to be supported by bones depends upon the volume
of the body, while their strength depends upon the area of their transverse section, it follows that the femur of an animal twice as large as
another must be quite disproportionately stout. Considerations of
stature, therefore, enable the field of possibles, in an individual case for
determination, to be greatly narrowed.

In all ruminants, the axis of the head and neck of the femur tends to
make a smaller angle with that of the shaft (i.e., closer to a right-angle)

than in the groups already described. The articular area of the head may extend far on to the 'saddle' between the head proper and the great trochanter. The latter process is high and very prominent laterally. The digital fossa at its base is extremely deep and is bounded posteriorly by the trochanteric ridge, joining the two trochanters, of which the curve, in posterior view, varies slightly between species.

The shaft is straight and more or less cylindrical, the distal articulations very large, the condyles being placed far to the rear of the axis of the shaft. They are connected with the front of the shaft by a very long and elevated patellar area (femoral trochlea). Both this and the condyles are set very obliquely to the axis of the shaft, so that the intercondylar notch, as seen from behind, runs upwards and laterally, as does the patellar area in front. As in the Perissodactyla, the medial lip of this area is the more prominent anteriorly, but it is not developed in such strength and thickness as with these. The trochlea is longer, narrower and less ruggedly modelled.

The tibia is very long in proportion to the femur and much more slender even than in the horse. Its proximal articular areas for the condyles are not so steeply inclined axially to form the inter-condylar crest, nor is this so high and prominent. The upper part of the shaft of the tibia is more bent, transversely, in the ruminants than in the horse, with a medial convexity. The prominent anterior crest, therefore, seems to be more sharply oblique medially. Where the posterior surface of the tibial shaft in the horse is marked by four or more raised lines, running obliquely distally and medially, these, though often clearly traceable, are far less prominent in the ruminants. The whole bone seems more gracefully proportioned and the shaft tapers more noticeably in its distal third.

The distal articulation for the astragalus consists of two grooves, not so deep as in the horse, set parallel with a sagittal plane instead of obliquely to it. The medial malleolus is more strongly developed than the lateral, which is a fused-on vestige of the fibula.

The fibula is a mere rudiment proximally, where it is preserved at all, and is seldom recovered in archaeological circumstances.

Cervidae. As with the other long bones, the hind-limb bones of deer tend to be very long and slender. Even in the large and comparatively heavy elk (*Alces*) this feature is apparent and distinguishes the bones at once from those of most of the Bovidae. Qualitative differences are only slight and, in the present state of our published knowledge, it is impossible to say how constant and reliable for species as a whole may be such differences as can be observed in individual specimens. Only the study of considerable series can suggest dependable distinctive features.

Considerations of size are most helpful in reducing the number of possibilities in a doubtful case. Measurements of the specimens figured by Hue (1907) are as follows:—

MAXIMUM OVERALL LENGTHS PARALLEL
TO THE AXIS OF THE SHAFT IN SAGITTAL VIEW

	Femur	Tibia
Elk (*Alces*)	398 mm.	440 mm.
Red deer (*Cervus*)	274	310
Fallow deer (*Dama*)	252	248
Reindeer (*Rangifer*)	248	278
Roe deer (*Capreolus*)	198	224

The same caution applies to these measurements as to those given above for metacarpal cannon-bones (p. 155). They may, nevertheless, be useful as giving some guide to size.

Bovidae. This family is, on the whole, more heavily built than the Cervidae. The shaft of the femur is slender in comparison with that of the Perissodactyla, but in the larger Bovidae is, none the less, very stout, the trochanters high, thick and laterally prominent, the distal condyles large and wide. Thus, in these cases, no possible mistake could be made between Bovidae and Cervidae. In some lighter species, however, notably the saiga and chamois (*Rupicapra*), the femora are very deer-like in proportions, save that their shafts tend to a rather greater thickness distally. Sheep and goats, again, with their shorter limbs, are easily recognized as bovids, though their similarity among themselves is very great.

Measurements, taken from the same source, may be helpful in differentiating at least some of the genera:—

MAXIMUM OVERALL LENGTHS PARALLEL
TO THE AXIS OF THE SHAFT, IN SAGITTAL VIEW

	Femur	Tibia	
Domestic cattle (*Bos taurus*)	483 mm.	383 mm.	(smaller
American bison (*Bison bison*)	441	403	indiv.)
Musk-ox (*Ovibos moschatus*)	350	376	
Saiga 'antelope' (*S. tartarica*)	194	222	
Chamois (*Rupicapra rupicapra*)	195	250	
Domestic sheep (*Ovis aries*)	194	234	
Domestic goat (*Capra hircus*)	204	258	
Ibex (*Capra ibex*)	203	242	
Mouflon (*Ovis musimon*)	181	190	

In these measurements femur and tibia are not necessarily taken from the same individual, so that even relative proportions based on these figures are unreliable.

11

The Hind-extremity (pes)

THE MAMMALIAN PES comprises, like the manus, three groups of bones: the *tarsus*, corresponding with the carpus, the *metatarsus*, consisting of a group of up to 5 long bones, frequently reduced in number, and the *digits*, composed each of 3 phalanges save digit I (*hallux* or great toe), which, as with the pollex, has but 2.

THE TARSUS. The full mammalian complement of bones of the tarsus is 7 irregularly-shaped bones, closely united by ligaments which permit practically no movement between them (Fig. 49). They are derived, by fusion and suppression of two members, from a primitive group of 9 bones, arranged, much as are those of the carpus, in two rows, a proximal and a distal, with one bone occupying a central position. This arrangement still persists in some lower, non-mammalian, vertebrates.

Flower's classification of the tarsal bones, with their synonyms, is as follows:

Tibiale + Intermedium }	=Astragalus	prox. row {	=*Talus*
Fibulare	=Calcaneum		=*Os calcis*
Centrale	=Navicular		=*Scaphoideum*
Tarsale 1	=Internal or medial cuneiform		=*Entocuneiforme*
Tarsale 2	=Middle or Inter-mediate cuneiform	dist. row	=*Mesocuneiforme*
Tarsale 3	=External or Lateral cuneiform		=*Ectocuneiforme*
Tarsale 4 Tarsale 5 }	=Cuboid		=*Cuboideum*

As before, the names in the middle column will be used here.

The proximal row of tarsals is represented by two biggish remaining bones, the astragalus and calcaneum, which have special functions.

The *astragalus* forms the sole articulation with the tibia and fibula, for which purpose it has a more or less deeply-grooved pulley-like superior articular surface, with lateral and medial facets for the two malleoli. Below, it rests by three flat facets upon the calcaneum. Distally and medially it has a more or less rounded head, for articulation with the navicular bone. It thus forms a hinge-joint with the leg-bones, permitting movement of the pes at the ankle in one plane only, with very little lateral play.

The *calcaneum* supports the astragalus from below and projects posteriorly in a more or less long lever, the *tuberosity*, to the extremity of which is attached the very strong 'Achilles' tendon (*tendo calcaneus*) of the extensor muscles for the foot, which occupy the posterior part of the tibia ('calf' of the leg). These muscles extend the pes on the leg, as in leaping, so that the length of the calcaneal tuberosity is a measure of the leverage it can apply. Distally and laterally, the calcaneum extends forward in the pes almost to the level of the head of the astragalus, alongside which it presents a more or less rounded surface for the articulation of the cuboid bone.

These two strong bones are commonly found entire, or but slightly damaged, in archaeological contexts, and are sometimes characteristic of the species. They are thus of some importance to this study. The remaining tarsal bones are comparatively unimportant, but a brief account of them is included for the sake of completeness.

The central bone of the primitive tarsus is represented in mammals by the *navicular* (little ship). In man and other unspecialized members of the Class, this is a somewhat boat-shaped bone, of which the hollow proximal surface articulates with the head of the astragalus, the distal side with the three more medial members of the distal row, the *internal* (*medial*), *middle* and *external* (*lateral*) *cuneiform* (wedge-shaped) bones. The cuneiforms, respectively, afford articulations to the 1st, 2nd and 3rd metatarsals. Laterally to them lies the *cuboid bone*, articulating proximally with the calcaneum, medially with the navicular and lateral cuneiform and distally with the bases of the 4th and 5th metatarsals. Save for certain reductions and the occasional fusion of two adjacent tarsals, this arrangement holds good for all the groups of animals which we are considering.

THE METATARSUS, when fully represented, consists of 5 long bones, numbered I to V from the medial side of the pes, of sub-equal development. Their number is, however, frequently reduced by atrophy and suppression of some of the corresponding digits, and such reductions are of importance in classification. Each metatarsal is articulated with the tarsus and with its neighbours by joints at which no more than a slight elastic or gliding movement is possible. The tarsus and metatarsus thus form together a more or less elongated lever, with the fulcrum at the ankle-joint and the load on the heads of the metatarsals. The motive force is applied at the extremity of the calcaneal tuberosity.

The distal end of each metatarsal presents a *head* with a more or less cylindrical articular surface with a raised median sagittal ridge, which is greatly developed in the more specialized quadrupeds and prevents any lateral displacement. In these, the metatarso-phalangeal joints are strict hinge-joints, while, in the Primates, for example, the joint surfaces are more globular so that the pes may readily adapt itself to supports of various shapes and sizes, such as branches. A metatarsal is generally longer than the corresponding metacarpal. Its shaft tends to be some-what flattened transversely, so that its lateral profile is deeper than in the corresponding metacarpal.

PHALANGES OF THE PES. The 1st phalanx, as in the manus, has a hollowed proximal joint-surface corresponding with the convex head of its metatarsal. It is the longest of the three phalanges, the 2nd and 3rd (ungual) phalanges being successively shorter.

Those of the pes are, in general, closely similar to those of the manus, being somewhat larger and stouter in the more generalized groups, often less strongly developed in the more specialized ungulates, with their heavy fore-quarters. They are hard to distinguish from one another, save where, as in man, the dimensions of the digits of manus and pes are clearly different.

SESAMOID BONES. Reference has already been made to the sesamoid bones, particularly in connection with the patella (p. 159) and the pisiform bone of the carpus (p. 147). They are, properly, not skeletal bones at all, but local ossifications in tendons, where these cross a joint and are subject to friction on the skeletal bones as the joint moves. In the sheep, for example, there are four sesamoids on the posterior (palmar or plantar) surface of each extremity, at the extended meta-carpo- and metatarso-phalangeal joints. The flexor tendons here cross the barrels of the metapodials (metacarpals or metatarsals). There is another, wider, pair of sesamoids, in both manus and pes, at the joints of the second and ungual phalanges. In the horse, there is one pair at the barrel of the metapodial and a single, very wide and short sesa-moid, at the 2-3 inter-phalangeal joint. This cannot have any great range of movement with respect to the bones and is, in effect, an addition to the articular surface of the wide hoof-core with the second phalanx.

The sesamoids are generally small, rounded, pea-like bones (cf. 'pisiform') with only a single, or two closely adjacent, articular facets. Owing to their small size (save only for the patella) they are seldom recognized as bones and recovered by excavators in archaeological circumstances. It is, however, necessary to be aware of their existence so as to avoid confounding them, if found, with (say) the carpal or tarsal bones of an animal much smaller than the species to which they really belong. As with caudal vertebrae, they may offer a trap to the uninitiated and cause much loss of time spent in attempting to identify them. The more peculiar sesamoid bones have already been mentioned in connection with the limb to which they belong.

The pes in different mammalian groups

INSECTIVORA (Fig. 46b, c). The tarsus has its full complement of bones and all 5 digits are generally present, the hallux being the shortest.

The ungual phalanges bear curved, pointed, simple claws. The mole (*Talpa*), which has such extraordinary adaptations for burrowing of the fore-limb and manus, is quite normal in the development of the pes.

CHIROPTERA. The pes, unlike the manus, which forms the skeleton of a wing, is, save in one particular, an entirely normal hind extremity, very like that of the insectivores with 5 sub-equal small-clawed digits. The sole peculiarity is an enormously elongated slender calcaneum which serves as a strut for the hinder margin of the wing-membrane. The bone is thus nearly as long as the tibia.

The pes, in a bat, serves to support the hinder part of the body in shuffling awkwardly on the flat, supported in front on the carpus. Normally, however, it is a hook for suspension when asleep in the usual head-down position.

RODENTIA. The pes is very variable, according to special adaptations, from the short, broad strong paddle of the beaver (*Castor*) (Fig. 46d) to the immensely elongated bird-like pes of the kangaroo rat, or jerboa (*Alactaga jaculus*), a biped, leaping, desert and steppe dweller, in which three very slender metatarsals are fused together to give the long digitigrade lever. The remaining digits in *Alactaga* are vestigial or absent. The hallux is wanting in the hares.

PRIMATES. The foot in man (Fig. 49a) is a feature peculiar to his zoological family, the Hominidae. In his nearest living relations, the arboreal great apes, the pes, with a widely separated hallux, forms a grasping hand admirably adapted to climbing. The possession of a relatively flat-soled foot and a great toe parallel with the rest of the digits and not separable to any great extent, is the mark of a long palaeontological history of terrestrial bipedism, of which we have not yet the morphological links to connect him with a presumably arboreal ancestor in common with the apes. That the sole held flat to the ground is indeed, likely to be derived from an originally quadrumanous pes is seen in the primitively inturned sole of the human infant, which only later assumes its typically human attitude, when bipedal progression has been learned. The apes are poor walkers on the flat and never achieve the flat-soled stance, their weight being supported on the lateral edge of the pes.

The tarsus in man is complete and of even development. In view of the shortness of the foot-lever, the calcaneal tuberosity is short, though very strong and stout. The articulation of the astragalus with the tibia and fibula is broad and simple, permitting a small degree of *inversion* (plantar surface turned medially) and *eversion* (sole turned laterally) of the foot, whereby it is enabled to adapt its posture to uneven ground while the leg remains vertical. Rotation at the ankle is possible only to a very slight extent. The extreme toes-out and toes-in positions of the foot are chiefly produced by rotation of the entire limb about the head of the femur.

The metatarsals are longer and stronger than the metacarpals,

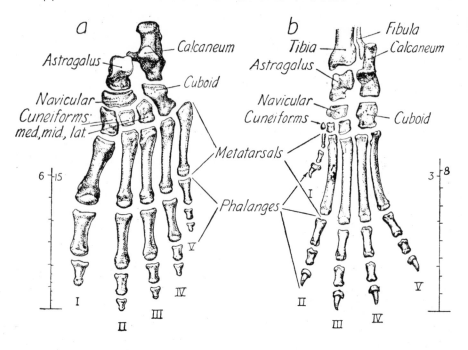

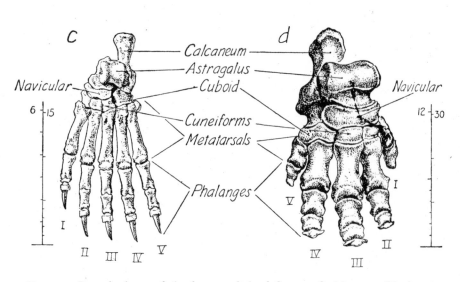

FIG 49.   Dorsal views of the bones of the left pes of: (a) man, (b) dog,
(c) bear; and of the right pes of (d) elephant.

especially that of the hallux. Their heads form the 'ball' of the foot.
The toes are short, the hallux not the longest but by far the strongest.
The axis of the foot as a load-bearing member thus lies close to the
hallux, not, as in many mammals, on the IIIrd and IVth digits. The

phalanges of the IInd, IIIrd, IVth and Vth toes are small and short. The Vth in particular is degenerate.

CARNIVORA. In the plantigrade families of the bears (Ursidae) (Fig. 49c) and martens (Mustelidae) the pes is flat and broad, with all 5 digits well developed, though the hallux is the shortest.

In the dogs (Canidae) (Fig. 49b), cats (Felidae) and hyaenas (Hyaenidae), all of digitigrade gait, the pes is long and narrow and the hallux is degenerate, represented only by a vestigial metatarsal. In all these the tarsus has its full complement of bones in their usual positions. In the plantigrades, the tuberosity of the calcaneum is short and stout, much as in man; in the digitigrades it is more elongated, a feature necessary to give adequate mechanical advantage to the extensor muscles of the pes, when the heel is permanently off the ground in the standing position. The 4 metatarsals are of almost equal development, the weight borne by the limb falling on their heads and on the digits, which are flat to the ground. The ungual phalanges are like those of the manus.

In the seals (Phocidae) (Fig. 46f) the pes forms part of a trailing rudder and is no longer of use in terrestrial progression. It is completely extended and inverted, the plantar surface turned medially in contact with that of its opposite member. Since the pes sustains little or no load in extension at the ankle-joint, the tuberosity of the calcaneum is scarcely apparent, though all the tarsal bones are present and, otherwise, normal. Digits I and V are long and strong, forming the marginal spreaders of the 'steering-oar' membrane, while the middle three digits (II, III, and IV) have only the subsidiary function of intermediate fin-rays and are both shorter and much more slender.

The sea-lions (Otariidae) and walrus (Odobaenus), on the other hand, do use the flexed pes for progression, so that, in these, the calcaneal tuberosity is fairly long and the digits of more or less equal development.

PROBOSCIDEA. The elephants have the pes (Fig. 49d), like the manus, very short and broad, but narrower than the manus and with digits I and V less fully developed. The astragalus is low and flat and does not meet the cuboid. The medial cuneiform projects distally beyond the other tarsals, as does the trapezium in the manus (p. 150). In the conformation of the tarsus, therefore, the pes of the elephants approaches the condition seen in the Perissodactyla. The metatarsals are even shorter than the corresponding metacarpals.

PERISSODACTYLA (Figs. 50a, c, d). As in the manus, digit III is in the axis of the limb and is the most strongly developed. II and IV, flanking it, may be almost as large (Rhinoceros) (Fig. 50a) or only rudimentary (Equus) (Fig. 50c). The hallux is invariably missing.

Rhinoceros (Fig. 50a). The pes is short and broad. The astragalus is very wide with a rather deeply grooved tibial articulation. The calcaneum is stout, standing very far to the lateral side, owing to the width of the astragalus. The tuberosity is very prominent and stout. The other tarsal bones are also much shortened and very broad. The astragalus has only a small contact with the cuboid. The middle cuneiform is very small. The rather short metatarsals and the very short phalanges resemble those of the manus.

Horse (*Equus*) (Fig. 50c). The pes is greatly elongated. As in the manus, digit III is the only one remaining in function. The astragalus is fairly wide and rather high and its tibial articulation very deeply grooved. The calcaneum, because of the elongation of the loaded segment of the lever, has a long tuberosity, but it is also very deep sagittally, though not thick transversely. In this, a horse calcaneum differs from that of an Artiodactyl bone of comparable size, which is relatively slender. The navicular and lateral cuneiform are very broad and short, the middle cuneiform small and relegated to the extreme medial side of the tarsus. The cuboid is small on the lateral side. The medial cuneiform is missing. These reductions are, of course, the concomitants of the reduction of digits II and IV, to which the middle cuneiform and the cuboid, respectively, correspond.

The metatarsal cannon bone resembles the metacarpal, but is even more elongated. It also differs from the latter in the section of its shaft, of which the antero-posterior axis is greater in proportion than in the metacarpal, which is far wider transversely. The 'splint-bones', the vestigial metatarsals II and IV, lie closely alongside III and somewhat to the rear. Even when missing, the niches for the articulation of their proximal ends, on either side of the main metatarsal III, show that they were present.

The phalanges of the sole remaining digit closely resemble those of the manus.

An equine cannon-bone is distinctive and can scarcely be confounded with a bone of any other beast. It is very strong, thick-walled and dense and so is frequently reasonably well preserved when much else has perished beyond recognition. The presence of but a single distal articulation for a digit and the notches at the proximal end for the splints make its determination a simple matter.

ARTIODACTYLA. The pes has 4 or 2 functional digits and its axis runs between digits III and IV, which are equally and symmetrically developed. Because of the equal status of the two digits, the tarsal bone corresponding to IV, the cuboid, attains some importance, where, in the Perissodactyla, it was subsidiary to the navicular and lateral cuneiform, supporting the central digit, III.

Suidae (Fig. 50b). The tarsal bones are all distinct. The astragalus has a fairly broad, rather shallow, tibial articulation and is rather more elongated than the astragalus of a ruminant. Its head meets the navicular over perhaps the medial two-thirds of its area. The rather pulley-like surface of the distal articulation is apparently turned medially through a small angle with respect to the axis of the tibial articulation

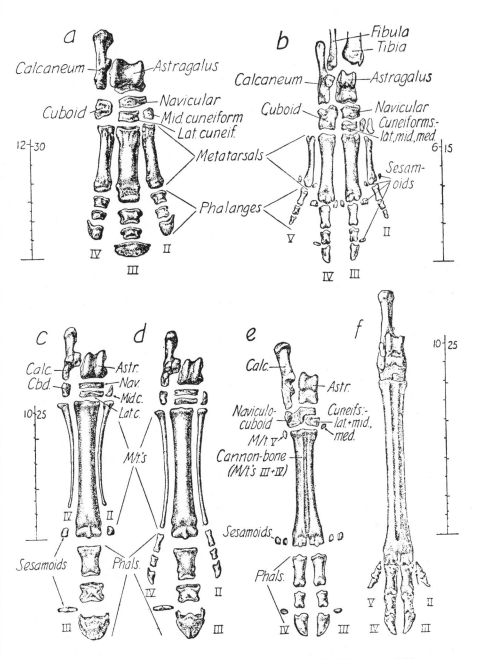

FIG 50.   Dorsal views of the right pes in ungulates: (a) rhinoceros, (c) horse,
(d) *Hipparion* (extinct 3-toed horse) (Perissodactyls); (b) pig, (e) ox,
(f) red deer (Artiodactyls). (c), (d) and (e) all on the same (left lower,
scale.

while that of a ruminant almost follows the axis. This feature exemplifies the 'twistiness' of many bones of the pig in comparison with those
of the more specialized ruminants. The calcaneum has a long tuberosity
of which the neck is markedly narrow transversely in comparison with
its extremity. The navicular and the lateral cuneiform (c^3), with the
cuboid, occupy the whole of the dorsal aspect of the tarsus, since the
intermediate and medial cuneiforms ($c^2, ^1$) are relegated to the medial
side of the plantar aspect.

In the hippopotamus, metatarsals II and V are more strongly developed than in the pigs, approaching more closely to the degree of
development seen in III and IV. All of them are very short and stout,
even more so than the corresponding metacarpals. Digits II and V
are nearly as long as the main digits and in all the phalanges are very
much shortened, especially the broad, rounded unguals.

In the pigs, metatarsals III and IV are much more strongly developed
than II and V, which are shorter, thinner and much reduced in thickness
proximally. The principal phalanges of the pigs are shorter and stouter
than those of sheep or other smaller ruminants. Those of digits II
and V are short and slight with very simplified articular surfaces and
degenerate, small unguals. These do not reach the ground when the
animal is standing on a hard surface, but do function as reversed
'barbs' to prevent the limb sinking too deeply in marshy ground.

Ruminants (Fig. 50e, f). The pes is very much elongated and slender,
especially in the lightly built deer. The astragalus is fairly short, though
longer than in the Perissodactyla. Its tibial articulation is a rather
deeply grooved, pulley-like surface, its head similar, but with a shallower, less well-defined groove, of which the axis falls almost in line
with that of the tibial articulation (difference from pig—see above).
The calcaneum is slender, elongated and its tuberosity more 'waisted'
in lateral view than that of the Equidae.

The cuboid and navicular are fused into a single large, wide and very
short bone, which receives the articular surfaces of the astragalus and
calcaneum. This bone, the naviculo-cuboid, is typical of the ruminants
and is not uncommonly recovered in archaeological contexts. Cuneiforms 2 and 3 (the intermediate and lateral) are also fused, but c^1,
though small, is always distinct and is relegated to the plantar aspect
of the pes.

The metatarsus, like the metacarpus, consists of a single 'cannon-
bone', formed by the fusion of the shafts of the metatarsals III and IV.
Metatarsal I is always entirely missing and II and V are also atrophied,
being represented, if at all, only by small proximal or distal vestiges,
which are of little importance in the present context.

The metatarsal cannon-bone has a number of proximal facets for
articulation with the tarsals and, distally, a pair of epiphyses, each drum-
like with a median circumferential ridge for the proximal phalanges.
Its shaft is rather square above, more or less transversely flattened

below, in contrast with the metacarpal cannon-bone, which tends to be wider transversely and flattened antero-posteriorly. The metatarsal is, moreover, longer and more slender than the metacarpal, apart from the evident difference in the number and distribution of the facets for the tarsal and carpal articulations respectively.

Cervidae (Fig. 50f). All bones of the pes are comparatively narrow and slender. The calcaneal tuberosity is very long indeed. The metatarsal cannon-bone is very long and narrow, even in a comparatively heavily built beast such as the elk (*Alces*). The shaft is much flattened from side to side and, in compensation, deep sagittally. Its anterior aspect bears a marked half-round flute along its entire length, joining the small foramen below the proximal articulation with the larger just above the distal epiphyses. In posterior view, the shaft is somewhat deeply channelled, especially about the middle of its length. These features, combined with the proportions, instantly distinguish a deer metatarsal from that of one of the Bovidae.

Elk (*Alces*). The metatarsal, like the metacarpal, is rather short in proportion, but otherwise altogether deer-like. The distal epiphyses are comparatively narrow and their median ridges parallel. There is a well-marked pair of transversely salient shoulders, if anything above the level of the suture between the epiphyses and shaft, so that the maximum transverse breadth of the bone comes at this point. This is distinctive for the genus.

Red deer (*Cervus elaphus*) (Fig. 50f). The metatarsal is slender, narrow and deeply grooved behind. The distal epiphyses are narrow, their maximum width near to the centres of the epiphyseal barrels. The median ridges are not very salient and parallel (difference from reindeer).

Reindeer (*Rangifer tarandus*). The metatarsal is much like that of a red deer, save that the distal epiphyses are wide, the median ridges of their barrels salient and divergent distally, to give the characteristic splay toes of this species, an adaptation to snow and soft marshy ground. There is an abrupt shoulder at the level of the suture, but the widest point is low, on the barrels themselves.

Fallow deer (*Dama*). The metatarsal is light and slender, not so deeply grooved behind as in red deer or reindeer. The narrowest point of the shaft is close above the distal anterior foramen and thence widens with sloping shoulders. The epiphyses are wide and the maximum breadth is low on the barrels, though their median ridges do not diverge and are not very prominent.

Roe deer (*Capreolus*). The metatarsal is very small and slender, rather square in section for a cervine metatarsal and not deeply grooved behind. The distal epiphyses are small and narrow, the breadths almost equal on the gently sloping shoulder and low on the barrels of the epiphyses. Their median ridges are very narrow, acute and salient, but parallel.

Some cervine metatarsals figured by Hue (1907) gave the following maximum overall lengths:—

Elk (*Alces alces*) metatarsal cannon-bone	385 mm.
Red deer (*Cervus elaphus*)	322
Reindeer (*Rangifer tarandus*)	245
Fallow deer (*Dama dama*)	209
Roe deer (*Capreolus capreolus*)	185

Bovidae (Fig. 50e). The calcaneal tuberosity is, on the whole, shorter, stouter and more 'waisted' than in the deer. The metatarsal is very square in the shaft above, transversely flattened below. The anterior flute of the shaft is usually less well marked and the groove behind shallower and less well defined than in the deer. The distal epiphyses are wider in the barrel, as is the deep notch separating the two barrels. These differences vary in degree with the build of the animal concerned. The comparatively long-legged, light chamois and saiga are more deer-like in the general proportions of the metatarsal, but they are decisively bovid in detail.

Bos and *Bison*. These genera are very difficult to determine with any confidence from the metatarsals, as from the other long bones. Differences in stature between *Bos primigenius* and *Bison priscus* are negligible and are often confused by differences of sex and individual build within the genera. In both the cannon-bones are long, heavy and stout. In comparable individuals, the shoulders at the suture of the distal epiphyses are said to be more marked in *Bison*, while those in *Bos* are more sloping. The difference is often clear in particular individuals, but is hard to recognize in the presence of sex differences also. The median ridges of the barrels are perhaps somewhat divergent in frontal aspect in *Bison*, not in *Bos*. Exact measurements and indices derived therefrom, are probably the only reliable criteria in most cases.

Musk ox (*Ovibos moschatus*). Both the dimensions and the relative proportions of metatarsal and metacarpal distinguish this species. The form is distinctly bovine, though small, but the metatarsal is relatively short and broad in comparison with the metacarpal, as in sheep.

Saiga (*Saiga tartarica*). The metatarsal is exceedingly long and slender in comparison with the metacarpal, very narrow proximally and in proportion broad at the distal epiphyses, with sloping shoulders.

Chamois (*Rupicapra rupicapra*). The metatarsal is fairly long and slender, not as extremely as in the saiga. The distal epiphyses are very broad in proportion, with markedly square shoulders.

Sheep (*Ovis*) and goat (*Capra*). These genera are usually mutually indistinguishable from the long bones. The metatarsals are square in the shaft, little longer than the metacarpals, broad and square-shouldered at the epiphyseal suture. In general proportions they are intermediate between the saiga and chamois on the one hand and the heavily built bovines on the other.

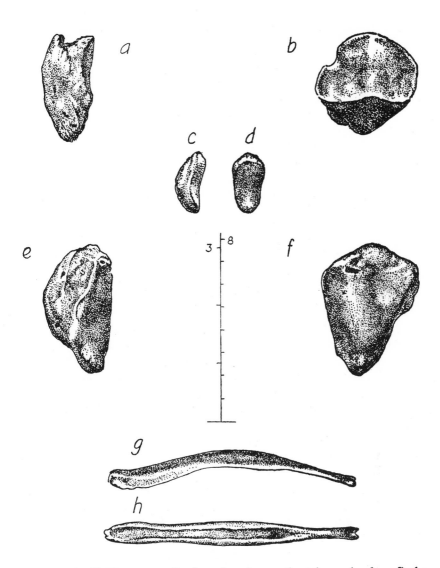

FIG 51. (a, b) Human patella, lateral and posterior views: (c, d, e, f) the same views of patellae of dog and ox respectively. (g, h) Right lateral and ventral views of the os penis of a wolf. All on the same scale.

Some length measurements of specimen bovid metatarsals, taken from Hue's figures, may be some rough guide to stature:—

Bison (*Bison bison*)	236 mm.
metatarsal cannon-bone	
Domestic ox (*Bos taurus*)	230
(not the same individual	
as the metacarpal on p. 155)	
Musk ox (*Ovibos moschatus*)	187
Saiga (*Saiga tartarica*)	182
Chamois (*Rupicapra r.*)	150
Ibex (*Capra ibex*)	132
Domestic goat (*Capra hircus*)	132
Mouflon (*Ovis musimon*)	148
Domestic sheep (*Ovis aries*)	151

To these may be added some measurements from actual bones:—

Urochs (*Bos primigenius*) (♀)	293
Celtic ox ('*Bos longifrons*')	178-218
	(range of several)

Phalanges of the Pes. These are hardly to be determined, save on the basis of size, without very complete comparative material. The phalanges of pes and manus are very alike in the ruminants and the digits of one limb are also distinguishable from those of the other only on close scrutiny and comparison. For those wishing to attempt these unrewarding tasks there are some fairly adequate illustrations in Hue (1907), Plates 180-186.

One point of general interest arises from a study of these illustrations. All the phalanges of the manus in the Cervidae and Bovidae are thicker and stronger, and sometimes also longer, than those of the pes in the same individual. This might be expected in males from the greater load falling on the fore-legs owing to their bearing heavy antlers or horns. To what extent it may apply also to the females is not stated—it is at any rate unknown to the writer.

The matter is thus seen to be of some complexity and our exact knowledge on the subject of phalanges is limited. Until sufficient new work has been done and published the only solution is to appeal to the comparative material of some unusually well-stocked museum, if the urgency of a particular case seems to warrant it.

THE OS PENIS (*Fig.* 51g, h). There remains but a single bone, once more not properly a skeletal bone, which must be mentioned, lest its occurrence in an archaeological context should constitute an insoluble problem.

In most less specialized mammals, Insectivores, Rodents, Chiroptera, Primates (save man) and Carnivores there is a local ossification called *os penis* of a soft structure which supports the penis in the males.

In a large dog, for example, the os penis is 4 inches long or more, a bilaterally symmetrical bone of anteriorly tapering form, rounded dorsally, and deeply grooved longitudinally below. It is somewhat bent ventrally in the M.S.P. towards its anterior end.

While not often recovered, should such a bone appear in a collection it would perhaps not even be recognized as mammalian unless its existence had been referred to.

12

Determination of Species from Bones

THE FOREGOING DESCRIPTIONS of the mammalian skeleton in general and the principal characteristics of the bones in the various zoological groups leads on to the real purpose behind the study of bones by an archaeologist—the determination of the species represented in an excavated collection.

Few people with even a nodding acquaintance with mammals—not zoologists only—would find great difficulty in assigning the entire skeleton of an animal at least to the correct Order within the Class Mammalia. Unfortunately, save for those of men and their domestic dogs, it is a rarity for archaeologists to unearth complete skeletons. Most collections from archaeological sites consist overwhelmingly of fragments. Complete bones are rather few. The reason for this is evident.

Man's chief concern with his mammalian contemporaries was to hunt for food and clothing those which he was able to overpower, and to shun those which he regarded as worthless for these purposes, or in hunting which he was more likely to lose his life than gain a meal or a pelt. Only the remains of the former group will be found in any quantity at his habitation-sites. Those of the remainder, naturally buried in peat or river-gravel, will have suffered the ravages of scavengers and of decay, so that only the more massive and durable parts are likely to have been preserved.

Later, when the arts of agriculture and the domestication of animals had been learned, the herdsmen lived chiefly on their domestic stock and hunted as much for pleasure as for meat. However acquired, the remains of animals which we find at archaeological sites have mostly been butchered and carved, the bones even deliberately smashed for their marrow or to obtain industrial material. What was left was either dropped underfoot, wherever the diner or craftsman happened to be, or, in later and tidier societies, was consigned to the lake, the river, the bog or the midden. In favourable circumstances the material is found much as it was discarded by man, but very often natural agencies have further affected it, so that, again, only the more resistant fragments are available to be examined. How far the smaller pieces may be useful for study will be considered below. This chapter is concerned with the determination of entire, or at least fairly complete, single bones.

Determination is by a number of steps and systematic eliminations.

A. What part of the skeleton is it?

The essential preliminary step in any determination is to decide what part of the mammalian skeleton the specimen represents. Unless a confident decision on this point can first be made, all sorts of ridiculous errors may follow, such as, for example, mistaking a finger-bone of a larger species for one of the main limb-bones of a smaller.

In the case of a tooth, this step will obviously be unnecessary from the outset, but until preliminary recognition of a bone and its assignment to the correct part of the skeleton becomes axiomatic, serious mistakes can hardly be avoided if it is omitted. It is specially important when the specimen is fragmentary.

The following is an attempt to construct a 'Key' to the bones of the skeleton, on the lines of those used in other branches of biological science for the recognition of species. Under each main head there is a number of alternatives, and by following up those which correspond with the observed characters of the unknown specimen its identity should be readily recognized.

Key to the bones
of the mammalian skeleton

1. (a)	The specimen is clearly a 'long' bone	SEE PARA. 2
(b)	It is *not* clearly a long bone	,, 7
2.	It has (a) Both articulations convex	,, 3
	(b) Both articulations flat or concave	,, 4
	(c) One articulation convex, the other flat or concave	,, 5
	(d) A clear articulation only at one end	,, 6

3. (a) The rounded head has a distinct neck and a small pit in its articular surface. The other end has a pair of knuckle-shaped condyles, separated by a deep notch, and a patellar facet in front

Femur
(Figs. 45, 46, 47)

(b) The head has no distinct neck. The other end is a pulley-shaped trochlea with more or less deep fossae above it, before and behind, occasionally perforated

Humerus
(Figs. 39, 40, 41)

4. (a) The shaft is triangular in section above.
        The proximal joint-surface consists of
        two flattish facets with a raised crest
        between them. The distal articulation is
        concave and more or less pulley-shaped.
        There may be a fused-on vestige of a
        fibula   *Tibia*
                                                        (Figs. 45, 46, 47)

   (b) The shaft is very slender, flattened or
        polygonal in section. The articulations
        at both ends are flattish small facets   *Fibula*
                                                        (Figs. 45, 46, 47)

5. (a) The largest articulation is a deep,
        rounded notch, not right at the end of
        the bone but in one side of its length.
        The shaft tapers to a small articulation
        at the other or is broken off close to a
        point where it is fused with another
        bone   *Ulna*
                                                        (Figs. 39, 40, 41)

   (b) (i) The convex head is usually more or
        less cylindrical with a slightly concave
        facet on the end of the bone. The other
        end is wider, with a hollow articulation.
        Unspecialized (e.g., human or carni-
        vorous)   *Radius*
                                                        (Figs. 39, 40, 41)

   (b) (ii) There is no distinct head. One arti-
        culation is hollow and pulley-like, the
        other end has a complicated surface of
        several convex and concave facets. The
        shaft is D-shaped in section, with a scar
        on its flat face for the ulna or a fused-on
        vestige of the ulna—specialized quad-
        ruped (e.g., bovine)   *Radius*
                                                              (Fig. 41)

   (c) One articulation consists of a number
        of almost flat facets, the other of one or
        two almost cylindrical 'barrels' or
        'knuckles', transverse to the shaft, each
        with a more or less raised median
        ridge   *Metapodial*
                                                  (Metacarpal or metatarsal)
                                                  (Figs. 43, 46, 49, 50)

(d) One articulation is hollow, the other a more or less prominent knuckle, without a median ridge. The bone may be very short (elephant) or very long (bat), but is generally not more than 3 or 4 diameters of its shaft in length

Phalanx of manus or pes.
(Figs. 43, 44, 49, 50)

6. (a) The articulated end is convex and forms something of a knob. The shaft tapers to a more or less sharp point

Degenerate *Fibula*, *metapodial*
(Figs. 47, 50)

(b) The articulation is concave, or a more or less rounded notch

Degenerate *Ulna*
(Fig. 41)

7. (a) The bone is bilaterally symmetrical, i.e., lies in the midline of the body

SEE PARA. 8

(b) It is *not* symmetrical, is, therefore, one of a pair which are mirror-images of one another, lying laterally to the M.S.P.

,,   9

8. (a) It is pierced by a large foramen, or is even ring-like (*atlas*). Has a body, transverse processes and neural spine, with two pairs of articular facets

Vertebra
(Figs. 28-30)

(b) It is relatively narrow, flat or keeled, and bears the impressions at either side of costal cartilages or sternal ribs

Sternum
(Fig. 33)

(c) It is a more or less long, rigid tube, consisting of two distinct halves which meet on the one side in the plane of symmetry and on the other are joined by a wedge-shaped sacrum

Pelvis
(Fig. 36)

(Probably of a carnivore, in which the sacro-iliac joints and symphysis pubis are early ankylosed).

(d) It is somewhat wedge-shaped, evidently consists of several vertebrae fused together and has areas at both sides for the articulations with the ilia

Sacrum
(Fig. 31)

(e) It is narrow and elongated, tapering towards one end and deeply grooved throughout the greater part of its length on the inferior (concave) side of its slight longitudinal curve, transversely rounded above

Os penis (probably of a carnivore) (Fig. 51)

(f) It is an entire skull or an unpaired bone of the skull

Frontal, occipital, sphenoid, palatine, ethmoid, maxilla or mandible (Figs. 6, 7)

(g) It is sub-cylindrical in section, somewhat waisted, and otherwise almost featureless, save, possibly, for small processes or longitudinal ridges

Caudal vertebra

(h) It is sub-rectangular in section, waisted, and shows a half-facet at each end on either side for a costal cartilage or sternal rib

Sternebra (segment of sternum)

(i) It is disc-like, one surface smooth (clearly an articular surface, perhaps marked with indistinct concentric circles), the other surface rough (with the crystalline texture typical of an unfused epiphysis). The discoid may be more or less flat or more or less deeply dished, with the articular surface either convex or concave

Vertebral epiphysis (Fig. 30)

9. (a) It is tabular in structure, bounded by denticulate sutures, finely cellular in section where fractured

(parietal or temporal, probably human).

Paired bone of cranial vault

(b) It is of irregular shape, thin and plate-like, or more or less coarsely cellular in structure or cavernous

Cranial bone

(c) It answers the foregoing general description, but is more or less conical,

curved or twisted, the surface more or
less clearly marked by ramifying
grooves of blood-vessels and small
foramina   *Ruminant horncore*
                                           (Figs. 11, 12)

(d) It is more or less cylindrical in section
or palmate, branched, and the branches
terminating in points. Close to the
thicker base, a 'burr' or 'coronet'. The
whole surface more or less clearly
marked with the ramifying grooves of
vessels. In section it is seen to consist
of a thick outer layer of dense bone,
the interior being finely cancellous or
cellular—much more finely than in a
skeletal bone of comparable size   *Deer antler*
                                           (Fig. 10)

(e) It is more or less flat and blade-like,
or sub-rectangular in section, curved
longitudinally, with two articular prominences close together at one end. A
groove for vessels and nerves runs
along its length near one edge, inside
the curve   *Rib*
                                           (Figs. 3, 4, 29)

(f) It is flat and blade-like, with a median
crest or spine at right angles to the plane
of the main blade. Generally sub-triangular or sub-oval in outline, the most
acute angle having a large, more or less
oval, shallow articular surface. The end
of the spine nearest this may be more or
less expanded and overhanging the edge
of the articular surface   *Scapula*
                                           (Figs. 33-5)

(g) It is superficially somewhat rib-like, but
has a double S-curve, unlike the single
C-curve of a rib, with clear articular
facets at both ends   *Clavicle*
                                           (Fig. 33)

(h) It has a large, more or less expanded,
fan-shaped projection with a circular,
cup-shaped articular surface at its base.
Two other branches diverge from the

articular cup and rejoin to enclose a
large, more or less oval, space

Os innominatum
(Figs. 36, 37)

(i) It is an irregular-shaped, compact bone,
with two or more rather flat or shallow
articular facets

*Carpal or
tarsal bone*
(Figs. 43, 44, 49, 50)

(j) While answering the general description
under (i), it has a more or less prominent lever-like process, roughened
at its extremity for the attachment of a
strong tendon

Calcaneum
(Figs. 49, 50)

(k) While answering the general description under (i) one of its surfaces is a
rather prominent pulley-shaped articulation

Astragalus
(Figs. 49, 50)

(l) It is rather small and pea-like, with one,
or two closely adjacent, articular facets
on one side only

Sesamoid bone
(Figs. 43, 44, 49, 50)

(m) While answering the general description
under (l), it is generally larger, approximately heart-shaped and is marked by
roughened areas at base and apex for the
attachment of strong tendons

Patella
(Fig. 51)

(n) The bone has but one clear, somewhat
deeply concave, articular facet. Its part
opposite to this may be distinctly claw-
or hoof-like in shape, but in any case,
has the rough, vascular surface, full of
small foramina, which shows it to be the
core of a horny structure

Ungual phalanx
(Figs. 43, 44, 49, 50)

(o) The bone shows clearly in one part an
articular surface or surfaces, but in another has a surface more or less regular
but characteristically rough and crystalline in texture

*Loose epiphysis
of a long bone*
(Fig. 38)

(Refer to the bone or bones suggested
by the form of the articular surface).

(p) The bone shows no articular surface
but only that characteristic of a still-
growing epiphysis

> *Epiphysis
> of a trochanter, tuberosity,
> or other process for the
> attachment of a tendon,
> which is ossified separately
> from the main part of its
> parent bone.*

This 'key' is a rather clumsy expedient, introduced only to make the book as self-contained as possible, for those who have no ready access to personal demonstrations in osteology. Rapid recognition of bones and their correct attribution to the part of the body to which they belong comes only with practice and after handling a certain amount of bone material. No illustrations, however complete, can be an adequate substitute for the actual bones in the round. With all these limitations, however, the key may make it possible for the reader to take the first steps unaided. After having gained a little experience, he will, in most cases, soon be able to abandon these crutches and only occasionally have to go through the whole system to arrive at a conclusion, in the more difficult and uncommon instances.

Once armed with the correct location of the bone in the skeleton, the next step may be taken, towards the determination of the species to which it belonged.

B. First elimination—
what could it be, in point of size?

All determinations consist in a process of elimination. The most obvious first elimination is by size. A femur (Fig. 52) 360 mm. (14″) long and 38 mm. (1½″) in diameter in mid-shaft evidently belongs to an animal of some moderate size. One can, therefore, immediately eliminate as possibilities the small mammals (Insectivora, Chiroptera, Rodentia, Primates—save man—and the smaller Carnivora) on the one hand and, on the other, the very large and heavily built (elephants, rhinoceroses and hippopotamuses). Increasing familiarity with the material will lead to this elimination, and those which follow, becoming, to some extent, automatic and subconscious. At first, however, it is as well deliberately to eliminate even the obvious impossibilities, in order to arrive at a complete short list of conceivable possibilities. Omission of this step may lead to jumping to premature conclusions. When eliminating any group, one should conscientiously ask oneself the question: 'How do I *know* that this group cannot have owned the bone in question?' It is one thing to *know* that a particular specimen is not horse, it is more permanently useful (and communicable!) to be able to explain in detail *why* it could not be horse.

To return to our 'sheep': for the femur under examination we are now left with the following list of possibilities:—Man, a large carnivore (bear or lion), horse, pig, a large deer (e.g., elk) or one of the larger bovids (*Bos, Bison, Ovibos*).

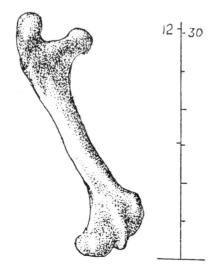

Some further eliminations from this list, on the basis of dimensions, are possible, on closer consideration.

No adult man has a femur as short as 14″. If, therefore, the femur in question is clearly adult, with completely-fused epiphyses, man can forthwith be counted out. Conversely, the pig, though comparable with man in body-weight, has very short legs and its femur is, therefore, too short to come into the question here.

As to the claims of the remaining candidates, the next set of eliminations will have to be based on morphological considerations.

FIG 52.

C. Second elimination—
to what Order does the bone belong?

Beginning with the larger zoological groups, reference may be made to p. 162 where the femora are described in turn. Under Carnivora, it is there stated that the femur approaches the human form and that the great trochanter seldom projects above the head, save in the family of cats (Felidae). On reference to the specimen, it is seen that the great trochanter does project far beyond the head. This does not eliminate the Felidae, but it may be observed, in addition, that the head is not so rounded or so well detached, the shaft so slender and, at the distal end, the patellar area is much more extensive and elevated than in the cats. Moreover, the whole bone is much shorter and stockier than in the Carnivora, so that this Order may safely be excluded.

The bone clearly belongs to a somewhat more specialized terrestrial quadruped.

The list is now abbreviated to horse, large deer or one of the larger bovids. Of these, the horse belongs to the odd-toed group of ungulates, Perissodactyla, in which a constant feature of the femur is a prominent third trochanter. The specimen has no such process, so it cannot have belonged to a horse.

Under Cervidae, it is shown that the two largest (*Alces, Megaceros*) have femora 400 mm. or more long, and withal slender. The next in size (*Cervus elaphus*) is much shorter than our specimen and even more slender in proportion. Evidently, then, the femur is not part of any deer in our list.

We have thus eliminated all but a single zoological Family—the Bovidae.

D. Within the Order or lower category identified, what species does the bone best fit?

In view of the comparative difficulty of distinguishing morphologically between members of the same Family, a review of the sizes of the possible claimants is, once more, worth while. At 360 mm. or so, our specimen is more than half as long again as the femur in sheep or goats, but notably smaller than those of the bison, urochs or modern domestic cattle. The nearest match for size is *Ovibos*, the musk ox. Now, unless our femur comes from a Pleistocene site where the presence of musk-ox is conceivable, this conclusion must also be rejected.

Assuming that *Ovibos* must be discounted, as at a Roman or Iron-Age site, we seem to have reached an *impasse*, having considered everything in our list without reaching a conclusion. Presently we remember, however, that prehistoric domestic animals were frequently much smaller than our modern breeds, so that the specimen would probably fit a Celtic ox, the so-called '*Bos longifrons*'. This determination is obviously likely to be correct.

E. Comparison with known material

Until the student of bones comes to know his material pretty well, such a determination *faute de mieux* is not good enough. The final test for every determination is comparison with known and labelled material. The larger and more varied this is, the firmer are the conclusions to which the student may have to append his name in an eventual publication. Until our femur has been compared with at least one from a known prehistoric ox and found to be identical save in very minor details, the task is not finished. If a whole series of comparative specimens is available, showing a range of variation within the race, into which range the specimen can be fitted without discrepancy, so much the better. Sex, age, heredity, and environment all have an influence on the stature of animals, which must be taken into account where, as here, a determination rests largely on dimensions of the specimen and on probabilities.

It is not every case, even of an entire bone, which permits a process of elimination so complete as to exclude all but a single species. In the dog Family, the Canidae, for example, there is always likely to be some doubt as between the long bones of a large dog and those of a wolf,

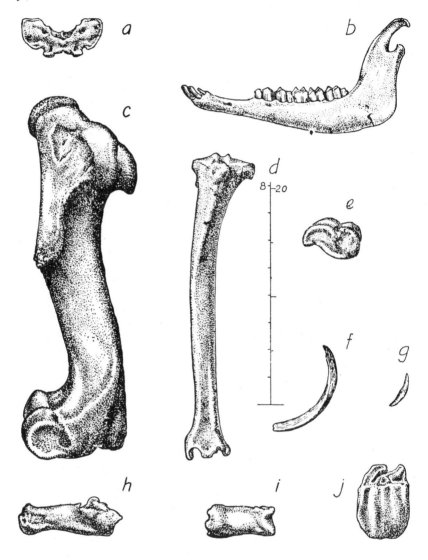

FIG 53.   Examples (a) to (j) for initial practice in determination of entire bones and teeth. All the pieces are drawn to the same scale. Try it yourself first—only then refer to Appendix A (p. 248) for description of the recommended procedure for determination in each case.

or between small dogs and two species of fox. The sheep and goats are notoriously difficult to distinguish, save from good skulls or horn-cores. The rest of the small bovids will only be known apart from these by the use of comparative material at first and, later, by skill in memorizing minor differences in proportions and morphology. A visual memory, a sound knowledge of the mammalian skeleton in general,

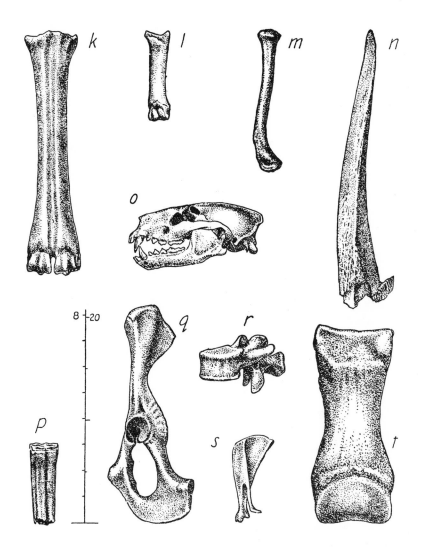

FIG 54. Examples (k) to (t) all to the same scale, for practice in determining bones and teeth. See Appendix A (p. 248) for results—but try them unaided first.

with its modifications in the main Orders, and some understanding of the habits and environments of the living animals are all helpful and can be cultivated.

In order to assist the beginner a few examples for practice in determination of entire bones are illustrated in Figs. 53-4. The solutions, with the detailed arguments leading to them, are given in Appendix A.

13

Fragmentary bones

+ +

IT HAS ALREADY been pointed out, at the beginning of the preceding chapter, that the vast majority of animal bones from archaeological sites is found, for reasons there discussed, in a more or less fragmentary condition.

There will be many of these too small or too damaged to give any useful information. With a little luck in the preservation of significant details, however, and by reconstructing in the mind's eye what is missing, a surprising number, even of fragments, will yield their probable identities to a practised student. A quantity will always remain undeterminable, or, what amounts to the same thing, not worth the labour of determination. There are, thus, two main points to be considered here:—

(i) What kinds of fragments are at all determinable?

(ii) What is worth the expenditure of some time and labour in arriving at a determination?

What is determinable?

Absolute size is no measure of importance. A rodent molar 2 mm. long may enable the exact species to be determined, while a piece weighing several pounds from the shaft of a long bone of some large species may tell us nothing certain but that it is of a large animal.

How, then, is the excavator to know what is worth keeping and what should be discarded?

We have seen that bones are recognized largely by the form of their articulations. Unless a bone can first be identified, the species to which it belonged cannot be determined. It is important, therefore, to recover the articular surfaces, and this includes loose epiphyses of immature bones. At the same time, a fragment of a shaft alone may retain the evidence for its determination. The radius of a horse, showing the ankylosed vestige of the ulnar shaft, cannot be mistaken for anything else, even when its articulations are missing. A single inch of the shaft of a human femur, with its characteristic raised linea aspera, is sufficient to determine man.

Shaft-fragments should, therefore, be examined for excrescences, pits, ridges, grooves, foramina, etc., which may betray their nature directly or enable a match to be found among the comparative material.

Much of zoological classification is based on teeth and toes. No tooth, or even a piece of enamel showing any possibly characteristic sculpture, should be thrown away. Considerable fragments of meta-podials are always valuable. Even loose phalanges may be informa-tive, although they do not always enable exact determination between species of similar size. The often insignificant, multi-faceted carpals and tarsals are also important when they are recovered, especially the astragali and calcanea, since different zoological groups have different equipment and arrangements at wrist and ankle, which may serve to distinguish them.

Horn-cores, hoof-cores and antler fragments are always worth preserving. In the case of horn-cores, there may be no other way of distinguishing readily between sheep and goats. The bony pedicle, the burr, beam and brow-tine of an antler are important in determining deer remains.

It is well worth while considering fragments in their context, as found. Several undistinguished chips and flakes of bone, found to-gether, may have joins preserved which will enable something signifi-cant to be rebuilt. If a badly broken skull is found in position, it may be quite useless merely to collect the biggest and strongest pieces, for important contacts will certainly be lost. If, on the other hand, every-thing which might belong to the find is scrupulously gathered and kept together, a skilled and patient preparator may be able to strengthen and rebuild from it a really valuable specimen. Fragments which evi-dently belong together should never be separated.

Though whole skulls and skeletons may be rare, every effort should be made to recover, and preserve unbroken, considerable portions which may be discovered.

Any bones found in their correct articulated positions are interesting, for this means that at least some of the muscles and ligaments still held them together when they became buried. A femur and a tibia of a deer found separately mean no more than that man hunted and ate that species of deer, but the same bones, found lying in their correct anatomical relationship, may represent a funerary offering of an entire haunch of venison, a foundation-deposit or other evidence of con-temporary piety.

The importance of recovering the whole of a find, even when badly broken or decayed, may be seen when it is realized that species-determination often rests on proportions rather than on differences of anatomical details. A broken bovine thoracic vertebra, for instance, may equally well belong to ox or bison. If the whole of the neural spine is recovered, however, or even its original length recorded (when it cannot be lifted in reconstructable fragments), a definite de-cision one way or the other becomes possible. So also for the skulls of these genera. Horn-cores are often in poor condition, owing to their light, cellular structure, but they are distinctive as between *Bos* and *Bison* if enough can be recovered. The base of the horn-core and the presence or absence of a buttress of bone supporting it is said to distinguish a wild *Bos primigenius* from a large domesticated *Bos taurus*. The most important distinctive feature between sheep and goat lies on the vault of the skull, just behind the bases of the horns, where the course of the coronal suture is specific.

Separate teeth have already been mentioned, but their value is much enhanced if they are still in their alveoli in maxilla or mandible. One suggested significant difference between dog and wolf rests on measurements of the last three upper cheek-teeth *in situ*. The cave-bear's dentition, apart from mere size, differs from that of the brown bear only in the total absence of a degenerate premolar, which is present as a vestige in the latter.

Cases could be multiplied almost indefinitely. The principles to be followed in all are the same—careful excavation, noting any possibly significant spatial relationships between bones, careful lifting of any which seem worthy of preservation for study or exhibition and the collection of all fragments which might possibly be associated with a single specimen, to ensure the best possible restoration if that should be attempted.

What may safely be discarded on the site consists only of the numerous splinters and fragments of shafts of long bones which bear no characteristic features, broken vertebrae and ribs, small skull-, mandible- and pelvis-fragments which are unrelated to any particular portion worth reassembling.

What is worth determination?

Many sites of permanent human settlements yield bones in great profusion. These are generally overwhelmingly of the usual domestic animals and the number of specimens determinable with certainty, or at least with a high degree of probability, often runs into hundreds, if not thousands.

In these circumstances, it is clearly waste of time to attempt the determination of any fragments which are not sufficiently complete to give an unequivocal answer quickly. This does not mean that everything not recognizable at the first glance should be discarded. In such an assemblage, it is the occasional wild mammal, fish or bird which holds considerable interest, as supplementing the basic menu of beef, mutton and pork, which the bulk of the collection usually represents. Only those doubtful fragments which could most readily belong to the list of common species at the site should be jettisoned forthwith. The remainder is worthy of a second review, in case the original element of doubt should have resided in their being unusual rather than altogether inscrutable.

In the case of a site where the collection of bones is small, the value of the smaller and less easily determined fragments is increased and a greater effort should be made to identify them. If any guess can be made as to their attribution, a decision can often be obtained by matching the fragments against complete bones belonging to the possible species. Small details of surface relief, hitherto unexplained, shallow muscle-impressions and hitherto unnoticed small foramina for nutrient vessels will fall quite accurately into place as soon as the correct match is found.

The same care is usually worth while also where remains of Pleistocene wild faunas are the subject of the inquiry. Not only is bone material of any sort, in this case, much rarer than on sites of permanent occupation, but what does survive is probably much broken, worn and more difficult to recognize. The variety of species present, on the other hand, is likely to be much greater than when domesticated species form the bulk of the material. It is, therefore, important to determine every single fragment if it be at all possible.

It is here that a 'feeling' for bones, the intuitive perception which leads straight to the selection of a likely match for a difficult specimen, amid so many possibilities, comes into its own. No great palaeontologist is without it and it is doubtful whether it can be developed at all if the student lacks a certain essential sense of solid form, but there is no question that it is based, in the first place, on an intimate acquaintance with finer details, as well as the basic anatomical points. This can only be acquired by practice, by handling and comparing bones and by studying the methods of leading palaeontologists in the published literature.

Every fragment displaying some characteristic features which eludes the primary identification as a specific part of the skeleton should be treated as a challenge. If only its location in the skeleton can first be ascertained, it is likely that it may prove to be determinable. Since its nature was not, at first, obvious, the eventual determination may add an uncommon, and therefore, important, species to the list. To acknowledge defeat without a struggle is often to miss a 'plum' of this sort in a rather arid waste of 'suet'!

Some common fragments

Damaged and broken bones are infinitely variable in their state of preservation between the extremes of near-completeness, when their character should fairly easily be recognized, and relatively fine comminution. Any attempt to identify them in the latter condition is certainly doomed to failure. The point at which this lower limit is reached, of course, varies, to some extent, with the skill of the worker, but for everyone there must be a stage, short of actual crumbs, at which he must admit defeat.

It is, therefore, impossible to offer any systematic method for attempting to determine an individual fragment, but the parts of the skeleton vary in their capacity to withstand violence and chemical attack, so that it is possible to indicate some more durable parts which are not infrequently recognizably preserved as distinct fragments.

SKULL. Teeth are, of course, of prime importance in all species. Under natural conditions the enamel is extremely durable, but it is a curious fact that it is more susceptible than the dentine to destruction by fire, so that in a cremation, for example, or any assemblage of burnt bones, a watch should be kept, not so much for the crowns as for the *roots* of teeth.

In the smaller mammals, with thin skulls, the mandible and the teeth alone survive, in most cases. In man, the more durable fragments are of the thicker parts of the vault (frontal, parietals, occipital), especially the central part of the occipital squama, where it is thickest, the frontal eminences and the upper margins of the orbits. The base and face generally disintegrate first, but, of the base, the dense petrous parts of the temporals, containing the inner ear mechanism, may be well preserved. The mandible is denser than most parts of the skull and, though frequently broken at the mental foramen, to one side or the other of the symphysis, enough may be left to be useful.

In the very large ungulates, on the other hand, the skull, for the sake of weight-saving, is often extremely cellular and porous, and is, therefore, easily decayed. The denser parts are, once more, the mandible, the very durable large teeth and those parts which support horns, antlers and the nasal horn in the rhinoceroses. The large and prominent occipital condyles, the condyles of the mandible and the sigmoid notches in front of them, are not uncommon loose fragments. Horn-cores, antlers and the dense frontal bones supporting them are next in order of importance.

AXIAL SKELETON. Vertebrae are seldom preserved entire. In the large animals with heavy heads, however, some of the cervicals, and especially the atlas and axis, are very heavy and solid. Even though much broken, the details of their function are often present in fragments and permit their recognition. Pieces of rib-shafts are common, but not often very informative, save as to the general size of the animal. Sacra, where they are well ossified, may be preserved and caudal vertebrae, where there is a strong tail, may survive recognizably owing to their initial lack of prominent detail. In man, the atlas and axis often outlast even the large lumbar vertebrae, and the sacrum, transmitting the whole weight of the trunk, is denser and more often preserved than it is in most quadrupeds.

SHOULDER-GIRDLE. The blade of a scapula, though thin, is often dense and strong enough to be largely preserved. The vertebral margin is often less well ossified—is, indeed, largely cartilaginous in ungulates (Fig. 35e)—and is generally very eroded. When even most of the blade has perished, the strong neck with the glenoid cavity may survive, with enough of the spine to permit determination. Even the shape of the glenoid surface and the development of the coracoid may be sufficient to identify the species. The absence of a prominent acromion and coracoid in ungulates assists the preservation of a recognizable fragment. In man, the processes have often decayed, but the blade, in contrast, is well ossified throughout and its outline and strong spine will identify it. The clavicle is a considerable and strong bone in the Primates, and often outlasts the ribs and vertebrae.

HIP-GIRDLE. Whatever else may fall away, the acetabulum and the portions of the ilium, ischium and pubis immediately adjacent to it are the last parts to disappear. The ilium, or at least its neck, generally survives to some extent, though the iliac crest and fan-like expanse are first attacked, even before the ischium and pubis.

LONG BONES IN GENERAL

The shafts generally outlast the articulations, so that the recognizable shaft-features are important.

HUMERUS. The head and tuberosities seem to decay first, but the upper part of the shaft and the deltoid ridge are generally in fairly good condition. Owing to the deep coronoid and olecranon fossae, the weakest part of the distal end of the humerus is just above the trochlea, so that this is not uncommon as a separate fragment. Where nothing but a shaft remains, its distal end may show the base of the division of the epicondyles supporting the trochlea on either side of the olecranon fossa. This identifies a humerus.

ULNA. The strength of this bone is mostly concentrated round the trochlear notch and in the olecranon process. Even where it is well developed, the shaft may disappear before the more proximal parts. In domestic species the olecranon will often be found to be broken across. It has, of course, an epiphysis, which in youth is loose, but even in an adult bone this break is often seen. Owing to the comparative strength of the bone this is not a place where one would expect to see a natural fracture and, indeed, it appears to be a feature of pre-historic, as of modern, butchery. It seems that it is easier to break the olecranon than neatly to detach the triceps tendon from it, when butchering a carcase.

Where the shaft of the ulna is weak or degenerate, it is often broken off a little in front of the coronoid process.

RADIUS. In man and unspecialized animals the radius is often broken a little beyond the tuberosity for the biceps, so that the head and this tuberosity remain as one recognizable piece and the strong distal end with its tapering fragment of shaft forms another. In the specialized quadrupeds, the radius is equally developed at both ends and has a very strong dense shaft. This normally shows a trace of the degenerate ulna, either as an ankylosed stump of the shaft (horse) or as a scar where the ulnar shaft made contact but was not ankylosed (ruminants). In aged individuals, even among the ruminants, the ulna may be firmly ankylosed at this point, but is almost inevitably broken in fossil material. The two ends of the radius, and especially the loose distal epiphysis, having no considerable prominences, are well preserved as separate fragments and are easily recognized.

CARPAL BONES. These are generally not well preserved, or not recovered, but examples attributable to the largest mammals are not uncommon because they are big enough to be readily recognized as bones. They are valuable indicators, if available, and are often not seriously damaged.

METACARPALS AND METATARSALS. These are often very strong cannon-bones and, with the emphasis on toes in classification, are very valuable evidence. Shafts may be broken in the middle, but both ends of a cannon-bone are easily recognized and give a good idea of the proportions of the entire bone to a practised eye. Even loose or broken distal epiphyses are useful guides to size.

PHALANGES. The shorter and stronger phalanges are commonly well preserved and a good guess at their specific nature may be made from their size and proportions. Where these are not sufficiently distinctive we are in difficulties, and more study is needed to enable us to make the most of this sort of material. If not deeply decayed they are seldom broken, but the palmar wall of the shaft is often thin and is easily perforated. This is a feature of which prehistoric man took advantage to make 'phalange whistles'. Owing to the natural weakness at this point, it is likely that many examples of supposed 'whistles' are due to natural decay and not to adaptation by man. Evidence of working should be adduced before concluding that such an object is an artifact.

The ungual phalanges are more valuable than the rest for distinguishing the major zoological groups. Those of the carnivores with the reflected basal plate are especially distinctive.

FEMUR. As with other long bones, the shaft is usually better preserved than the ends. Trochanters, especially, are rather susceptible to decay, so that the evidence to be gained from their height above the articular head is frequently lost. The head itself is a fairly common object as a loose epiphysis. It is easily distinguished from other epiphyses by the presence of a pit in the middle of its surface for the round ligament, in all species which concern us save the elephants.

The circular section of the shaft is shared with the humerus, but in many ungulates there is a more or less well-marked lateral supracondylar fossa. This is often preserved even when the joint surfaces have been lost, and identifies the femur in these species.

The third trochanter of the Perissodactyla, or its broken base, is specific for this group, among the ungulates. The distal epiphysis, with the femoral condyles and the patellar area, is frequently found loose. The surface for its attachment on the shaft is characteristic, consisting of four rather pyramidal eminences, with the usual granular or crystalline surface (Fig. 30).

TIBIA. The rather slender shaft, in most species, especially in its distal third, results in frequent breakages, whereby the distal end with the articulation for the astragalus is found as an isolated fragment. The proximal fragment, when this occurs, is easily known by the triangular section of its shaft. Both proximal and distal epiphyses of young individuals occur loose. The former, not so frequent because it is fused with the shaft at an earlier stage of growth, is unmistakable with its two oval facets and intervening crest. Comparison will usually permit its approximate determination. The distal epiphysis, with its two more or less deep grooves for the astragalus and protecting malleoli on one or both sides (the lateral, when present, a fused vestige of the fibular epiphysis) is equally easy to recognize. The form of the articular surface, whether deep or shallow, specialized or generalized, is a helpful clue as to its nature.

FIBULA. Degenerate in most species, the fibula survives in the fragmentary state usually only as a vestige more or less ankylosed with the tibia. Even when fully represented, the slender shaft does not lend itself to preservation. In man, its quadrilateral section betrays the nature of the fragment.

TARSAL BONES. Astragalus and calcaneum are not often found broken. Where the rest of the tarsal bones are distinct they are seldom recognized, save in the case of large animals, but the fused cubo-navicular of ruminants and the short and flat navicular and lateral cuneiform of the horse are generally recovered when found.

Metatarsals and phalanges have already been treated under metacarpals and those of the fore-limb.

It is hoped that these hints will assist in the identification of some of the commoner fragments. Success in this field is mostly a matter of practice, a good knowledge of the details of entire bones and the quality of imagination which will enable the investigator to restore in the mind's eye such parts as may be missing. Once identified, determination is a matter of elimination and comparison, as for entire bones.

No determination is possible until the identity of a fragment has been established. In difficult cases a systematic listing in the mind of the bones of the skeleton to which the fragment *could not* belong narrows down the field.

It is nearly always unwise to jump to a conclusion on the strength of a 'hunch'. In the earlier stages of apprenticeship in bones 'hunches' are generally wrong. The student should be able to explain to his own satisfaction *why* he concludes that a fragment belongs to a particular bone. When he knows this answer, the problem is solved once and for all.

14

Bones in the Field & in the Laboratory

Properties and structure of bone

FRESH BONE is a complex structure of mineral and organic materials, in the approximate ratio by weight of 2:1. The mineral fraction is chiefly calcium phosphate with some calcium carbonate and other salts in small amounts. The organic matter is a protein called ossein, with fats and other components in the marrow filling the shafts of the long bones.

The mineral substances can be removed from fresh bone (decalcification) by soaking (macerating) for a considerable time in dilute mineral acids, when the organic structures remain and are perfectly pliable, so that a completely decalcified fresh long bone can be tied in a knot! Conversely, the organic matter can be completely destroyed by fairly prolonged heating to red heat (calcination), when the mineral salts alone remain and the bone, while retaining its shape, becomes dead white, light in weight and extremely porous and friable, crumbling to powder if subjected to any stress.

The mineral salts thus confer on fresh bone its hardness and rigidity; the organic matter, toughness and a certain resilience.

Bone occurs in two forms: the compact substance and the cancellous or spongy tissue of which the articular ends of the long bones are constructed, save for a very thin outer skin of compact substance. Even this so-called compact substance is highly porous, being permeated, in life, with minute nutrient vessels which occupy a network of fine channels, averaging 0.05 mm. in diameter, the *Haversian canals*. These run approximately longitudinally in the shaft of a long bone, ramifying and rejoining one another at small angles. They are interconnected by a still finer system of capillary vessels running in *canaliculi*, radiating from the canals and reaching all the tiny cavities (*lacunae*) in which reside the living bone-cells.

Fossilization

Natural conditions suitable for the preservation of bones as fossils are exceptional. If this were not so the face of the earth would be paved metres deep with the remains of dead creatures. A first prerequisite is that the body of a dead animal should be rapidly covered, otherwise the remains are accessible to scavengers and the processes of weathering, both of which make short work of reducing it to its original chemical elements or at least simple compounds like carbon dioxide, water, ammonia and mineral salts.

Quick burial, away from these destructive agencies, can take place if the body falls into a river, lake, bog or sea, where it may come to rest and be covered with rapidly accumulating water-formed sediments. Volcanic eruptions yielding quickly formed ash deposits of all particle sizes, from boulders down to the finest dust, may also preserve fossils, as may other wind-borne sediments like loess and dune sand. Lime-saturated water in caves or surface springs may cover them with drip-stone or tufa. In any case, it will be obvious that chance plays the largest part in preservation, and that for every specimen preserved, millions of contemporaries perish completely.

With the coming of man the chance of preservation of animal remains is increased. The abundant bones of cave-earths, kitchen middens, prehistoric rubbish-pits or ditches testify to the accumulated food-refuse of the inhabitants and yield interesting evidence of their environment, habits or economy.

When a fresh bone becomes buried in the earth it undergoes chemical changes, differing in nature and degree with the chemistry of the surrounding matrix. Save in extremely acid soil-conditions, it is the mineral constituents of the bone which are most resistant to change and, if there is reasonable access of atmospheric oxygen, the organic substances are gradually and more or less rapidly broken down into relatively simple compounds, such as carbon dioxide, ammonia and water. Their removal from the pores of the bone allows free access to the innermost recesses of soil-water, bearing in solution mineral salts, such as iron and calcium compounds, which it may have been able to dissolve out of the surrounding soil. Seasonal drying out of the soil and the contained bone causes these minerals to be deposited in and even on, the bone substance, so that, in a soil rich in such salts, a bone may gradually become completely mineralized and concreted, or 'fossilized', gaining weight and hardness and becoming less porous, without significant change of form. These conditions are provided by soils containing an excess of chalk, limestone and iron and manganese salts. Depending on the exact conditions, this process of natural impregnation or incrustation with minerals will generally take place rather slowly, so that a high degree of mineralization is taken to be an indication of considerable age.

In a well-aerated, acid soil, poor in bases, not only is the organic matter of a bone somewhat quickly decomposed, but even the mineral part will soon be attacked and the specimen may disappear without trace in a comparatively short time. It is for these reasons that Bronze-Age barrows, for example, when built on chalk or other calcareous soil, are generally found to cover reasonably well-preserved human burials, while, under those on a porous sandy soil, the grave is almost invariably empty and even chemical traces of phosphate from the bones may have disappeared.

Waterlogged conditions, by excluding oxygen from the remains, will favour an entirely different set of reactions. In the presence of plentiful bases, as in the ooze on the bed of a deep lake in limestone country, the bones will be well preserved and hard. In certain circumstances, even the soft parts of a body may be converted in a few years into a stable mass of a wax-like substance called 'adipocere,' (fat-wax).

Another case is that of the waterlogged conditions met with in lakes on acid rocks and in peat-bogs. Here the surroundings are extremely poor in minerals and the soil-water is highly acid with dissolved products of plant decomposition (humic acids). In these circumstances the mineral components of the bone will be gradually dissolved out, as by acid-treatment in the laboratory, but the exclusion of air will prevent total disintegration of the organic portion. This is, doubtless, considerably altered, but some proteins, notably the keratin, of horn, hoof, hide and hair seem to persist relatively unchanged for thousands of years in these conditions. The bones will thus be found in a soft and pulpy state, more or less decalcified and perhaps deformed, yet retaining their general shape and proportions. In a complete body, even the external details of skin and hair may be to a large extent preserved, as in the case of the Iron Age man of Tollund, a bog in Denmark, or the famous Starunia (Poland) woolly rhinoceros carcase.

Exclusion of water, preventing chemical change, is a rare condition in our Western European climate. In dry countries, as in Egypt, entire bodies with their stomach-contents still identifiable have been preserved wonderfully well by natural dehydration in the desert sands.

These are all extreme instances. Depending on the exact surrounding conditions, all intermediate stages of decalcification, mineralization and loss of organic content will be encountered. Thus, the mammalian bones of the famous Great Interglacial site of Swanscombe, Kent, are somewhat decalcified and may be of a pulpy consistency when wet. They harden and may shrink considerably on drying, when they tend to become flaky and extremely brittle, requiring preservative treatment before they may safely be handled.

One more case of special interest to archaeologists should be mentioned—that of cremated bones.* As stated above, complete calcination of bone renders it light and fragile. Before this stage is reached, the organic matter which it contains becomes charred, but, still filling the pores and spaces to some extent, helps to hold the mineral constituents together. A burnt, but incompletely calcined, bone is often still fairly strong. Moreover, once carbonized, the organic fraction becomes exceedingly stable and resistant to chemical change, so that the additional strength conferred by charring is permanent.

Completely to burn out the carbon from a large bone requires that it be held at at least a low red heat for a considerable time in a fire with free access of air. The amount of fuel and labour required completely

* In man ($\male$) bone is a little less than 6·9 per cent of living body-weight; (6·9 per cent represents total ash).

to consume a fresh human body is considerable. Our prehistoric ancestors, fortunately for us, were not often concerned to prolong the process of cremation to complete calcination of the bones. Once the body was reduced to the bare bones the pyre would be allowed to die down and, since it was customary to inter the ashes in an urn, or at least in a bag of some sort, the remains would be collected, perhaps separated by washing from charcoal and wood-ash, and broken into fragments small enough to be conveniently packed into the vessel or bag. The comminution was often done very thoroughly, so that it is seldom possible usefully to reconstruct anything from the remains, but the fact that eventual breaking up was intended made it unnecessary to have the bones burnt completely white, so that such fragments as can be recognized at all are often very perfectly preserved. Thus the condition of skull-sutures can often be seen clearly, enabling an estimate to be made of the age of the individual. Brow-ridges, mastoids and the central part of the occipital squama may still be recognizable, so that a reasonably good guess may be made as to the sex. Any search for teeth, however, is almost certain to be something of a failure. For some reason, the enamel, in other circumstances the most durable part of a tooth, is almost invariably destroyed in a cremation, so that little recognizably remains of a tooth but its roots, the dentine of which is more resistant. These should always be sought, however, for the condition of the roots, whether open or closed, will at least decide whether the individual was immature or adult.

Excavation

On dwelling-sites of the later prehistoric and historic periods, bones are often found in great profusion and may be fairly strong and well-preserved. It is, nevertheless, worth while taking a little care in their excavation if they seem to be reasonably complete, avoiding unnecessary breaks by rough handling or by levering them out of the deposit before they have been properly cleared. In the case of a midden or ditch-filling, where no bone is likely to be in any way related to its neighbours, no special precautions beyond these are called for.

Anything suggesting that two or more bones are in their correct anatomical positions in relation to one another should be taken as a warning to go carefully, for an entire skeleton may be present. In such a case, the whole body will have to be gradually exposed without displacing any part, cleaned and prepared for a photograph *in situ*. If the remains are human, there may be ornaments or grave-goods.

The normal excavator's tool, a pointing-trowel, is used to clear away the deposit, the loosened earth being frequently scraped and swept away for disposal by bucket or barrow. The greatest care is essential, even in the spaces between and around bones, to avoid damage to or displacement of associated objects.

As far as possible, the bones should be undercut and stand out clearly from their background, props and pillars of earth being left undisturbed to support them at strategic points. When clear, they must be carefully cleaned. If possible, this is best done after the adhering deposit has had time to dry, when gentle brushing with a 1 inch paintbrush will remove most of it. Any resistant small masses still sticking and small awkward corners can best be broken up and cleared by gentle stabbing with the point of a stout mounted needle, followed by brushing. Unless it is essential, the use of water should be avoided, but if the weather should be wet or it be impossible to shelter the skeleton and get it reasonably dry before photographing, the minimum of water may be applied by splashing with the brush or with a fine spray.

Directors of excavations are often working against time and it is distressing to them to have to spend longer than necessary on preparing skeletons. The body may, moreover, be lying on an area of deposit which it is desired to clear, so as to expose what lies underneath. Within reason, the longer the bones can be allowed to dry out *in situ* the better chance is there of lifting them without breakage and transporting them to the laboratory for proper treatment. The Director, however, will probably be anxious to have them photographed and removed as soon as possible. Thus, every effort should be made, short of hasty or careless work, to comply with his wishes.

Measurements in the Field

It may happen that a considerable number of skeletons comes to light on an excavation, most of them in such poor condition that complete treatment and lifting for removal to the home base is impossible, for reasons of finance and economy in the time of the excavators. It may also be technically impracticable.

In such a case it is worth while to attempt the taking of at least some measurements of the bones *in situ*. The results will not be as reliable as those of a properly-equipped anthropological laboratory, could the material be safely conveyed there, but even rough measurements would be preferable to none at all.

Skulls are always worth lifting and treatment, if not too deformed by earth-pressure or so comminuted as to present insuperable difficulties in mending. In these cases, they are of little value for measurements, however carefully lifted.

Whatever the condition of the skulls, it is unusual for the main long bones to be so broken or compressed that nothing of value can be obtained from them. If it is decided not to attempt to lift them, the ends should be cleared as they lie in the earth until a *maximum overall length* can be taken with callipers. This, of course, involves the sacrifice of the articulated ends of the adjacent bones, without removal of which it may well be impossible to get the callipers into position.

Some strategic planning here will minimize the losses. After drawing or photography the extremities may be cleared away, which will expose the necessary distal points for measurement of ulna, radius and tibia. The ulna may be measured forthwith, for the extreme point of the olecranon at its other end is free of any articulating bone. The ulna can then be scrapped if it lies uppermost and will not lift in one piece without treatment. If the radius is uppermost, it will have to be dealt with before removing the ulna. Its proximal end, close to the capitulum of the humerus, will not be reachable by the point of the callipers, but if the space once occupied by the articular cartilages is carefully cleared of earth the desired point will be visible. Its position may be marked by setting a thin nail (of which the head has been nipped off) or a stout wire, as an index, so that its end coincides with the extremity of the radius. If the same is done with the distal end of the bone, its overall length can be measured after its removal, with a steel tape or straight edge. If the forearm is in such a position that even this device will not serve, the bone must be scrapped unmeasured.

This exposes the trochlea of the humerus. It may be possible to find the extreme point of the head of the humerus with the callipers without more ado, but it is likely that the scapula will first have to be removed.

As to the tibia, the removal of the foot will allow the one leg of the callipers to be adjusted to the medial malleolus of the tibia, but the articulating femur will make it impossible to find its other extremity; moreover, the form of the articular surface will in most cases make it hard to overcome this difficulty by means of the nail or wire index. One answer may be to tackle the femur first. The head of the femur may be reached by picking away the margin of the acetabulum, if exposed, or, in the case of the under-limb in a skeleton lying on one side, by carefully opening the acetabulum from the *internal* surface of the os innominatum and picking away the surrounding bone until the callipers will reach the extremity of the head. For the other end of the femur, the medial condyle is more easily fixed than the extreme point of the tibia by the nail-index. Once the femur has gone, measurement of the tibia presents no great difficulty.

Directions cannot be given to cover all possible cases. There will be times when one or other bone will have to be sacrificed unmeasured in order to clear the way for a proper measurement of its neighbour, but every effort should be made so to plan the lifting that these losses are reduced to the minimum. At the same time, a few really reliable measurements are better than a whole page full of what amount to guesses within a 'few millimetres'.

If time permits, girth measurements, at the midpoint of the maximum length, are valuable. In conjunction with the over-all length of a long bone they permit the calculation of an 'index of robusticity'. This is worth while because it not only exemplifies the general build of the long bones but also may point, if the index is unusually low, to chronic deficiencies in nutrition affecting the population concerned. Such an indication is of interest as bearing on their economics and environment as well as to the historian of nutrition.

Girth measurements should be taken, after undermining the measured midpoint of the bone, with a strong linen (not steel) tape, of which the accuracy has been checked and is from time to time re-checked.

Since the accuracy of stature-estimates depends on the number of bones of an individual available for measurement, as many as possible should be recorded, having regard to the necessity for making some sacrifices of individual bones in the interests of the accuracy of measurement of the rest. In each case it should be stated whether the bone belongs to right or left limb and the sex of the individual should be given also, where this is determinable.

The working up of the results is properly a task for an anthropologist, but the onus of recording the measurements lies clearly on the excavators.

In comparison with those of the main long bones other measurements are unimportant, at least in the field and in the circumstances quoted. In the case of fully-extended burials it would be worth while as a check to measure the approximate stature directly, even though differences of attitude would introduce some errors. Crown to heels, the erect standing height, is the proper measurement, so that the normally somewhat extended feet should be carefully allowed for. When the body is at all flexed the likely inaccuracy of any direct measurement is so greatly increased that the attempt to estimate the standing height in this way is valueless.

Treatment in the Field for Preservation

It is best to get the bones thoroughly dry and to lift them without any treatment, if they will stand it. If it is clear that some or all will disintegrate when moved, and it is desired to preserve them, they will have to be treated on the spot to strengthen them and the block of earth on which they lie.

If well dried, a dilute plastic solution (polyvinyl acetate in toluene) may be sprayed or painted on and be allowed to harden before attempting to lift the bones. If they are still wet, and there is no hope of getting them dry enough to be impregnated in this way, an emulsion of the plastic solution in water, using a wetting agent, will penetrate where the pure solution cannot. Here, also, the solvent and the added water must be allowed time to evaporate before the specimen is moved, and the drier the whole surroundings the better will be the chance of success. Individual bones may be lifted, with any related fragments carefully preserved, as soon as they will stand handling and packing. Groups of small bones, as in hands and feet, are best lifted on an undisturbed block of earth if not strong enough to be taken individually.

No strengthening treatment is very effective unless the solvent has had time to evaporate fairly completely before moving the specimen.

If there is no time, treatment is better omitted, or the result is sure to be a nasty sticky mess of bones, earth and plastic, without the gain or any advantage over an attempt to lift the specimen as it is, wet or dry.

In the case of a really unique specimen, such as a Palaeolithic human skull, it would be necessary to suspend all other operations, assemble expert witnesses and concentrate on extracting the find as completely and as skilfully as possible. This would be an expert undertaking, not to be contemplated by the inexperienced.

The proper place for preparation and preservation of valuable fossil bones is an adequately equipped laboratory. Treatment in the field should be strictly confined to extracting the specimen in as complete a state as the conditions permit and to ensuring its arrival under proper care without further damage.

Packing and transport

Bones from archaeological deposits are seldom as strong as the pottery finds. The latter are normally parcelled up in strong paper bags and packed as tightly as possible in tea-chests or other cases, when they travel perfectly safely if handled with reasonable care. It is not for a moment suggested that the frequently large quantities of bones should be individually wrapped in tissue paper and cotton wool, but some attention should be paid to their nature and condition before treating them in exactly the same way as the pottery. It is not to be expected that bundles of human long bones and ribs, fragments of the pelvis and vertebrae together with the skull, still full of heavy loam, can be stowed in bags at the bottom of a case with a weight of other material above them, and arrive without fresh multiple fractures. Any major break will loosen the whole mass and permit shifting during transport, so that the lower strata may well be *en miettes* when unpacked.

Even if reasonably dry and hard, ancient bones are comparatively brittle. Long bones should be supported all along their length, packed in layers on and under pads of wood-wool faced with soft paper. Bones of left and right limbs and extremities should, if possible, be packed separately. Skulls should, preferably, have individual boxes, be wrapped in paper first and be well wadded with shavings, crumpled paper or other packing. Sawdust is, at all costs, to be avoided. It becomes compressed with jolting and sifts between the objects, which are certain to work loose and be injured.

Vertebrae, with their irregular shape and often long spines and other processes, will certainly suffer if lumped together in a bag. They will, in fact, occupy less space laid out in layers between pads.

Wherever wood-wool, cotton wool or other fibrous packing is used, especially if the bones have been hardened with plastic before lifting, they must first be wrapped in paper. Failure to do this may present a difficult and unnecessary problem to the preparator in the form of a skull, for example, 'tarred and feathered' with polyvinyl acetate and cotton lints!

While the method of packing in bags simplifies labelling and makes less likely the confusion of finds from different layers and trenches, the layer method requires more care in packing and unpacking if mistakes are to be avoided. Each layer must be unpacked completely into a tray with its label, before another is exposed. The better condition of the remains makes this extra trouble well worth while.

Large and heavy bones, such as pieces of fossil tusk and other remains of large animals, travel satisfactorily lying on a bed of crumpled newspaper in open trays or boxes on the back seat of a car. If such a consignment has to go by rail, however, it will need very careful packing and tight wedging into a case with wood-wool. For export or import, expert packing in double cases is essential.

Small and delicate specimens, on the other hand, are easily transported. The very small, e.g., rodent teeth or shells, are best packed in corked glass tubes properly labelled. The tube may be padded at the bottom and under the cork with a pledget of cotton-wool wrapped in tissue paper. Two-ounce flat tobacco tins are excellent for larger teeth, etc. Tissue paper makes the best packing. The containers should neither be overcrowded nor too loosely filled. Any vacant space must be filled with soft padding of some sort. Cylindrical or square deep tins are less convenient than flat boxes, but will serve at need. Cardboard boxes are generally useless by themselves, but small corrugated cartons individually packed with care are adequate if not crushed in transit.

The tea-chest is the container of choice for any quantity of bone finds. It is itself light, very rigid and not easily dented or stove in. The contents, however packed, if protected from crushing and friction during transport, will travel in perfect safety from the site to the laboratory.

Archaeologists should need no urging as to the importance of adequate marking and labelling of bones, as of other finds. Labels for individual specimens, boxes and packed layers could usefully be supplemented, in a varied collection, by a packing-list in the top of the case, especially where the recipient is not the excavator himself or one of his staff, with personal knowledge of the material and the circumstances of its discovery.

Cleaning, strengthening, mending and reconstruction

Few bony remains are so well preserved that they will stand much handling or can be put on exhibition without further treatment.

In the case of domestic animal bones from later sites, where it is desired only to list the species represented and to report on their relative frequency and importance in the human economy, the material will certainly, for the greater part, be discarded once the report is written, so that no special care is needed in its treatment unless any pieces seem to have particular interest. Some few perfect, or almost perfect, specimens may be retained as comparative material for future studies and any uncommon items, even though very fragmentary, may be required for exhibition. Whole skeletons are always worth preserving, so that the bodily proportions of an entire individual may be not only recorded at the time but remain available for fresh studies in the future.

In these latter cases something more is required than mere superficial cleaning to permit recognition and determination, which is enough for those pieces to be discarded. If the material is strong enough to stand it, such cleaning may take the form of careful brushing with a not too hard brush and quick rinsing in a basin or under a running tap. Soaking should be avoided and as much moisture as possible should be drained and shaken off each specimen at once. Drying ought to be slow, to avoid warping and splitting—exposure in trays to the outside air in a shady place is perhaps best. Direct heat or sunshine may cause too rapid and unequal drying.

Many bones, particularly the more decalcified, and especially Pleistocene fossils, will not stand wet treatment at all. If muddy, they should be allowed to dry slowly and evenly and the adhering matrix be needled and brushed off when it has shrunk and become brittle. The bones generally harden considerably on drying and become more fit to handle. Even so, a large specimen should be moved and handled as little as possible, and then only with great care by several pairs of hands together, to ensure support at all necessary points lest they break under their own weight. If the material is at all soft and 'cheesy' when moist, the increased hardness acquired on drying is deceptive and is usually accompanied by brittleness and 'short' fracture. Some much-decalcified specimens may shrink, crack and flake away at the surface, however carefully and slowly they are dried. In this case impregnation while still wet must be undertaken. The shrinkage is due to partial loss of the mineral lattice of the bone which allows the organic residue to contract on drying. The introduction of a hardening agent into the pores before complete drying replaces this stiffening to some extent.

A suitable plastic solution, emulsified with water by means of a wetting agent, is used. A ready-made preparation, among others, of this kind is sold under the name 'Vinamul'. It is of a thick creamy consistency and may be thinned with water. A polyvinyl acetate solution in toluene may be temporarily emulsified by the operator himself, by the addition of water with a wetting agent and vigorous shaking, but this tends to separate on standing and is inferior to the mechanically dispersed product. The latter consists of exceedingly minute globules of plastic solution dispersed in water and therefore penetrates the very fine canals of the bone more readily.

Impregnation may be achieved to some extent by painting with the emulsion and allowing it to percolate by gravity and capillarity, or by simple immersion. By far the most effective way is to immerse the specimen completely in the emulsion and to enclose the containing vessel in a space which can be partially evacuated. By this means air is drawn out of the pores, escapes as bubbles and is replaced by the emulsion on restoring the normal air-pressure. Save on a very modest scale (when it can be done in a large vacuum desiccator, in which the pressure is reduced by a laboratory water filter-pump attached to a running tap) this requires special heavy apparatus and a power-driven vacuum-pump. The principle is exactly the same, but a tank to contain sizable bones is costly both in money and space.

Dry bones are easily impregnated with plain polyvinyl acetate dissolved in toluene in the same ways as with the wet emulsion. While the vacuum treatment is speedier and more complete, simple immersion for some time is reasonably effective in the case of fully dry material.

Whether wet or dry, the impregnated bones must next be allowed to drain in an atmosphere saturated with the vapour of the plastic-solvent. This generally means the enclosed space above the surface of the solution in the impregnating-tank. As the solution is fairly viscous and the excess takes some time to drain from the surface of the specimen, it must not be suspended in the open air. If the solvent is allowed to evaporate before the specimen is completely drained, the solidifying plastic may form unsightly drops and blobs, or at least present an unnaturally and unevenly glazed and varnished appearance. When well drained in an atmosphere of the solvent and afterwards dried, the impregnated bone shows little superficial evidence of the treatment or even change of colour—only greatly increased mechanical strength.

Drying out after impregnation should be slow and complete. Though shrinking and flaking is largely prevented by the presence of the plastic in the pores, the strength of a bone is scarcely improved at all until the solvent has evaporated, allowing it to harden. Impregnation procedures are nowadays almost routine treatment for fragile fossils, and fragments of all sizes, before reassembly or mending is attempted.

If properly and conscientiously collected, the main portion of any fossil will be accompanied by as many detached fragments as could be recovered—even some very small ones. These should be carefully cleaned, dried and impregnated in the same way as the main portion.

Mending bones, like mending pots, is a matter of patience, practice and skill, plus anatomical knowledge—about in that order of importance—but in an even higher degree. Patience is by far the largest factor in the successful reassembly of much-broken remains. A single job may take weeks or months before the operator can satisfy himself that no more can be done to it. Of course, it is a question, in every case, to what extent the result is likely to be worthy of the time and trouble certain to be spent on a major reconstruction. This decision will rest rather with the excavator and the museum or institution which is to have the specimen than with the student of bones or the preparator. Space, both for museum- and teaching-collections, being generally limited, exhaustive mending and reconstruction of missing parts will only be attempted when the specimen is rare or even unique, or because it happens to fill a gap in the particular collection. One does not spend days reconstructing the commonplace when a perfect specimen may easily be available a week or a year hence. On the other hand, some repair is often necessary before the material can be most fully studied. This is especially the case with human skulls, which may, when mended, show ancient fractures indicating the immediate cause of the violent death of the individual. Such evidence is often unrecognizable, or at least not easily noted, when there is only a mass of fragments to examine. Moreover, anthropological studies are largely based on measurements, so that a skull in any way crushed or deformed by earth-pressure is useless until it can be restored to a close approximation to its original dimensions and proportions.

Rebuilding skulls and shattered bones from many small pieces, even when most of them are known to be present, requires some considerable acquaintance with the detailed anatomy of the species concerned. Sheer persistence alone will do much to find the joins, but a great deal of time will be saved if the approximate location and attitude of a fragment can be recognized at an early stage. Even so, the operation calls for a high order of patience, and if there should be a large part missing altogether the difficulty and uncertainties are much increased.

As the joins are recognized the pieces may be reunited as accurately as possible. The best adhesive for dry bones has been found to be a well-plasticized cellulose nitrate solution.* If, as is often the case, the fragments have first been strengthened with polyvinyl acetate, these solvents 'bite' into the impregnation and enable the dry joint to adhere very strongly. The adhesive should be used sparingly and the uniting surfaces very carefully fitted. When joined, the united fragments are stood in an attitude of balance in a sand-bath until the adhesive has set. Only if the shape of the fragments absolutely demands it should more than two be stuck together at one time. Correct balance while hardening is very hard to find for two loose pieces simultaneously, so that errors are more likely to occur than in a well-balanced single joint. Impatience in this matter nearly always leads to disaster, or at least to a setback and time wasted in the long run. Never was the advice to hasten slowly more appropriate than here—or harder to follow! Mending errors are in any case hardly to be avoided; with undue haste they are certain, and sure to be greater than need be. Any errors are cumulative, so that it is the final joining of the main rebuilt pieces which is the most difficult task of all.

If a skull is in many fragments this accumulated error may amount to a centimetre or more to be adjusted, before the final joint to make a

* HMG, made by Henry Marcel Guest, Collyhurst, Manchester 9, or 'balsa cement', as used by model-makers, are recommended.

presentable whole is possible. Such adjustment requires the softening of some joints already made, if not their complete dismantling. Solvent may be painted on the joint to be softened, or, in the thicker parts, a rag moistened with the solvent be laid on the joint. Judicious manipulation when the adhesive softens sufficiently, having regard to the strength of the fragments, may suffice to correct the greater part of the error. Where several joints are involved, it may be necessary to correct them successively, since simultaneous softening of too large an area of the work may endanger the whole.

Detection of mending-errors and the estimation of the amount of the necessary correction is a matter of skill and practice, joined to an eye for form and symmetry.

In the mended specimen, there will almost inevitably be some missing fragments and areas so comminuted by accident or decay that their rebuilding from the existing 'crumbs' would not repay the time and trouble necessary. If the specimen is required for exhibition or for teaching, it may be desired to reconstruct the missing parts. Indeed, if the gaps are many, considerations of mere strengthening may dictate the filling in of at least some of them with new material.

Materials used for this purpose in the past, such as plaster, gesso or wax compounds, have been entirely superseded by modern plastics in most laboratories. The preparation now most in favour is 'BJK' (Butvar, jute and kaolin) dough, which is light, strong, adhesive and clean to work with, dries hard and may be worked down and finished with files and rifflers when dry. It may be re-softened with solvent if alterations are required after it is hard.

BJK dough is not obtainable commercially, but must be compounded in the laboratory. I am indebted to my colleagues, Miss I. Gedye and Mr. H. W. M. Hodges, for the following formula and directions.

800 gms	Butvar B98 (Polyvinyl butal)	100 parts by weight
1260 ml	Acetone	120
504 ml	Industrial Methylated Spirits	50
370 ml	Amyl Acetate	40

Stir and leave for 24 hours in covered container.
add:

928 ml	Xylene (Benzene or Toluene will do)	100

Stir well.
add:

480 ml	Water	60

Stir till emulsified, then stir in with a wooden spoon jute flock and dry kaolin, 2:1 dry measure, until too stiff to stir. Turn out on to slab and knead in more jute and kaolin, in the same proportions, until the dough does not stick to the hands. Good kneading is essential. Store in a closed container.

The dough may be worked just like clay. In filling in gaps, it should be well kneaded against surfaces and edges to which it is required to adhere and be roughly modelled to the required shape in position.

The material shrinks slightly in drying, so should not be applied in masses more than a quarter of an inch at one time. Thicker portions of the work should be built up in several layers, allowing one to dry out thoroughly before applying another. Considerable areas of restoration, such as large parts of a human skull-vault, may sag out of shape by their own weight if unsupported while drying. Strips of material modelled to the correct curvature in the dough and allowed to harden separately may be luted into position with fresh dough and, when set, form a scaffolding for the intervening areas, which will then be adequately supported.

Plasticene supports may be used, as for plaster-work, but should be covered with polythene film to prevent adhesion of the dough to the support.

Where large gaps have to be filled in, for example in the middle of the shaft of a long bone, an armature of iron or zinc rod, bar or wire, preferably of square or other angular section, should be built in to reinforce and support the filling material. The ends of the armature, in the above example, would be firmly grouted into the marrow cavities of the original fragments with the filling compound and the reconstructed part afterwards built up round it.

Methylated spirits (poisonous!) may be used as a solvent to soften the material for alteration or adjustment.

Butvar B98 may be obtained from Shawinegan, Marlow House, Lloyd's Avenue, London, E.C.3. Jute flock may be obtained from Cullaflox Ltd., Fibril Works, Dartford, Kent.

15

Estimation of Age, Sex & Stature from Bones

✦✦

IT HAS ALREADY been indicated that the progress of ossification of the bones and the stages of calcification, eruption and wear of the teeth may be used to estimate the age of an individual of a species in which these processes have been sufficiently studied.

It is scarcely incumbent on the archaeologist to study the bone material statistically and exhaustively for its own sake. This is properly the province of the zoologist or anthropologist, but it is not out of place for the archaeological student of bones to be able to form an opinion on the site as to the composition of the animal and human population, in respect of age, sex and stature. Matters of strictly archaeological, economic and historical weight may hang on such conclusions.

If a group of human skeletons should be revealed by the excavators, it becomes at once important to know whether they represent war-casualties, a family or tribal group stricken all at once by plague, famine or massacre, or the occupants of peaceful graves in a cemetery used over a long period of time by the community concerned. The stratigraphy may show unmistakable evidence of contemporaneous interment of the whole group. One of the first two possibilities would then appear to offer the simplest explanation: the remains themselves will indicate which. Warriors slain in battle will consist overwhelmingly of men, and men largely in the prime of youth and vigour, while a plague would spare neither youth nor age and make no distinctions of sex. A massacred population might include only men and boys, while the women and young girls were carried off as the prizes or slaves of the victors. The Iliad and Odyssey yield eloquent evidence of this custom in Bronze-Age Troy. The nature of any bone-injuries observed may indicate whether resistance was offered by the victims or whether they suffered a violent death passively. A cemetery, on the other hand, would be expected to yield rather the remains of those dying from natural causes—predominantly the very young and the elderly of both sexes, with a comparative dearth both of men and women in later youth and middle life.

As to the animals, the conclusions to be drawn from the bones are, perhaps, less striking. Many of the regular food animals will be young, for then, as now, tender joints would be preferred to tough. Any species, such as the horse, kept mainly for transport or draft, or for sport and protection, like the dog, might, therefore, be expected to show greater maturity than those, such as the sheep or pig, reared solely or mainly for food.

Hunted meat, also, would, both by chance and design, tend to be, on the whole, of younger and less experienced individuals, the leaders of the herds being both more wary and dangerous and less fitted for food. Nevertheless, the sporting instincts of the hunter and his desire for trophies, as well as the need for strong industrial materials, might encourage occasional selection of the noblest stag, the fiercest bull or the heaviest tusker, despite the gastronomic inferiority of such quarry. He is no true fisherman who can sneer at a 'walloper', on the ground that a creelful of half-pounders makes better eating—unless it is the other fellow who has landed the 'big un'.

As in other matters, it will be found that the developmental aspect of osteology and dentition is far better understood in relation to humanity than is the case in the lower mammals. Indeed, apart from the domestic animals, the literature on the subject is very scanty and, even for these, the readily available information falls far short, in detail, of what is known about man.

It is, therefore, with man that we must begin and, if the actual data applicable to man will not serve for any other species, the principles remain the same for all mammals.

Age Determination in Man

Information from the bones as to the age of a human individual is to be gained from three main sources:

(a) The degree of ossification and bony fusion of the bones of the skull, especially those of the vault.

(b) The state of eruption and wear of the teeth.

(c) The state of ossification in the various epiphyses of the long bones.

Of these, the last process is completed with the attainment of full stature and, therefore, yields no evidence much beyond the age of 20 years. The others show characteristic changes to an advanced stage of maturity and even into old age.

A. CHANGES IN THE
HUMAN SKULL WITH INCREASING AGE

(i) BEFORE BIRTH. Some bones, still maintaining their independent identity in adult lower mammals, but normally synostosed with their neighbours in human adults, originate in man also from distinct centres of ossification, and may remain separate in youth.

The bones are pre-formed in membrane. Their ossification begins at one or more centres for each bone and proceeds until, at a later stage, adjacent bones meet at their sutures. An incompletely ossified cranial bone has a thin, irregular 'feather-edge' and a characteristically spicular or crystalline appearance, where the mineral salts are in the process of deposition.

Frontal. Begins to ossify at the end of the second intra-uterine month from two centres above the supra-orbital margins. In the foetus the two halves do not meet.

Parietals. Ossified radially from centres near the parietal eminences. In the full-term foetus they do not meet in the mid-line.

Occipital. Four parts unite to form the occipital squama (= supra-occipital) early in intra-uterine life. This remains separate, until much later, from a pair of condylar parts (= exoccipitals) and a basilar part immediately in front of the foramen magnum (= basi-occipital).

Temporals. These are also represented by the homologues of the primitively separate squamosal, tympanic and periotic bones, the last comprising the petrous and mastoid parts in man. In the foetus the tympanic ring is still separate from the temporal squama.

Sphenoid. The pre-natal ossification is very complex, since the human sphenoid comprises four primitively distinct bones, of which the ossification is not simple.

Ethmoid. Mostly cartilaginous in the foetus.

Nasals. Ossification begins in the third intra-uterine month.

Maxilla. Ossifies from two centres on each side (= maxilla + pre-maxilla) which unite in the third intra-uterine month. The inter-maxillary suture, separating the two halves, may persist into middle life.

Malars. Each ossified from a single centre, beginning towards the end of the second intra-uterine month.

Mandible. Very incompletely ossified.

(ii) AT BIRTH. The base of the skull and the facial parts are very small in comparison with the vault. Many of the bones are still incompletely ossified and have not everywhere made contact with adjacent bones. This is the case, in particular, with the angles of the bones of the vault, which are most remote from the primary centres of ossification. These centres are situated near the thickest parts of the completed bones—the two frontal eminences, the two parietal eminences and the centre of the occipital squama, so that in vertical view, the outline of the infant cranium is markedly pentagonal. The greatest breadth is at the parietal eminences.

At the still unossified angles of the bones there are considerable gaps, closed only by membrane, known as *fontanelles*. These are 6 in number:

1. Anterior (at the bregma)
2. Posterior (at the lambda)
3. | Antero-lateral (in the two pterion regions)
4. |
5. | Postero-lateral (in the regions of the two asteria)
6. |

Frontal. The two halves are still separate, though just meeting in the middle of the forehead at the metopic (forehead) suture. There is, as yet, only an incomplete external angular process.

Parietals. Just meet their neighbours, save in the aforementioned fontanelles.

Occipital. The squamous, two condylar and basilar parts are still separate but in joint-contact.

Temporals. The tympanic ring and squama are normally just united, but the circumference of the ring is incomplete, leaving a foramen in the floor of the auditory meatus.

Sphenoid. In three parts: one, central, consisting of the body and lesser wings (= basisphenoid + presphenoid + orbitosphenoids) and two lateral, each comprising a greater wing and a pterygoid process (=alisphenoid + pterygoid). The greater wings are not completely ossified in the antero-lateral fontanelles.

Maxillae. In close contact with the malars and meeting, but not united, in the inter-maxillary suture. There is no contact yet between the frontal processes of the maxillae and the frontal bone, the whole region of the root of the nose being still cartilaginous.

Malars. Closely joined to, but not ossified with the maxillae, their temporal processes meeting the zygomatic processes of the temporals to complete the arch, but their frontal processes still incompletely ossified, showing a considerable gap between these and the equally incomplete external angular processes of the frontals.

Mandible. The body, or horizontal ramus, is a mere shell, with incompletely partitioned alveoli. The germs of the deciduous teeth may be found. The angle between body and ascending ramus is about 175°, the condyle nearly in line with the body. The two halves are still separate at the symphyseal suture.

(iii) IN INFANCY AND CHILDHOOD. The fontanelles close and fill out as the bones thicken along their sutures, giving the cranium a more rounded contour. The posterior and antero-lateral fontanelles are obliterated between two and three months from birth, the postero-lateral at the end of the first year and the anterior towards the middle of the second year.

Frontal. Union of the two halves begins in the second year and the metopic suture is generally obliterated, save in its lowest part, near the glabella, by the eighth year. In a small percentage of individuals a metopic suture persists into middle age and runs in families.

Parietals. No important change takes place after the closing of the fontanelles, save for normal growth and filling out in thickness, until the beginning of the obliteration of the sutures in adulthood.

Occipital. The squama unites with the two condylar parts in the fourth year. The basilar part is united to the rest in the sixth year.

Temporals. The petromastoid part unites with the squamous during the first year and the mastoid processes appear towards the end of the second year. The foramen in the floor of the auditory meatus normally persists until the fifth year, but is permanent in a small number of cases.

Sphenoid. The three parts (see above) unite during the first year.

Ethmoid. The perpendicular plate (= mesethmoid) and *crista galli* ossify in the first year and join the superior conchae early in the second year. *Mandible.* The two halves unite at the symphysis during the first year, save for a small part near the alveolar border. Growth takes place mainly by the addition of bone on the posterior border of the ascending

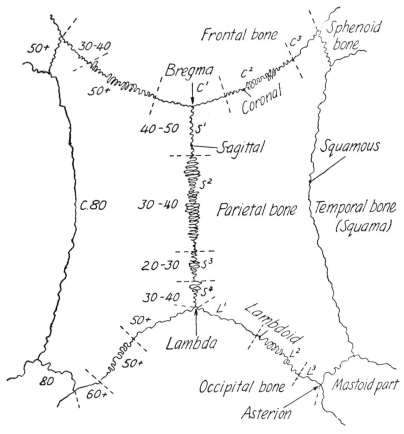

Fig 55. *Homo sapiens,* plan of vault of skull and ages at which sutures are obliterated (After H. V. Vallois). For more exact description, the sutures are sub-divided into regions. Thus C^1 means the most medial region of the coronal, S^4 the most posterior of the sagittal.

ramus and by absorption on its anterior border. The angle between the horizontal and ascending rami thus closes, becoming about 140° by the fourth year.

(iv) IN ADOLESCENCE AND YOUTH. Changes in the skull are mainly matters of growth and proportion. Narrower age determination during this period rests more on the evidence from the teeth and long bones.

(v) IN ADULTHOOD. With the attainment of the full skull-dimensions and proportions few further changes take place. Age determination from skulls of age 20 years and upwards depends almost entirely on the progress of obliteration of the cranial sutures, which, fortunately for our purpose, is a somewhat protracted process and does not take place simultaneously in all regions.

Synostosis between bones at the cranial sutures begins at the inner table and proceeds outwards. The course of the suture is thus clearly to be seen externally even when all trace has disappeared on the inner table and after the bones are effectively and rigidly fused for the greater part of their thickness.

The accompanying diagram (Fig. 55), redrawn and adapted from a publication of Vallois, is more eloquent and more useful for reference than pages of verbal description. With its aid, the age between 20 and 50 of a given individual may be estimated within ten years, more or less. There are, of course, individual variations, so that even such an estimate may be wide of the mark in particular cases, though, on an average, over many individuals, it will not be very far out.*

The cartilaginous joint between the basilar part of the occipital and the sphenoid is obliterated by synostosis before the age of 25. The angle between the rami of the mandible varies, in adults, between 110° and 120°.

(vi) IN MATURITY AND OLD AGE. After the main sutures have been obliterated, skull-changes are degenerative in nature. The bones become thinner and lighter. Loss of teeth may cause the complete disappearance of their alveoli and resorption of the alveolar parts both of maxilla and mandible. The mandible, in particular, undergoes regressional changes, the angle between ascending ramus and body opening out again to 140° as in the child, with narrowing of the ascending ramus.

These features are less reliable than the foregoing in suggesting an absolute age, but they are general indications of senility, of use in support of evidence from the degree of wear of the teeth.

B. AGE DETERMINATION IN
MAN FROM THE STATE OF THE DENTITION

In comparison with the lower mammals, man has a protracted period of immaturity. This is exemplified by the fact that he may live for a quarter of a century before developing his full dentition, completed in the dog, for example, soon after the age of 6 months. While most individuals have cut their third molars by age 20, in some these teeth may never erupt at all.

The usual dates of eruption and replacement of the teeth in modern Europeans are shown diagrammatically in Fig. 56. This mode of representation has been chosen because the diagram may be used directly to determine approximate age from the state of development of the dentition. If a straight edge is aligned vertically on the particular combination of teeth found in an individual of unknown age, a reason-

* But see Genovés & Messmacher (1959).

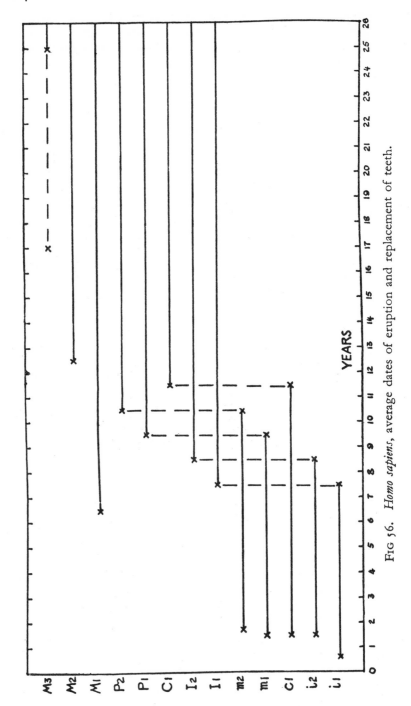

Fig 56. *Homo sapiens*, average dates of eruption and replacement of teeth.

ably good estimate, between birth and adulthood, can be read off the scale at the foot of the diagram.

There are fairly wide individual variations in the dates of eruption and replacement of teeth, so that the error in a particular case may be considerable. The possible extent of such error is indicated by dotted lines. The successional *order* of these dental events, however, is fairly constant and reliable.

Upper teeth generally follow the lead of the corresponding lower teeth, after a short interval.

Once the full adult dentition has come into use, the only guide to the age of its possessor is the degree of wear which the teeth have sustained. A first molar deeply worn, a second much worn but a third scarcely worn, in the same jaw, suggest a probable age in the early 20's.

The feature of wear in teeth has no absolute value in the archaeological context, for environmental factors, such as the nature of the diet and the ways in which the food was prepared, must be taken into consideration. Early-Iron-Age Britons, for instance, habitually ground grain on sandstone querns. Their molars may have been worn literally to the gums by the time they were 30 years old, through the chewing of siliceous grit from the quern in their meal. Modern civilized peoples, with a diet largely well cooked, soft and free from dirt and foreign bodies, may retain little-worn teeth to a good old age, if any escape the ravages of decay.

Within any population from a single environment, in which the state of tooth-wear at different ages is known from other evidence—the degree of obliteration of the skull-sutures, for instance—the age of an individual represented only by teeth can well be estimated by comparison of the degree of wear which they show. It would be extremely hazardous to extend the comparison to a different group of men, without other evidence of similarity of environment and habits.

C. AGE DETERMINATION FROM THE STATE OF OSSIFICATION OF THE EPIPHYSES OF THE LONG BONES AND OF SOME OTHER PARTS OF THE SKELETON

Most of the epiphyses of the long bones in man have begun to ossify before the age of 5 years. Those of the knee-joint, in particular, begin at, or even before, birth. The dates of their final fusion with the shafts of the bones are useful, because they sub-divide to some extent the pause in development of the dentition between the eruption of the second molar at about age 12 and that of the third, generally about 20.

The approximate dates are indicated diagrammatically in Fig. 57.

Some other useful indications of age in bones are given below. They are by no means exhaustive.

Vertebrae. At birth they consist of three separate parts: the centrum and the two halves of the neural arch. The latter are united in the midline between the first and third years, beginning in the lumbar region and

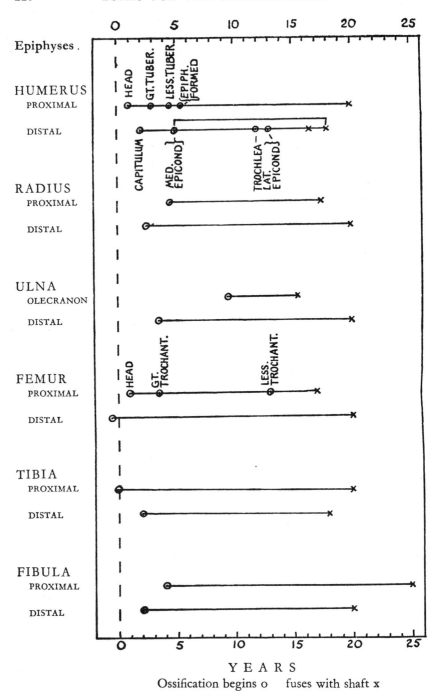

FIG 57. *Homo sapiens*, dates of synostosis of epiphyses with the shafts of the main long bones.

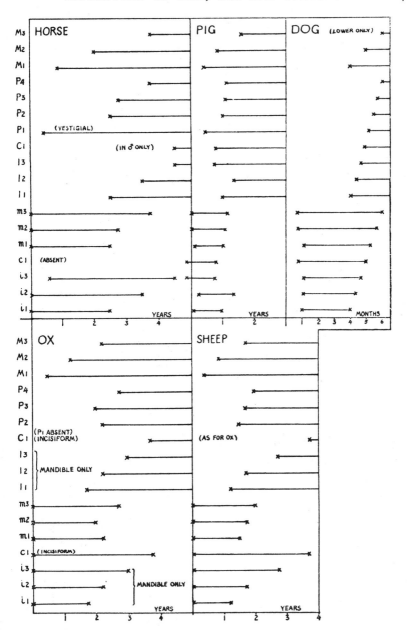

FIG 58. Deciduous and permanent dentitions of domestic animals. Average dates of eruption and replacement. Milk molars are replaced by permanent premolars.

proceeding upwards. The centra unite with the arches from the third to the sixth years, from the cervical region downwards. The epiphyses for the centra appear about the sixteenth year and fuse at about age 25.

Sternum. Sternebrae 4 and 5 unite soon after puberty; 2, 3 and 4 between puberty and age 25. The manubrium (= sternebra 1) unites, if at all, only in old age. The xiphoid process ossifies at about age 40.

Ribs. Secondary centres of ossification for head and tubercle appear at 16-20 years and unite about age 25.

Scapula. The coracoid process, independently ossified, is united about the fifteenth year. The extremity of the acromion begins to ossify about the seventeenth year. Ossification of the bone is completed at about age 25.

Os coxae. The triradiate cartilages in the acetabulum begin to ossify about the twelfth year. Ilium, ischium and pubis fuse completely about puberty.

Extremities. The heads of the metacarpals, metatarsals and phalanges fuse with their shafts between the seventeenth and twentieth years.

Age Determination in Domestic Animals

A much smaller amount of information than that available for man can be found to help in determining the age of animals from bone remains. A great deal of work has still to be done in this field.

The average dates of eruption and replacement of the teeth in the common domestic animals are summarized in Fig. 58.

For the long bones, the tables opposite give the approximate dates of fusion of the epiphyses with the shafts. The figures represent the age of the animal in years, where not otherwise stated.

Sex Determination in Man

The whole skeleton, in human beings, is affected by the sex of the individual. The differences between the sexes are, for the most part, diffuse and only of degree, so that there are few qualitative features the individual presence or absence of which may be taken as a guide to sexing.

Males, owing to their generally larger bodily dimensions and greater muscularity, tend to have longer, stouter, heavier and more rugged bones, larger and thicker skulls. Female skeletons are, on the whole, of smaller, lighter, more gracile build, with less distinctly developed muscular impressions. Nevertheless, there are infinite intergradations, so that, while the sex may be determined from these considerations with reasonable ease and certainty in the more extreme cases, there will be many instances where the general appearance is not distinctive and only close examination of several separate features and balancing of their evidence will lead to a probably correct determination.

Osteometric (bone-measuring) methods are here excluded. The sex-ratio in a fairly numerous population may be determined by statistical methods, based on measurements of the long bones of the various individuals. The relative proportions of the limb bones differ, on the average, between the sexes. Such methods properly belong to

	HORSE		OX	
	EPIPHYSES		EPIPHYSES	
	prox.	dist.	prox.	dist.
Humerus	$3\frac{1}{2}$	$1\frac{1}{2}$	$3\frac{1}{2}$–4	$1\frac{1}{2}$
Radius	$1\frac{1}{2}$	$3\frac{1}{2}$	1–$1\frac{1}{2}$	$3\frac{1}{2}$–4
Ulna	$3\frac{1}{2}$	Fused with radius before birth	$3\frac{1}{2}$–4	$3\frac{1}{2}$–4
Femur	3–$3\frac{1}{2}$	$3\frac{1}{2}$	$3\frac{1}{2}$	$3\frac{1}{2}$–4
Tibia	$3\frac{1}{2}$	2	$3\frac{1}{2}$–4	2–$2\frac{1}{2}$
Metapodials	Before birth	$1\frac{1}{2}$	Before birth	2–$2\frac{1}{2}$
Phalanges	1	Before birth	$1\frac{1}{2}$–2	Before birth

	PIG		DOG (age in months)	
	EPIPHYSES		EPIPHYSES	
	prox.	dist.	prox.	dist.
Humerus	$3\frac{1}{2}$	$1\frac{1}{2}$	12	6–8
Radius	1	$3\frac{1}{2}$	6–8	18
Ulna	3–$3\frac{1}{2}$		15	15
Femur	$3\frac{1}{2}$	$3\frac{1}{2}$	18	18
Tibia	$3\frac{1}{2}$	2	18	14–15
Fibula	$3\frac{1}{2}$	$2\frac{1}{2}$		
Metapodials		2		5–6
Phalanges				
Calcaneal Tuberosity	2–$2\frac{1}{2}$			

the province of the physical anthropologist and lie outside the scope of most archaeologists, who are seldom also competent statisticians. The present writer hastens to align himself with that majority!

Three parts of the skeleton especially lend themselves to qualitative sexing. In order of importance, they are: the pelvis, the skull and the thorax.

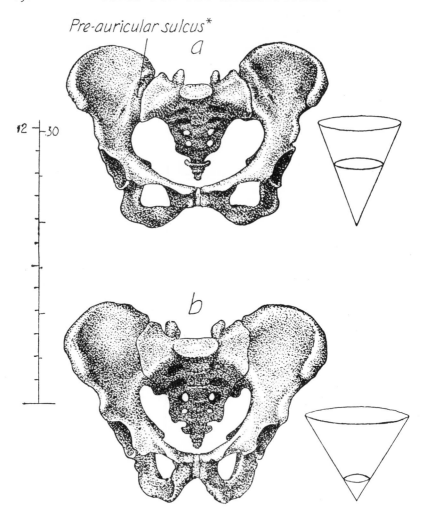

FIG 59.   (a) female and (b) male human pelves, with diagrams illustrating
their similarities to a short section of a long cone and a long
section of a short cone, respectively (p. 232) (re-drawn from
Gray's 'Anatomy').

THE PELVIS. Since the function of child-bearing is peculiar to women
and since the foetus has to pass through the opening of the pelvis
during parturition, it is not surprising that, among all the bones, the
pelvis shows the most distinctive sex-features.

The typical female pelvis differs characteristically in form from
that of a typical male (Fig. 59). As with other parts of the skeleton,
there are cases in which the pelvis as a whole is not distinctive.

* The pre-auricular sulcus is generally most clearly developed, not, as
illustrated in Fig. 59a, *above* and before the auricular area on the ilium, but
below and before it, i.e. out of sight in the drawing.

One qualitative feature, alone, stands out as a very constant indication of female sex—the presence of a *pre-auricular sulcus* (Fig. 59a). This is a roughened groove, lying in front of and below the auricular area on the ilium, at which it meets the sacrum in the sacro-iliac joint. The joint is maintained, in both sexes, by strong, short ligaments between the bones, but owing to the greater forward inclination of the female sacrum and the less obtuse posterior angle which it forms with the lumbar part of the vertebral column, the lower fibres of the anterior sacro-iliac ligament are more strongly developed in the female, to make them equal to the task of bearing up the weight of the trunk imposed at this angle. The attachment of these very strong ligamentous fibres marks the female ilium with a more or less deep, rough groove along the anterior margin of the auricular area. This is the best single indication of female sex.

For the rest, the features of the female pelvis as compared with the male are as follows:

	FEMALE	MALE
As a whole	Pelvis more gracile and less rugged. Relatively more expanded laterally and anteriorly.	More heavily built, with strong muscular impressions. Ilia less expanded. Pelvis narrowing to the pubic symphysis.
Inlet	More nearly circular.	Inlet heart-shaped.
Outlet	Less obstructed by the hinder part of the sacrum and the ischial spines.	Narrowed by the long sacrum and inwardly-projecting spines.
Sacrum	Shorter and wider, the auricular area covering only the vertebrae S.1 and S.2. Somewhat tilted forwards, making the angle with the lumbar vertebrae more acute.	Longer and narrower, the auricular area extending fully over S.3
Symphysis pubis	Depth small.	Depth greater.
Sciatic notches	Wider and shallower, with ischial spines not projecting inwards.	Notches deeper and narrower, the ischial spines noticeably inturned.
Pubic arch	Margins less everted.	Margins more everted.

	FEMALE	MALE
Acetabulum	Smaller, widely separated and looking more forwards. Horizontal diameter never as great as the distance of its anterior margin from the pubic symphysis.	Larger, directed more laterally, its horizontal diameter often equal to the distance of its anterior margin from the pubic symphysis.
Obturator foramen	Smaller and more angular.	Larger and more rounded.

The characteristic general proportions of the female pelvis have been summarized by likening it to a short section of a long cone, while that of the male resembles rather a long section of a short cone (Fig. 59).

These proportions and the features detailed above are distinguishable in pelves of all ages—even of young children.

THE SKULL. In contradistinction with the pelvis, the features indicative of sex in skulls (Fig. 60) are all secondary—developed only after puberty.

Most adult females have a skull thinner, lighter and with lesser muscular impressions, about one-tenth less in capacity than that of a corresponding male. The whole aspect of the skull is more youthful. Male sex is generally indicated by the following features (Fig. 60b):

Frontal region. More or less prominent brow-ridges and glabella, with a more extensive frontal sinus. This makes the forehead more sloping and blunts the upper margins of the orbits, which tend to be sharp in the female, owing to the more vertical, smooth forehead and frontal eminences not masked, as they may be in the male, by these outgrowths of the forehead.

Parietal region. Here, also, the general thickness of the bones and larger capacity, by raising the midline of the vault, tend to lessen the prominence of the parietal eminences, which stand out clearly in females and children. The temporal lines are better marked, in keeping with a strong jaw-musculature.

Occipital region. Owing to the more powerful nape-musculature, the impressions of the muscles on the occipital bone are deeper and more extensive. There may be a very prominent inion and well-marked nuchal lines.

Temporal region. The stronger lines delimiting the area of the temporal fossa of the male have already been noted. The mastoid processes are more strongly developed in the male—again, a function of musculature.

Masticating equipment. Strong male jaw-muscles, indicated by the development of the temporal lines, generally correspond with a heavier, more powerfully-chinned mandible with marked muscular relief. The teeth are larger, the ascending ramus wider, the horizontal ramus deeper and the gonial angle square, rugged and even everted.

Large teeth require a longer dental arcade and consequently a large palatal area.

All these features of the male human skull, save the large mastoids, are primitive and are seen, much exaggerated, in the skulls of many lower Primates. Human evolution has tended to the reduction, and even suppression, of many such secondary skull-features. In this re-

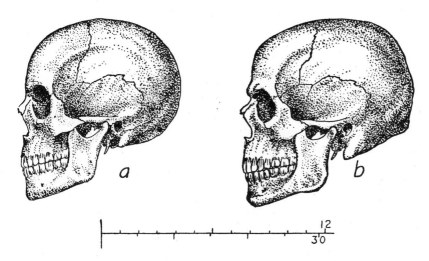

FIG 60.   Typical female (a) and male (b) adult human skulls.

spect woman is more highly-evolved than man—though the apparent advantage is, perhaps, nullified by the ten per cent. deficiency in cranial capacity!

THE THORAX. In females, the thorax as a whole is relatively less capacious. This probably has to do with the less athletic and muscular habit of the whole body, dependent as it is for stamina in violent exertion on capacious lungs and voluminous heart.

Sternum. The female sternum is shorter, its upper margin level with the lower part of the centrum of the third thoracic vertebra. In the male, this margin falls opposite the second thoracic.

Ribs. The movements of respiration in the female are predominantly thoracic, while in males the diaphragm and abdomen play a larger part. The upper ribs are, therefore, more mobile in the female, allowing a greater expansion of the upper part of the thorax.

Sex determination from bones in animals

For investigating ancient domestic animals, for example, it is just as desirable to discover the sex-ratio of the group as it is in the case of the human population.

As in man, the sex-differences are mainly of degree rather than of kind, though a few groups offer qualitative differences which are striking—such as the antlers in male deer, borne by the females also only in the case of the reindeer.

It is obvious that bulls have, on the whole, stouter horns than cows, and boars longer tushes than sows, but it is difficult, without a large material and statistical treatment, to discover where the line between the sexes is to be drawn in a given population. It does not follow that such a line, defined for one species or race, will be equally valid for another of different geographical and temporal provenance.

In this field a very great deal of work remains to be done before any general recommendations for sexing individuals of animal species can be offered.

The quantitative method—defining measurements, and indices based on such measurements, followed by statistical study of a series of adequate size—is likely to be the most fruitful, though it cannot be said that the more qualitative approach, as outlined above in the case of human bones, has been exhaustively explored, even in the common animals.

For the present, then, archaeologists for the most part must wait upon the results of specialist workers in these fields, though there is nothing to prevent a mild excursion into statistics by any archaeological student of bones who has sufficient material to hand and the time, patience and interest to work it up. Archaeology stands to gain more from his results than any other branch of knowledge—which is probably the reason why so much remains to be done, the zoologists having found the prospect somewhat unrewarding.

Reconstruction of living stature from dry long bones

In examining the excavated skeletal remains of prehistoric and early historic peoples, it is often of value to estimate the living stature of individuals and groups.

It must be emphasized at the outset that the exhaustive study of such material is properly the province, in the first place, of the trained anthropologist, aided, if required, by specialists in forensic medicine and general and dental pathology.

In view of the possible difficulty of enlisting, in a given instance, the assistance of the limited number of such specialists available, it is not altogether out of place to suggest here how the archaeologist himself may, at need, extract at least some valuable information from the bones.

Quite apart from the anthropological interest of the results, the ability to estimate living stature from isolated long bones may be of assistance on the site or in the laboratory in assigning scattered bones to a particular individual, or of distinguishing the remains of particular individuals in a mixed collection representing several.

It is, of course, evident that a collection yielding two left femora must include remains of at least two individuals, but it is not so clear which of them, if either, owned, respectively, a possibly associated humerus and radius, unless an estimate of their living dimensions can first be made. Even so, it may not be possible to single out with certainty remains of a particular individual from such a collection, unless the differences in stature are sufficiently large, but the possibility of so doing is worth pursuing.

Theoretical difficulties in reconstructing living stature from dry bones are many. For example, it has been shown that the standing height of an individual may change during the day by as much as 0.9 in.; that the recumbent height is greater than the standing height by as much as 1.2 ins.; that nutrition and old-age affect it materially; that corpse-length exceeds living stature by perhaps 0.8 in. These, and other critical considerations are expounded in a recently-published work*, from which the following instructions and data for obtaining living stature from dry long bones have been obtained.

1. The bones must be measured, to the nearest 1 mm. or 0.1 in. by a uniform technique, preferably with a proper Hepburn osteometric board†, or between squared wooden blocks resting on squared paper, if this is not available. The use of tapes, callipers or slide-gauges is excluded.

2. Measurements:

(a) Femur. The greatest overall length from the medial condyle (in contact with the fixed vertical plane) to the head. The bone lies with its anterior surface uppermost and is moved from side to side until the maximum reading is obtained.

(b) Tibia. Greatest length, exclusive of the inter-condylar eminence, from the lateral condyle (in contact with the movable vertical plane) to the tip of the medial malleolus. The bone lies with its anterior surface uppermost and its long axis parallel to that of the board.

(c) Humerus. Greatest overall length from the most distal margin of the trochlea (in contact with the fixed vertical plane) to the head. The bone lies with its anterior surface uppermost and is moved from side to side until the maximum reading is obtained.

(d) Radius. Greatest length from the tip of the styloid process (in contact with the fixed vertical plane) to the head. The bone lies with its posterior surface uppermost and its long axis parallel to that of the board.

3. Armed with these measurements, a set of stature/bone-length coefficients, with constants to be added in each case, given in the following table, can be applied to obtain estimates of stature. The coefficients

* Boyd, J. D. and Trevor, J. C. 'Race, sex, age and stature from skeletal remains.' In *Modern Trends in Forensic Medicine*, ed. by Keith Simpson, London, Butterworth, 1952.

† Hepburn osteometric board obtainable from Messrs. Andrew H. Baird, 31-39 Lothian St., Edinburgh.

and constants have been calculated for bones of the right side. Despite individual variations, which are difficult to assess, the measurement of a left bone may be substituted where the right is missing. It is necessary to know the sex of the individual. Accuracy is increased when measurements of several bones are available, to be used singly and in combination in several formulae. The results may then be averaged.

DUPERTUIS AND HADDEN'S GENERAL RECONSTRUCTION FORMULAE FOR STATURE FROM LENGTHS OF DRY LONG BONES WITHOUT CARTILAGE

Sex	Formula	Stature/bone-length co-efficients Femur (f), Tibia (t), humerus (h) and radius (r)	Constant term to be added after calculation in previous column	
			cms.	ins.
Male	a	2·238 [× length of] (femur) [+]	69·089 [or]	27·200
	b	2·392 (tibia)	81·688	32·161
	c	2·970 (humerus)	73·570	28·965
	d	3·650 (radius)	80·405	31·655
	e	1·225 (f. + t.)	69·294	27·281
	f	1·728 (h. + r.)	71·429	28·122
	g	1·422 (f) + 1·062(t)	66·544	26·198
	h	1·789(h) + 1·841(r)	66·400	26·142
	i	1·928(f) + 0·568(h)	64·505	25·396
	k	1·442(f) + 0·931(t) + 0·083(h) + 0·480(r)	56·006	22·050

Sex	Formula	Stature/bone-length co-efficients	Constant term to be added after calculation in previous column	
			cms.	ins.
Female	a	2·317(f)	61·412	24·178
	b	2·533(t)	72·572	28·572
	c	3·144(h)	64·977	25·581
	d	3·876(r)	73·502	28·938
	e	1·233(f + t)	65·213	25·674
	f	1·984(h + r)	55·729	21·941
	g	1·657(f) + 0·879(t)	59·259	23·330
	h	2·164(h) + 1·525(r)	60·344	23·757
	i	2·009(f) + 0·566(h)	57·600	22·677
	k	1·544(f) + 0·764(t) + 0·126(h) + 0·295(r)	57·495	22·636

Example: To find the stature in life of a male with a femur measuring 40·8 cms. and tibia 33.6 cms.

Formula

(a)	$2·238 \times 40·8 + 69·089 =$	160·40 cms
(b)	$2·392 \times 33·6 + 81·688 =$	162·06
(e)	$1·225 (40·8 + 33·6) + 69·294 =$	160·43
(g)	$(1·442 \times 40·8) + (1·062 \times 33·6) + 66·544 =$	160·22

$$4\overline{)643·11}$$

Arithmetic mean 160·8 cms

$= 5 \text{ft } 3\frac{1}{3} \text{ ins}$

Applied even to many non-European people, good approximations to stature may be expected from these formulae.

Results based on the measurement of a single bone are probably seldom closer to the true height than 1 inch, but if measurements of several are available, greater accuracy than this should be obtained.

Boyd and Trevor (*ibid.*) give a table showing results calculated by these formulae from the above four main long bones of ten individuals whose height in life was known. The mean error was only one inch, though the 'known' heights were in cases 'presumed'.

Mention is made of attempts to use incomplete long bones, by reconstructing their original length from other measurements, but the authors are not enthusiastic about the accuracy of the conclusions reached. It is clear that unavoidable errors in the first reconstruction will be magnified during the calculation of the second.

16

Study and Interpretation

+ +

THE STUDY OF THE BONES associated with any archaeological remains should preferably begin on the site itself. Apart from the information intrinsic to the collection as seen on the laboratory bench, there may be much to be gleaned from an examination of the material while it is still in position.

The excavator is clearly responsible for recording the stratigraphical relations of the finds to the archaeological periods represented and for plotting their positions on his plans. In the case of any specially interesting group of bones, such as a skeleton, whether complete or disturbed by the activities of later occupants of the site, it is axiomatic that the excavator will also have photographs taken before anything is moved. Such records are nearly always punctiliously kept. Generally, this will be sufficient, but there are not infrequent instances where even the best photographs cannot be made to show everything which the worker who is to report on the bones might be able to distinguish on the site.

Obviously, to extract everything possible from such remains as found, there must be somebody present who knows enough about anatomy to notice anything out of the ordinary about the position of the body or of the individual bones. This is specially the case where a burial or group of burials has been disturbed, so that there is doubt as to the correct attribution to individuals of bones not in their normal positions of articulation. Under these circumstances, nothing less than accurate scale-drawings or numerous close-up photographs will serve to record the position adequately. These must be made by, or with the advice of, a person with special knowledge of bones sufficient to judge as to what may be important, preferably the one who will eventually report on the finds.

Disturbed bones, as in a pit-filling or a common grave, may well extend some distance in depth, below the level at which the uppermost of them were first exposed. If one body lies even only partly over another it may be possible to work on the lower individual only after the upper has been removed.

It may thus be necessary to use some approximation to the technique of 'serial sections', clearing and recording each layer in turn on a separate plan of an area. On completion of the work the plans, super-imposed in order, should enable the exact disposition of the remains in three dimensions to be reconstructed.

Each layer as it is exposed should be described verbally in the note-book, adding such conclusions and interpretations, as may, at the time, suggest themselves, however mistaken they may later prove to be. Any detail not immediately comprehensible should be described with particular care. Its full explanation may well emerge in the succeeding layer and lead to no observation of special interest, but there is a chance that something, at first inexplicable, may lead to an eventual conclusion of importance, as to the state of the bodies when buried or disturbed, evidence of violent death, dislocations or other injuries or abnormalities. Once the bones have been lifted this evidence is lost if not noted and sufficiently recorded at the time.

It may be added at this point that, even for someone used to handling bones and confident of an ability to recognize them on the bench, it is a very different matter to decide what bone he is dealing with when only a small part of it is visible in the ground. The knowledge of what to expect, and therefore how to set about clearing a specimen without danger of damaging it, is most helpful in the field, but is only acquired by practice and many errors at first. It is a humbling experience for the consulting 'expert' to have no notion at first glimpse of a human bone as to what part of the skeleton it may represent and to have a first theory as to its nature only to have to abandon it as clearing proceeds! One is constantly filled with admiration for the skill of archaeological field-workers with no pretensions to any knowledge of bones, who nevertheless clear an entire skeleton by patience and steady application without serious damage.

If the group is at all complicated and disturbed, measured drawings on a sufficiently large scale are desirable. These should be of such a quality that individual bones may be readily identified. It is not enough to show that a particular bone is a femur. It should be clear that it is a *right* femur with its posterior aspect uppermost. Such a high standard of drawing may be impracticable. Not every excavation has a skilled draughtsman at hand, nor is every archaeological draughtsman suffici-ently well versed in osteology to make a recognizable portrait of each item in a group of bones. Any deficiencies in drawing must be made good by even fuller verbal description and by giving identification-letters or numbers to individual pieces in a diagrammatic drawing. Another way is to letter on the spot a rough photographic print.

The notebook entry might read:

'(5) in photo 1. R. femur (? of body A), prone, in articulation with pelvis, knee-joint not yet visible. Shaft fractured (? anciently) in upper $\frac{1}{3}$.'

Should there be any doubt that a long bone is (or can be made, by impregnation) in sound enough condition to be lifted, its ends should be cleared until callipers can be adjusted to take its maximum length while still in the ground (see p. 208 ff). If, eventually, the bone reaches the laboratory safely, another measurement can be taken in accordance with the correct osteometric technique. If it should not survive the move in measurable condition, the rough measurement is better than none at all.

Animal remains on a settlement site will certainly mostly represent food-refuse. Thus, their condition and exact positions in the field are less likely to be informative. It is not essential to have a specialist present to see them excavated. It would be well, however, that at least one of the excavators should be able to recognize the species ordinarily found and to exercise special care should anything outside his experience be discovered.

Dogs, for example, and sometimes even larger domestic beasts, were occasionally buried whole. To have all the bones of a single individual, instead of the usual disjointed fragments, affords more useful information about the race in domestication at the time than hundreds of loose examples. In communities more sophisticated than those of our prehistoric times such animal burials may represent blood-sacrifices or funeral offerings. In this role, the remains may throw some light on ancient customs and beliefs and are worthy of exact recording and closer study.

It is not necessary to urge the advisability of there being somebody with a good knowledge of bones on every excavation carried out at a Palaeolithic site. Every student of the period understands the importance of associated fossils in elucidating Pleistocene problems and in reconstructing the animal and climatic environment of the time. Once again, unless a whole animal, or at least groups of bones in articulation, are found, the recording of the finds in relation to the stratigraphy is all that need be done on the spot. If they are at all fit to travel, cleaning, preservation and mending are best postponed until the full resources of a laboratory can be made available. Field treatment should be confined to ensuring their arrival home without further damage.

Bench-work

When the collection reaches the laboratory, the course of inquiry to be followed will depend to some extent on what the excavator already knows about the site and hopes to learn from the bones.

Some understanding of the archaeological problems involved in the excavation and a knowledge of what the purely archaeological evidence is going to show about the site is very helpful. A study of the bones carried out *in vacuo* is almost certain to be sterile—of little value to the student and of only the slightest interest to the excavator.

If, for example, it is likely that the site was only seasonally occupied, it would be profitable to look for migratory or hibernating species, in order to discover during what part of the year it was inhabited. In a permanently occupied settlement the character and numbers of the domesticated animals may throw some light on the economics of stock-breeding. Where wild species only are represented, they may illustrate the natural environment of the human settlers.

In the case of midden-material and discarded meat-bones, a bare list of the species represented, with some comment on their relative proportions, is not all that can be usefully undertaken. Anything at all unusual should be noted—a preponderance of young individuals, uncommon species, any evident selectiveness in the parts of the body used, details of butchery-practice (White, 1952-6) which may be inferred from mechanical damage, evidence of seasonal food-habits, of dependence on wild game, of significant differences in the assemblages of species in the different archaeological levels and so on.

Before any of these features can be discerned clearly, a view of the material as a whole must be obtained.

It is an inviolable rule that collections from different areas and levels must be kept separate. Only one bag or packed layer must be opened at a time and the contents spread out for inspection. Unless this rule is observed as faithfully as it is in the case of archaeological finds of different periods, important evidence may be lost, or, what is worse, entirely fictitious conclusions be formed. Even if no significant differences between one collection and another are apparent, they should not be lumped together except after consultation with the excavator, when it has been agreed that to keep them separate would be artificial or unreal. It is better to make too many distinct groups, in the hope that some may prove significant, than too few, when evidence of real distinctions may be lost.

Provided that the bones have been adequately cleaned and packed on the site and that there are not too many fresh breaks, a list should first be made of all determinable fragments in each group, under the different species. Obviously, there is a likelihood of some duplication, since it cannot be assumed that each fragment represents a distinct individual. Unless the collection is quite small, there will not be enough time at the investigator's disposal to segregate, for example, all the left femora of a particular species, with a view to arriving at the minimum number of individuals represented. Save when fairly complete skeletons are in question, to have any validity, this would have to be done for every bone in the body of every species, lest some individuals should be represented (as is likely, in a considerable mixed collection) by single fragments only. Further, an effort would first have to be made to reunite all fragments of every broken bone. Where, on a domestic site, remains of oxen or sheep, for example, may be represented by hundreds of fragments, this would obviously be an unrewarding, if not impossible, task. Some such reduction of the material in the smaller groups may be possible at a later stage; the first necessity is to list the material in some such form as the following:

OX	SHEEP (GOAT)	PIG	HORSE	OTHERS
1 femur ribs (3) calcaneum 2 l-vert radius frag. r. scapula 3 metacarpals. 1 metatarsal 2 incisors 5 molars.	2 molars 2 scapulae femur (young) 3 phalanges Frags. of pelvis.	½ mandible 2 molars metapodial lower tush	2nd phal. up. molar & frags. of maxilla.	Dog: lower canine, radius (size of Irish terrier). Deer: Antler burr (shed). Birds: 2 wing- bones. Man: Frags. of infant skull.

This list is that of an imaginary group of quite modest size. It is clear that, apart from obvious differences in age or dimensions, there need be no more than two individuals under the heading 'ox', but the probability is rather that most pieces are the sole representatives of the individual to which they belonged. The excavated deposit may have taken many years, even centuries, to accumulate; the longer the time, the less likely that two or more fragments of the same individual are present. This applies, too, to the other species.

If, therefore, we assume that all species are equally subject to chance or deliberate fractures and to the hazards of preservation, we can take the number of recognizable fragments of each as representing the relative frequency on the site of that species.* From the above list we get:

Ox	Sheep or goat	Pig	Horse	Dog	Deer	Man	Birds
22	11	6	2	2	1	1	2

The first 3, comprising 39 pieces against a mere 8 for all the rest, are clearly the main food-animals, in the rough proportion 4 : 2 : 1. The 2 pieces of horse found are of relatively inedible parts, so there is no evidence here as to whether the horse, also, was eaten, or only kept for transport. The dog, as today, was kept as a guard, companion and for hunting. The deer-antler proves nothing. Being naturally shed, it was either picked up as material for tools or as a curiosity. It was certainly not a hunted animal. The two birds probably represent meals. The human infant is almost certainly an intruded burial, perhaps disturbed at a later date, since no more of the body was found.

One cannot, of course, extract much valid evidence from a single group as small as this. The analysis must be extended to cover several groups of the same period from different parts of the site. Where the excavation was large and the material sufficiently plentiful, it may even be possible to use some statistical methods. Results from groups of different ages must be kept apart—they may show significant changes in the habits of the occupants of the site.

When an over-all picture of the collection has been gained, the un-

* But see Chaplin (1971) on this and other methods.

determinable fragments should once more be examined, to make sure that they represent nothing unusual. They should not yet be discarded. Any interesting pieces which obviously belong together should be reassembled and mended. If important fragments, as of a skull, are missing, the undeterminable collection should be sorted through in case any of them lie, unrecognized, among the rubbish. Nothing should be finally discarded until it is certain that no more is worth mending. It is tantalizing to find later that the one small fragment which would have completed a mend has probably been thrown away. If even the discard pile fails to yield the needed fragment, it is worth casting an eye over collections from adjacent areas and levels, taking special care not to confuse them with material already spread out. It is not unusual to find joining pieces at some distance from the main group.

In this way the more obvious joins and whole bones clearly belonging to the same limb or other part of the same skeleton may be found. This will, to some extent, reduce the number of individuals figuring in the first list by the number of the reassembled fragments. As noted above, there is an economic limit to this process, on which valuable time should not be wasted.

The real study can now begin. It is hard to generalize about its course, as collections are infinitely varied, in the amount of their material, nature, and the sort of information which they may be expected to yield. A natural line of inquiry will probably suggest itself on reviewing the lists already made and trying to assess what any particular features mean. Some main heads under which research might be profitable are as follows:—

Environmental

Do the wild species found belong to any particular natural milieu—forest, river-valley, steppe, fen, tundra, coast?

Proportions of wild to domestic species. How far were the people directly dependent on natural environment?

Did they show preference for any particular species? Why? Was it, for example, a matter of availability only during certain seasons?

Any evidence that young beasts were preferred?

Are any normally associated species conspicuously absent?—any incongruous ones present? Why?

Are any non-mammalian species important?

Domestic animals

Are all the usual species represented: cattle, sheep, goat, pig, horse, dog? In what proportions? Is any missing? Why?

Are there any tame cats or other small carnivores?

How do domestic beasts compare in size and build with modern races? Are there any peculiar features in shape of horns or in bodily proportions?

Are many young individuals present? Of what sort of age? Were calves and lambs autumn-slaughtered because there was not enough winter feed to maintain them as well as the breeding stock? Were any kept to a considerable age? Any evidence of sex?—e.g. only bulls?

Racial affinities. How do the animals compare with those of other periods, both earlier and later? Are there any common features which would suggest the source of the stock? How do they compare with wild European species?

Butchery. Any evidence of fractures or cuts, to suggest how carcasses were jointed?

Use of bones, teeth, horns and antlers for industrial purposes. Signs of cutting, sawing, drilling or wear in use as implements?

Human remains

How many individuals? Of what ages and sex? Infant mortality?

Buried? Cremated? Naturally preserved? If disturbed, why?

Features of skull and stature. Bodily proportions. Racial and family resemblances?

Evidence of tooth-wear in relation to age estimated from other features. Indications of diet?

Cause of death? Evidence of violence in skulls, vertebrae or long bones? Other cuts and fractures, perhaps accidental? Healed wounds, including immobilized joints following damage? Trepanation?

Pathological lesions. Bone erosions, exostoses, arthritic joints, dental anomalies, caries, abscesses?

Deficiency diseases. Rickets, mineral deficiencies leading to imperfect calcification?

The list is not exhaustive. Other lines of investigation will suggest themselves. Obviously, only a few of the above suggestions will be profitable in any given case. It is at least worth while to consider whether the collection in question may afford positive evidence on any of these points.

It is not part of the archaeologist's task to supplant, for example, the palaeontologist, the physical anthropologist or the pathologist, but it is quite proper for him to offer a general report on the remains as found and on the points likely to be of interest to fellow-archaeologists, as illustrating the environment, habits and way of life, economics, industry, warfare, funeral customs and beliefs of the inhabitants of the place and period under investigation. All these points will neither be so clear, nor of particular interest, to any one specialist who may be called in, in due course, to study the material exhaustively by his own special methods. Unless some indication is first given by the archaeological student of bones that the material apparently affords information of specialist interest, it is unlikely that those best able to describe and evaluate it will ever be invited to consider it.

For many not particularly distinguished collections the summary study is all that is likely ever to be undertaken. It can, nevertheless, be a useful record if treated with imagination and understanding of the archaeological point of view and the special problems of archaeology. To this end, the closest co-operation between workers on bones and excavators is necessary. It is the excavator's responsibility to get a competent investigator on the site to see any unusual bone material in position and to explain to him the possible archaeological implications of the find. Armed with an understanding of the context of the remains, the latter will then be able to direct his attention specially to the points of greatest interest and importance to the excavator. There will often emerge results which constitute a contribution of real value to the excavation-report, and not merely a largely irrelevant Appendix.

What is wanted is a more widespread interest among archaeologists in the bone material found on their excavations and closer liaison between excavators and osteologists, to their mutual benefit.

In the past the difficulty has been that workers on bones were too few. More may be encouraged to undertake the task with a specially designed manual to help them.

It is with the hope that it may prove useful in that capacity that this book has been written.

Bibliography

The literature on human and animal osteology, fossil and recent, is enormous. A bibliography pretending to any sort of completeness would certainly run to some hundreds of pages. The following works are suggested as further reading and for reference because they have been freely consulted by the present writer and afford more detail on points which have often been referred to only briefly here. The more recent of them often contain large bibliographies of the subjects which they cover, to which the would-be researcher is referred.

ABEL, O. (1927). *Lebensbilder aus der Tierwelt der Vorzeit.* 2nd ed. Fischer, Jena. 714 pp.

ANDERSON, J. E. (1962). *The Human Skeleton.* Nat. Mus. of Canada, Ottawa. 164 pp.

BROOM, R. (1930). *The Origin of the Human Skeleton.* London, Witherby, 164 pp.

BROTHWELL, D. R. (1963). *Digging up Bones.* British Museum (Natural History), London. 194 pp.

BROTHWELL, D. R. & HIGGS, E. (eds) (1969). *Science and Archaeology,* articles 23-30, pp. 251-358. Thames & Hudson, London.

CHAPLIN, R. E. (1971). *The study of animal bones from archaeological sites.* Seminar Press, London. 170 pp.

CUVIER, G. (1825). *Ossemens fossiles.* Paris. 5 vols.

DAVISON'S *Mammalian Anatomy,* with special reference to the cat. 7th ed. (1947), revised by STROMSTEN, F. A., Philadelphia. 349 pp.

FALCONER, H. (1868). *Palaeontological Memoirs II.* London. Hardwicke. 675 pp.

FLOWER, W. H. (1876). *Osteology of the Mammalia.* Macmillan. London. 380 pp.

FLOWER, W. H. & LYDEKKER, R. (1891). *Mammals Living and Extinct.* London. 763 pp.

GENOVÉS, S., & MESSMACHER, M. (1959). 'Valor de los patrones tradicionales para la determinación de la édad por medio de las suturas en cráneos mexicanos (indígenas y mestizos)', Cuadernos del Instituto de Historia, Série antropológica, No. 7, México, 53 pp. (Univ. Nac. autónoma de México).

GRAY, J. (1953). *How Animals Move.* Cambridge. 114 pp.

GRAY H., *Descriptive and applied Anatomy* (1946). 29th ed. rev. T. B. Johnston and J. Whillis. Longman's. London. pp. 203-424.

HESCHELER, K. & KUHN, E. (1949). 'Die Tierwelt.' In TSCHUMI, O., *Urgeschichte der Schweiz.* Huber, Frauenfeld. pp. 121-368.

HUE, E. (1907). *Musée ostéologique.* 2 vols. Paris, Schleicher. 186 pls.

KURTÉN, B. (1968). *Pleistocene mammals of Europe*. Weidenfeld & Nicolson, London. 317 pp.

MEYER, H. von (1864). *Die Diluvialen Rhinoceros-Arten*. Palaeontographica, II, 233.

MURRAY, J. (1970). *The first European agriculture*. Edinburgh University Press. 380 pp.

OSBORN, H. F. (1943). *The Proboscidea*, vol. 2. New York, 1945. pp. 805-1675.

OWEN, R. (1846). *British Fossil Animals and Birds*. London. 558 pp.

REYNOLDS, S. H. (1902-34). *Monograph of the British Pleistocene Mammalia* (several parts). London. Palaeontographical Soc.

ROMER, A. S. (1941). *Man and the Vertebrates*. 3rd ed. Univ. of Chicago Press, 405 pp. (Also in Penguin Books—Pelicans Nos. *A 303-4*. 2 vols. London, 1954. 437 pp.).

RYDER, M. L. (1969). *Animal bones in Archaeology*. Mammal Society Handbooks, Oxford & Edinburgh. 65 pp.

SANDARS, E. (1937). *A Beast Book for the Pocket*. London. Humphrey Milford. 378 pp.

SCHMID, E. (1972). *Atlas of animal bones*. Elsevier, Amsterdam. 159 pp.

SISSON, S. & GROSSMAN, J. D. (1953). *Anatomy of the Domestic Animals*. 4th ed. London. 972 pp.

SOERGEL, W. (1913). *Elephas trogontherii Pohlig und E. antiquus Falconer*. Palaeontographica 60, 1.

UCKO, P. J. & DIMBLEBY, G. W. (eds.) (1969), *The domestication and exploitation of plants and animals*. Duckworth, London. 581 pp.

VLERK, I. M. van der & FLORSCHÜTZ, F. (1950). *Nederland in het IJstijdvak*. Utrecht. 287 pp.

WHITE, T. E. (1952-6). Several articles on primitive butchery, etc. *American Antiquity*, vols 17, 18, 19, 21.

ZEUNER, F. E. (1945). *The Pleistocene Period*. London, Ray Soc., pp. 253-278.

ZEUNER, F. E. (1963). *A History of Domesticated Animals*. Hutchinson, London. 560 pp.

(German-language edition 1967). *Geschichte der Haustiere*. Bayerische Landschaftsverlag, München. 448 pp. (Text unaltered, but additional notes and references by Boessneck, J. & Haltenorth, T.)

ZITTEL, C. A. von (1925). *Text book of Palaeontology*, vol. III, Mammalia. London, Macmillan, 316 pp.

EXAMPLES TO SHOW the process of determination of whole bones (See Figs. 53, 54 (a) to (t), pp. 194–5.

(a) 1. It is not a long bone. It is symmetrical—therefore, a bone lying in the M.S.P., part of the axial skeleton. It has a large foramen—*vertebra*.

It has transverse foramina—*cervical vertebra*. It has no centrum or body—*atlas* (C.1).

2. It belonged to a moderately small animal, in size between sheep and hare. Possibly a small ruminant, pig, carnivore of medium size, large rodent.

3. The 'wings' of the atlas are too wide-spread for a ruminant. The foramen is too small for a pig. It is too large even for a beaver, so the rodents are excluded. It must belong to a carnivore.

4. Of the carnivores in our list, it is too small for a bear or lion, too large for a cat. It is too small for a hyaena, too large for a fox, probably too small for wolf. It could be a badger, among the Mustelidae, but is too large for any other. It is probably a rather large dog.

5. Comparison shows it to be quite distinct in form from the atlas of a badger, almost identical with wolf and fox, smaller than the former, larger than the latter. It is identical with *dog*.

(b) 1. It is clearly half a *mandible* with 4 front teeth and 6 cheek-teeth.

2. It belonged to a mammal of medium size, nothing larger than a moderate-sized ruminant—say red deer—nothing smaller than a dog.

3. The high-crowned teeth wearing to a rasp-like chewing surface indicate a specialized vegetable feeder. The premolars are somewhat molariform, the canines indistinguishably like the incisors and ranged with them—a *ruminant* peculiarity. It could be a small deer (fallow deer, roe), sheep or goat, saiga or chamois. On the whole deer have (for ruminants) rather low-crowned teeth. The height of the crowns here rules out deer. In chamois and saiga Pm_4 (the 3rd cheek-tooth from the front) is markedly longer than M_1, mesio-distally. This feature is especially marked in the latter. There are also differences of proportion on comparison.

4. The mandible, therefore, belongs to *sheep or goat*. Distinction between these two is exceedingly difficult. Close study and an adequate comparative material would be necessary to determine the species within these genera.

5. Compare with the available material and check these findings.

(c) 1. It is a long bone, with two convex articulations—femur or humerus. The head has no distinct neck and no pit for a round ligament —*humerus*.

2. It belonged to a large animal, from the shortness and stockiness of the upper arm a specialized quadruped. It cannot, therefore, be man,

lion or bear, of which the humeri would all approximately fit as to length. It is too small to have belonged to elephant, rhino or hippo. It is too large for a pig or any of the smaller ruminants. This restricts the choice to horse, elk, *Megaceros*, ox or bison.

3. The bone has a very prominent deltoid ridge, which is not found in any of the ruminants. This shows that the bone belonged to an odd-toed ungulate, therefore, *horse*.

4. Having narrowed the determination down to a single genus, the context of the site will show whether the horse was a wild species or domesticated. In western Europe wild horses disappear with the steppe conditions to which most were adapted. Domesticated horses appear only in the Late Bronze Age.

5. Distinction between wild species will depend on comparison. The above conclusions should be checked by reference to the material.

(d) 1. It is a long bone, both ends with flat or concave articular surfaces—tibia or fibula. The shaft is triangular above and the proximal articulation consists of two facets separated by a crest—*tibia*.

2. It belonged to an animal of medium size, not so large as horse or ox, larger than dog or sheep.

3. There is no trace of a fibula, fused or otherwise. It cannot, therefore, be man, a carnivore or a pig. It is of the same general form as sheep or ox, with the astragalus articulation in line with the anterior crest. It is, therefore, a ruminant.

4. The bone is of the same stoutness as the tibia of a sheep, but much longer—nearly as long, absolutely, as that of a small ox, but much more slender than this. It is a *deer*.

It is too small for elk, too large for roe or fallow deer. The remaining possibilities are red deer or reindeer. The former is generally considerably the larger (sample measurements on p. 169).

5. Comparison shows that the specimen is of a *reindeer*, both from the dimensions and because in reindeer the medial malleolus is much longer, forming the point of extreme length of the bone.

(e) 1. It is not a long bone. It is not symmetrical and does not, therefore, belong to the axial skeleton (it is clearly not a rib!). It is not part of shoulder- or hip-girdle, is not a loose epiphysis or a hoof-core; must, therefore, be a carpal or tarsal bone, a phalanx or sesamoid. It has no shaft, however short and stout, and cannot be a phalanx. The articular facets are distributed all round, not only on one side, so it cannot be a sesamoid. It must be a carpal or tarsal bone.

It has no lever—not calcaneum—but a pulley-like articulation for a limb bone. This cannot be for ulna and radius, must, therefore, be for the tibia and the bone is an *astragalus*.

2. The animal owning it was larger than a dog, smaller than a red deer.

3. The low tibial articulation shows that it is not a carnivore. The medial twist of the head of the astragalus meeting the navicular shows

that it is not a ruminant, where the head is straight. The animal can only be a *pig*.

4. Since we have only one species of pig, whether wild or domesticated, this stage is unnecessary.

5. Compare and check these conclusions.

(**f**) 1. It is a curved, prismatic, rootless *tooth*. It is not a molar, premolar or canine, having no grinding surface, cutting cusps or sharp point, but a chisel edge of enamel. It is an *incisor*. Being rootless, the pulp-cavity a simple conical hollow, it is constantly being renewed in the alveolus and continually growing out. This is an adaptation to very severe wear.

2. It belonged to a relatively small animal—smaller than an average dog, larger than a rabbit.

3. The only group in our list having such incisors is the Order Rodentia.

4. For a rodent the animal was large—hare, porcupine, beaver, marmot.

5. On comparison, the dimensions show it to be *beaver*.

(**g**) 1. It is a tooth, curved, slender and pointed, with a strong closed root—a *canine*.

2. It belonged to an animal of moderate size—between an average dog and a hare.

3. Canines of such size are found in smaller Primates (e.g., gibbon) and carnivores only, in our list. Unless its date could be Early Pleistocene the Primates are excluded—and a Pleistocene monkey or ape with a canine of this size would be a find indeed! It certainly belongs to a carnivore.

4. It is too small for lion, bear, hyaena, wolf or seal, too large for most of the Mustelidae (save badger and glutton) and for the wild cat.

The list is thus reduced to: smallish dog, fox, badger or glutton.

5. Comparison shows that dog, badger and glutton all have canines much stouter in comparison with their height than our specimen, which must, therefore, be *fox*. Further comparison shows that of the two possible species, *Vulpes v.* and *Alopex lagopus* (arctic fox) it must be the former, since the roots of the canines are much shorter and more flattened transversely in the latter, which has a shorter muzzle.

(**h**) 1. It is not a long bone. It is not symmetrical, is, therefore, one of a pair. It is of irregular shape with a number of articular facets—carpal or tarsal bone. It has a long, lever-like process—*calcaneum*.

2. It belonged to a large animal, lighter in build, if not smaller in dimensions, than an ox, larger than a red deer.

3. Its long, slender tuberosity shows that the pes as a whole was slender and much elongated (opposite arms of a first-order lever). The animal owning it was a specialized terrestrial quadruped.

4. It is too slender for horse or ox, approaching a red deer in its lightness of build, but much larger. *Elk* or *Megaceros*.

5. Compare for decision between these two.

(i) 1. Though absolutely short, it has the features of a long bone. The shortness excludes all of the main limb bones, so it must belong to manus or pes. It is not a metapodial, since its proximal articulation is single and hollow, not consisting of several flattish facets. It must be a *phalanx*. Since the proximal articulation has no trace of a median groove for the head of a metapodial, which has a median ridge, it is a *second* phalanx.

2. It belonged to a large, heavy animal.

3. Its shortness and strength suggests that it was an animal with less than 4 equally-developed digits, i.e., a specialized ungulate or ruminant. It is too stout and short for a deer, even for *Megaceros*, and must, therefore, belong to a large bovid, *ox* or *bison*.

4. Size is no guide in distinguishing these genera.

5. Even comparison, without measurements and mathematics, is no guide. Determination can go no further on the evidence. Skulls, horn-cores and thoracic vertebrae only are an indication at sight of the individual genera.

(j) 1. It is a tooth, worn with grinding vegetable food. A premolar or molar.

2. It is the grinder of a large animal, larger than horse or ox. Elephant? Rhino? Hippo?

3. The grinder of an elephant has many transverse plates of enamel and is far larger than this tooth. That of a hippopotamus has a quatrefoil enamel pattern when worn, pig-like and unspecialized.

This tooth is selenodont (with two crescents of enamel) and indicates a somewhat specialized ungulate—Rhinocerotidae. The presence of cement covering the enamel and lining the pits on the chewing surface and the presence of three such pits, in a worn tooth, instead of only two, show *Tichorhinus*, the extinct woolly rhinoceros.

4 and 5 are unnecessary. The last details are specific. Nevertheless, compare the upper molars of several rhinoceros species and note the differences.

(k) 1. It is a long bone, with faceted proximal end and two distinct distal articulations—ruminant metapodial, consisting of two bones with their shafts fused. The shaft is almost square in section above, somewhat deeper antero-posteriorly than transversely—*metatarsal*.

2. It belonged to a large and heavy animal which, in the ruminant group, could only be a large bovid—ox or bison.

3. The shoulders, at the level of the sutures of the distal epiphyses, are not square, but rather of the sloping, 'bottle-neck' form. The bone probably belongs to *Bos* rather than *Bison*.

4. This step is unnecessary here.

5. Visual comparison can do no more than confirm the attribution to one of these genera, without deciding for either.

(l) 1. It is a long bone, though rather short and squat—not one of the main limb-bones, but part of manus or pes. The faceted proximal end and the bold, barrel-shaped distal articulation with a median ridge show it to be a *metapodial*.

2. It is far too stout to belong to any of the smaller mammals in our list, being twice as thick as that of a carnivore of the size of a wolf. It is too unlike the human form to belong to man—or to bear or lion, which share with him rather generalized characters of manus and pes. The high median ridge of the distal articulation indicates that the phalanges had little or no lateral play—a sign of some specialization as a terrestrial quadruped. It is too small to belong to any of the heavier animals, red deer and upwards.

3. The specialized ungulates (horse and ruminants) have stout cannon-bones, in the case of the latter consisting of two fused metapodials. Since the specimen shows no signs of fusion with its neighbours it indicates a relatively less specialized ungulate than these.

4. Horse and rhino are excluded by their size, so that this bone can only have belonged to an even-toed (Artiodactyl) animal. Hippo is similarly excluded, so we arrive at the only possible animal—*pig*. The pig has four digits, this bone being one of the main pair (M/ps. II and III).

5. Comparison will be necessary to decide whether the bone is a metacarpal or a metatarsal. Even comparison will not distinguish between a wild and a prehistoric domesticated pig. The latter was neither so large nor as heavy-bodied as modern breeds.

(m) 1. It is not a long bone, but is, at first sight, somewhat rib-like. Unlike a rib, it has a double (S) curvature and articular facets at both ends. It is a *clavicle*.

2. The possession of a functional clavicle is a primitive feature. It is present in Insectivora, Chiroptera, some Rodentia and the Primates. In the rest of the groups in our list it is a functionless vestige if present at all. The size of the present example marks it as unmistakably *human*.

3, 4 and 5 unnecessary.

(n) 1. It is not a long bone. It is roughly conical, terminating in a point. The base is fractured and shows a coarsely cellular internal structure. It is not symmetrical but forms one of a pair. Its external surface is more or less deeply marked with vascular grooves and small foramina. It is a cranial appendage—a *horn-core*.

2. In size, it clearly belongs to an animal smaller than ox or bison—one of the smaller Bovidae.

3. It is roughly triangular in section, slender and tapering and appears somewhat twisted on its own axis rather than curved—the curve is an extremely narrow helix of which there is not one complete turn in the length of the horn-core. *Goat.*

4. In our list for western Europe only two goats come into consideration: the domestic species, *Capra hircus* and the ibex, *C. ibex*. The long sweeping curve of the horn-core in the latter is distinctive. This specimen clearly belongs to the former.

5. Compare and check.

(o) 1. It is an entire *cranium*.

2. It belongs to an animal of the size of a smallish dog.

3. The dentition, with its strong canines, blunt-pointed premolars and reduced molar set, tells us at once that this is a carnivore. It is, however, one not highly specialized, as witness the P^4, M^1, and M_1, which are multi-cuspidate and frankly grinding—not flesh-cutting teeth. They indicate a varied diet.

4. The unspecialized carnivores in our list are the bear and the badger. The skull is manifestly too small to belong to the former and must, therefore, represent the latter. The long, low vault, small brain-case, blunt muzzle and powerful jaws mark the family of the Mustelidae—weasels, martens, etc. These features confirm the determination as *badger*.

5. Compare and check.

(p) 1. It is a tooth. The crown is very high, the roots short and small, the worn surface a complicated pattern of enamel, dentine and cement, with small, narrow, open pits in the cement. Despite the complications, the basic selenodont pattern of the ungulates is apparent. It is a cheek-tooth—whether premolar or molar does not appear clearly.

2. It is the tooth of a relatively large animal, but clearly not of elephant, rhino or hippo. It is, therefore, *horse or a large ruminant*.

3. The height of the crown, the amount of cement covering the enamel and filling its reëntrant folds suggest a design to resist severe wear—i.e., a tough, abrasive diet.

Of the above list, the horse is originally a steppe-dweller and these feeding-conditions would demand just the structure we observe. Ox and bison, on the other hand, are preferably parkland and river-valley animals. Their teeth are not so high or so heavily reinforced with cement. *Horse*.

4. The size of the tooth is some guide to the stature of the animal. Most wild horses are of pony dimensions, but one group apparently lived in the Pleistocene forests and attained a considerable size (*Equus robustus* group). Prehistoric domestic horses (*E. caballus*) were generally small, not approaching the 14-16 hands measurement (56 inches-64 inches) at the withers of some modern breeds.

5. Compare and check.

(q) 1. It is not a long bone. It consists of three branches radiating from a cup-shaped articular hollow (acetabulum), of which two (ischium, pubis) rejoin to enclose a large oval (obturator) foramen, while the third (ilium) widens to a fan-shaped extremity. It is one 'half' of a pelvis, the *os innominatum*.

2. It belonged to an animal of medium size, larger than a dog, smaller than a pony.

3. The margin of the acetabulum is notched below, but the notch is closed to a mere slit at the actual margin by overhanging lips of bone. This is a feature of the acetabulum in the ruminants alone, and especially in the Bovidae. (The notch is less completely closed in the Cervidae.) The bone is, therefore, that of a rather small bovid.

4. The size suggests sheep, goat, chamois or saiga.

5. In the last, the ilium is rather short, the tuberosity of the ischium large in proportion and the obturator foramen a wide oval. The chamois is considerably lighter and the bones more gracile than in the specimen. The acetabulum is smaller and the foramen a long oval. The specimen lies between these two in form, is larger and evidently belongs to an animal heavier than either. It is, therefore, certainly *sheep or goat*. As in other cases with these two genera, a distinction is very hard to make. The goats seem to be rather lighter in build than sheep, but the differences are of the same order of magnitude as variations due to sex, age and different geographical races. They are, therefore, quite unreliable.

6. Compare the material and check these observations.

(r) 1. It is not a long bone. It is symmetrical—part of the axial skeleton. It has a large oval centrum, arch enclosing a wide foramen, transverse processes and neural spine—a *vertebra*.

It has no transverse foramina (not cervical).

It has no rib-facets on body or transverse processes (not a thoracic).

It has no sign of fusion with its neighbours (not a sacral).

It has all its processes well developed (not a caudal).

It must be a *lumbar vertebra*.

2. It is of a biggish animal, not as big as an ox but larger than a sheep. This narrows the possible field very considerably: to man, bear, lion or a middle-sized ungulate.

3. In the ruminants the centra, even of the lumbar vertebrae, are somewhat opisthocoelous (hollow posteriorly), while in the specimen they are practically flat. This rules out the ruminants. In all quadrupeds there is an anticlinal vertebra towards the end of the thoracic series, of which the neural spine stands vertically in a dorsal direction. The spines of those in front of this lean back, those behind, including the lumbars, forwards. In man, with an erect posture, there is no anticlinal vertebra and all the neural spines point downwards. This rules out the carnivores. *Man*.

4. Unnecessary.

5. Compare and check.

(s) 1. It is not a long bone. It is asymmetrical, showing it to be one of a pair. It is blade-like, with a marked spine standing at right-angles to the plane of the blade. *Scapula*.

2. It belongs to a rather small animal, larger than a rat, smaller than an average dog. It could, therefore, be a large insectivore (e.g., hedgehog), a large rodent, a small primate or a small carnivore. The rest are ruled out.

3. The most striking feature of the bone is the end of the spine (acromion) overhanging the glenoid cavity. This is divided into two, the acromion proper and a posteriorly-extended metacromial process. The notch between the acromion and the spine is very deep. This excludes the hedgehog and the primates, in which the acromion is undivided. Though present in some small carnivores, the metacromial process in these is neither so long nor so slender. We are left with the *rodents*.

Only one of the larger rodents has the subacromial notch as deep as in this case and the same slender, acute-angled form of the blade, with a concave posterior border. These features indicate *hare*. The rabbit is supposed not to be pre-Norman in Britain, so for a bone in a prehistoric context the determination as hare is conclusive.

4. Unnecessary.

5. Compare and confirm the findings.

(t) 1. It is a long bone, absolutely short and very stout. The rather flat facets at the proximal end and the rounded, convex surface at the distal show it to be a *metapodial*.

2. As a metapodial, it must have belonged to a very large mammal.

3. Of the three largest mammals in our list—elephant, rhino and hippo—the metapodials are extremely large and stout. Those of the hippo, though short, are relatively slender, there being 4 well-developed digits in manus and pes. In the rhino, all the metapodials are relatively long, the principal (III) member of the trio being also extremely strong. The elephant, with 5 complete digits, has metapodials shorter than either, but the Mp III's are scarcely less stout.

4. Unnecessary.

5. Comparison of the present specimen with the relevant material shows it to belong to an *elephant*. It is a metacarpal, the corresponding metatarsal being even shorter and stockier. The material does not permit a specific determination without extensive study.

Index

Acetabulum, 128
Acromion, 117
Adaptation to environment, 32
  of mammals, 40
Age of individual, as determined by
  bones and teeth, 219 ff.
Akanthion, 50
Alisphenoid bone, 54, 62
Alveoli, dental, 59
Animal kingdom, classification and
  nomenclature of, 23
Animals, as food of ancient man, 23
  as indicators of environment, 20
Anthropology, physical, 21
Antlers, of deer, 67 ff.
Apertura piriformis (nasal aperture),
  48
Artiodactyla (Order), Axial skeleton,
  114
  fore-limb, 142
  hind-limb, 165
  hip-girdle, 130
  manus, 153
  pes, 176
  shoulder-girdle, 123
  skull, 66
  teeth, 100
Asterion, 50
Astragalus, 170 ff.
Atlas vertebra, 107
Auditory meatus, external, 48, 55
  ossicles, 57
Axial skeleton, 39, 105 ff.
Axis vertebra, 107

Basi-occipital bone, 52
Basion, 50
Basi-sphenoid bone, 54
Bone, composition and structure of,
  204
    natural preservation and decay
    of, 204
Bregma, 50

Calcaneum, 170 ff.
Calvarium or Calotte, 47
'Cannon-bone' (=ungulate metapo-
  dial), 153-4, 176 ff.

Carnivora (Order), 42
  axial skeleton, 113
  fore-limb, 138
  hind-limb, 162
  hip-girdle, 129
  manus, 150
  pes, 175
  shoulder-girdle, 120
  skull, 59, 63-4
  teeth, 86 ff.
Carpus, 146 ff.
Cattle (horns), 70 ff.
Cement (teeth), 74 ff.
Central bone (of carpus), 146
Centrum, vertebral, 105-6
Cerebellum, 62
Chiroptera (Order), 43
  fore-limb, 135
  hind-limb, 160
  manus, 148
  pes, 173
  shoulder-girdle, 118
  skull, 63
Classification of mammals, 24
Clavicle, 117 ff.
Condylar facets (tibia), 159
Condyles, femoral, 157
  occipital, 52
  of mandible, 59
Coracoid process (scapula), 118
Coronal suture, 52
Coronoid fossa (humerus), 133
  process of mandible, 54, 59
  of ulna, 133
Cranial bones, structure of, 47
Craniometric points, 50
Cranium, 47
Cribriform plate of ethmoid, 54, 62
Crista galli, 62
Cuboid bone, 170 ff.
Cuneiform bone(s), of carpus, 146 ff.
  of tarsus, 170 ff.

Darwin, Charles, 27
Dating evidence from bones, 20
Deer (antlers), 67
Deltoid ridge (humerus), 133
Dental formulae, 78-9

Dentine (=ivory), 74 ff., 93, 207
Diastema, 85 ff.
Digital fossa (femur), 157
Digitigrade gait, 42
Digits of manus, 146 ff.
    of pes, 170 ff.
Diploë, 47, 65

Ecology, 19
Elephant (skull), 59, 60
    (See also Proboscidea)
Enamel of teeth, 74 ff., 196, 200, 207
Entepicondylar foramen, 133
Environment, 19 ff.
Epicondyles of humerus, 133
Epiphyses, ankylosis of, 226–9
    of long bones, 131–2
    of vertebrae, 107
Ethmoid bone, 54
Ethmo-turbinal bones, 55
Evolution, 27 ff.
Ex-occipital bone, 52

Femoral trochlea, 157
Femur, 157 ff.
Fibula, 157 ff.
Foramen, entepicondylar, 133
    magnum, 48, 52
    obturator, 128
    transverse, 107
Fossa(e), digital, 157
    glenoid, 59
    of cranial base, 62
    temporal, 48
Fossilization of bone, 204
Frankfort Plane, 48
Frontal bone, 52
    crest, 60, 62

Geological record, 28 ff.
Germ of tooth, 74
Glabella, 50
Glenoid cavity (scapula), 117
    fossa (skull), 59
Gonion, 50

Hallux (=great toe), 170
Head(s) of astragalus, 170
    of femur, 157
    of humerus, 132
    of metapodials, 174
    of radius, 133

Hippopotamus (skull), 66
Horns of cattle, 67
Horse, skull, 46, 59, 66
    (See also Perissodactyla)
Human remains, fossil, 21
Humerus, 132 ff.
Hyoid bone, 57

Ilium, 128
Infra-orbital point, 48
Inion, 50
Insectivora (Order), 42
    axial skeleton, 112
    fore-limb, 135
    hind limb, 160
    hip-girdle, 128
    manus, 148
    pes, 172
    shoulder-girdle, 118
    skull, 63
    teeth, 80–1
Intercondylar notch, 157
Inter-parietal bone, 52
Ischium, 128
Ivory (=dentine), 93

Jugal bone, 55

Lachrymal bone, 57
Lagomorpha (Order), 81 fn., 112
Lamarck, 27
Lambda, 50
Lambdoid suture, 52
Limbs, development of, 39, 40
Linnaeus, 25
'Long' bones, 131
Lunar (lunate) bone, 146 ff.

Magnum, 147 ff.
Malar bone, 55
Malleoli, 159
Mammalian skeleton, as a whole,
    36 ff.
Mammals, description of skeleton of,
    40
        evolution of, 30
        list of groups treated herein, 33
Man, brain-specialization, 43–4
Mandible, 47, 59
Mastoid process, 55
Maxilla(ry) bone, 57
Maxillo-turbinal bones, 57

Median sagittal plane, 36
Meningeal vessels, impressions of, 60
Mental eminence of jaw, 59
Mesethmoid bone, 55
Metacarpal bones, 146 ff.
Metacromial process, 118
Metapodial (=metacarpal or meta-tarsal), 147 ff., 171 ff.
Metopic suture, 52
Muscular impressions on cranial bones, 53

Nasal aperture, 48
    bones, 55
    conchae, 54
    septum, 54
Nasion, 50
Navicular bone, 170 ff.
Neural arch, canal, spine, 105
Nomenclature, International rules of, 25–6
Normae (true-profile views of skull), 48, 50
Nuchal (muscular) impressions, lines, 54

Obturator foramen, 128
Occipital bone, 52
    condyles, 48, 52
    protuberence, internal, 62
        external, 54
Occiput, 48
Odontoid process (=dens), 107
Olecranon fossa, process, 133
Opisthion, opisthocranion, 50
Orbital fissure, 62
Orbito-ethmoid bones, 55
    -sphenoid bone, 54, 62
Orbits, 48
Os calcis (=calcaneum), 170
    centrale, 146
    coxae (=innominatum), 126
    magnum, 147
    penis, 182–3
Ossification, progress of, as indica-cation of individual age, 219

Palaeontology, 27
Palatine bone, 57
Parietal bones, 52
Par-occipital process, 52
Patella, 159, 160

Pelvis, 126 ff.
Periotic bone, 55
Perissodactyla (Order), Axial skele-ton, 114
    fore-limb, 141
    hind-limb, 163
    hip-girdle, 130
    manus, 151
    pes, 175
    shoulder-girdle, 122
    skull, 65
    teeth, 97
Petrous (part of temporal) bone, 55
Phalanges (manus), 146
    (pes), 170
Pig (skull), 66
Pisiform bone (see also Sesamoids), 147
Plantigrade gait, 42
Pogonion, 50
Pollex (=thumb), 147
Porion, 50
Posterior nares, 57
Post-orbital constriction, 48
Pre-auricular sulcus, 230 fn.
Pre-maxilla, 57
Preservation and fossilization of bone, 205–6
Pre-sphenoid bone, 54
Primates (Order), evolution of, 31
    axial skeleton, 112
    fore-limb, 135
    hind-limb, 160
    hip-girdle, 128
    manus, 148
    pes, 173
    shoulder-girdle, 119
    skull, 47 ff.
    teeth, 82 ff.
Proboscidea (Order), axial skeleton, 114
    fore-limb, 139–141
    hind-limb, 163
    hip-girdle, 130
    manus, 150
    pes, 175
    shoulder-girdle, 121
    skull, 60
    teeth, 93 ff.
Prosthion, 50
Pterion, 50
Pubic bone, symphysis, 128

Radial notch of ulna, 133

Radius, 132 ff.
Ramus, ascending, horizontal, of mandible, 59
Rhinoceros(es) skull (see Perissodactyla), 59, 65
Ribs, 105, 109 ff.
Rodentia (Order), 42
    axial skeleton, 112
    fore-limb, 135
    hind-limb, 160
    hip-girdle, 128
    manus, 148
    pes, 173
    shoulder-girdle, 118
    skull, 63
    teeth, 80–2
Ruminants (see Artiodactyla)

Sacro-iliac joint, 128
Sacrum, 105, 109, 126
Sagittal crest, 59
    sulcus, 60
    suture, 52
Scaphoid bone, 146 ff.
Scapula, 117 ff.
Sella turcica, 62
Sesamoid bones, 172
Sex-determination from bones, 228 ff.
Sigmoid notch of mandible, 59
Skeleton, mammalian, as a whole, 40 ff.
Skull, 45 ff.
Specialization, zoological, 31, 42 ff.
Sphenoid bone, 54
Spine, scapular, 117
    vertebral (=spinous process), 105
Squamosal bone, 55
Squamous part of occipital, 52
    part of temporal, 55
    suture, 52
Stature, living, reconstruction from bones, 234 ff.
Sternum, 39, 105, 111
Sulcus, pre-auricular, 230 fn.
    sagittal, 60
    transverse, 62
Supinator ridge, 133
Supra-occipital bone, 52
Supra-orbital (brow-) ridges, 52
Supra-trochlear perforation, 133
Sutures, of skull, 47, 52
Symphysis pubis, 127–8
    mandibular, 59

Synostosis (bony fusion) of skull-bones, 47

Tables of cranial bones, 47
Tarsal bones (Tarsus), 170 ff.
Teeth, 74 ff.
    milk-, 78
    order of eruption, 227
Temporal bone, 55
    fossa, 48
    lines, 52
    muscle, 54, 59
Tentorium cerebelli, 62
Terminology of bones, 20
Terms, technical, to describe position and attitude of bones, 36 ff.
Thorax, 39, 105, 112
Tibia, 157 ff.
Transverse foramina, 107
    process, 105
    sulci, 62
Trapezium bone, 147 ff.
Trapezoid bone, 147 ff.
Trochanters of femur, 157
Trochlea, of humerus, 133
    of femur, 157
Trochlear notch of ulna, 133
Tubercle of tibia, 159
Tuberosity of humerus, 133
Tympanic part of temporal, 55
Type-species, zoological, 36

Ulna, 132 ff.
Ulnar notch of radius, 134
Unciform bone, 147 ff.
Ungual phalanges, 147, 172
Ungulates, 42
Unguligrade gait, 42

Vertebrae, 39, 105
Vertebral discs, 106
    formula, 109
    ligaments, 106
Vomer bone, 57

Zoological nomenclature, International Rules of, 25–7
Zygapophyses (vertebral), 105–6
Zygomatic bone, 55

ANIMAL KINGDOM

Phylum Chordata

CLASSES

Cyclostomata (lampreys) — Pisces (fishes) — Mammalia — Reptilia — Aves (birds)

SUB-CLASSES

Prototheria (1 order, Monotremata) — † Allotheria (1 order, †Multituberculata) — Theria

INFRA-CLASSES

Eutheria (placental mammals, numerous orders) — † Pantotheria (2 † orders) — Metatheria (1 order, Marsupialia)

COHORTS

Unguiculata (3 orders, 2 †) — Glires (2 orders incl. Rodentia) — Mutica (1 order, Cetacea) — Ferungulata

ORDERS

Insectivora — Chiroptera — Primates — Edentata (sloths, anteaters)

SUB-ORDERS

Prosimii (many † of uncertain position) — Anthropoidea

INFRA-ORDERS

Lemuriformes (3 superfamilies 6 families 9 sub-families Tree shrews (Tupaioidea) 7 genera, 2 †. lemuroids (Lemuroidea) 30, 21 †. Daubentonioidea, 1 living species) — Lorisiformes — Tarsiiformes

FAMILIES

† Anaptomorphidae — Tarsiidae

Tarsius

SUPER-FAM.

Ceboidea (2 families of platyrrhine monkeys –all New World & all living) — Cercopithecoidea — Hominoidea

FAM.

FAM. Lorisidae

Cercopithecidae (Old World monkeys) —3 uncertain: { Moeripithecus Apidium Oreopithecus

SUB-FAMILIES

Lorisinae (5 gen. 1 † lorises, pottos.) — Galaginae (2 gen. incl. Galago) — Cercopithecinae (14 gen. 4 † of baboons, etc.) — Colobinae (8 gen. 2 †)

FAMILIES

† Parapithecidae Parapithecus, L. Olig. Egypt — Pongidae (apes) — 3 of uncertain position— {Pondaungia, Amphipithecus, Xenopithecus — Hominidae (men)

SUB-FAMILIES

Hylobatinae † Limnopithecus, Kenya † Pliopithecus, Europe Hylobates (gibbons) Symphalangus (siamang) — Dryopithecinae † Dryopithecus † 6 Indian genera — Ponginae † Gigantopithecus Pongo (orang) Pan (chimp.) Gorilla

GENERA

† Australopithecus (incl. Plesianthropus, Paranthropus, etc.) Plio./Pleist., Africa — Homo All extinct & living races — † Ramapithecus Mioc., Africa & Asia

ORDER Carnivora

SUB-ORDERS

† Creodonta — Fissipedia (separate-toed) — Pinnipedia (flippers – e.g. seals)

SUPER-FAMILIES

† Miacoidea — Canoidea — Feloidea

FAMILIES

Ursidae (bears) — Canidae (dogs, foxes, wolves) — Mustelidae (martens, stoat, otter)

FAMILIES

Felidae (cats) (4 subfam. Felinae only surviving) — Hyaenidae — Viverridae (civets, mongoose)

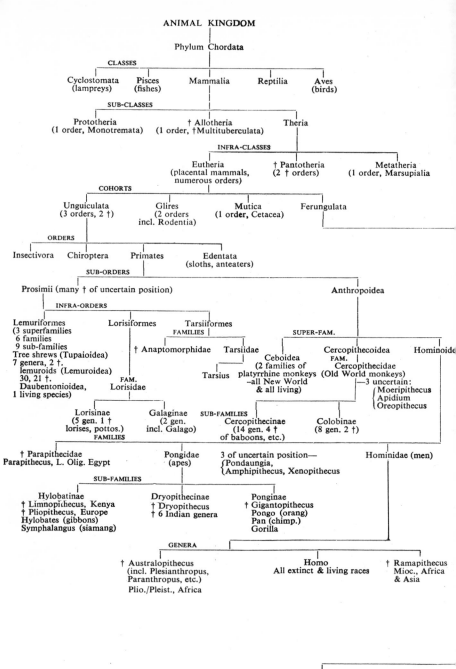
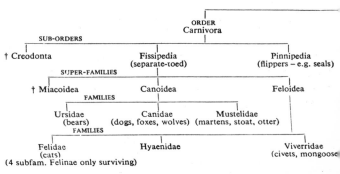